D1377378

LOYAL COMRADES, RUTHLESS KILLERS

LOYAL COMRADES, RUTHLESS KILLERS

The Secret Services of the USSR 1917–1991

SLAVA KATAMIDZE

LEWIS

INTERNATIONAL, INC.

First published in the United States in 2003 by
Lewis International, Inc.
Copyright © 2003 The Brown Reference Group plc

This book is copyright under the Berne Convention.
No reproduction without permission.
All rights reserved.

The right of The Brown Reference Group plc to be identified as authors of this work
has been asserted by them in accordance with the Copyright, Designs
and Patents Acts, 1988.

Lewis International, Inc.
2201 N.W. 102 Place, #1
Miami, F1 33172 USA

Tel: 305-436-7984 / 800-259-5962
Fax: 305-436-7985 / 800-664-5095

ISBN 1-930983-23-9

Editorial and Design:
The Brown Reference Group plc
8 Chapel Place
Rivington Street
London
EC2A 3DQ
UK
www.brownreference.com

Printed in China

Senior Editor: Peter Darman
Editor: Stephen Crane
Picture Research: Andrew Webb, Slava Katamidze
Design: Jerry Udall
Production: Alastair Gourlay

PICTURE CREDITS
Corbis:190
Corbis: Bettmann: 147, 205
Corbis: Hulton Archive: 128, 131, 167
Hulton Archive: 16, 164, 198
Robert Hunt Library: 8, 10, 12, 14, 15, 17, 20, 28, 33, 55, 59, 66, 68, 70, 72, 74, 79,
81, 82, 86, 90, 94, 95, 97, 98, 99, 100, 102, 103, 104, 107, 110, 112, 117, 118, 123,
124, 128, 134, 138, 140, 145, 150, 152, 154, 156, 159, 160, 169, 170, 172, 174, 178,
180, 183, 188, 190, 193, 194, 196
Slava Katamidze Collection: 13, 18, 19, 22, 23, 24, 26, 29, 30, 32, 35, 36, 37, 38, 40,
41, 43, 44, 45, 46, 47, 48, 50, 52, 53, 54, 55, 56, 57, 58, 61, 62, 63, 65, 67, 70, 72,
74, 75, 76, 78, 80, 81, 83, 84, 85, 89, 91, 92, 96, 97, 100, 101, 104, 108, 111, 114,
115, 116, 120, 121, 122, 125, 126, 132, 134, 137, 142, 145, 148, 161, 167, 175, 176,
183, 185, 207, 208
Novosti: 201, 212
Popperfoto: 128, 202
Press Association: 128
Rex Features: 215
Rex Features: Sipa: 198, 202, 204, 210, 211
Timepix: 157
Topham: 128, 214

CONTENTS

PREFACE

The history of the secret services of the Soviet Union is, to a large extent, the story of the Union of Soviet Socialist Republics (USSR). Consequently it reflects not only the main stages in the development of the Soviet state, but also events in the international arena between 1917 and 1991 (the year the USSR collapsed).

For their part, Western experts have few doubts that they deciphered the hieroglyphics of Soviet political history a long time ago, and assume that there are no black holes in their conclusions. But in the case of certain periods of Russian secret service activity in the twentieth century, this is being more than optimistic. There are still many unanswered questions. Take the bloody purges of the 1930s, for instance. Why were so many top-echelon Soviet military commanders, party bureaucrats and intelligence officers arrested, then shot or exiled? The explanation that Josef Stalin was ensuring that he remained in power by thus eliminating his rivals may be straightforward, but it is unconvincing. And why should so many ordinary Russians – millions – have been sent to prison camps?

In 1953, the man who had organized the stealing of atomic secrets from the West, Marshal of the Soviet Union Lavrenty Beria, was accused of being a Western spy and killed by Khrushchev and his military cronies. The history books say Beria had been plotting a coup. But there are no witnesses and no evidence of any coup at all; so why did he die? There are many questions of a similar kind; this book was written to provide some answers.

The memoirs of Soviet secret service officers, both published and in manuscript form, have been useful in reconstructing the events of the past century, and only two names have been changed in this narrative at the request of the writers' relatives, who still live in Russia. As well as published sources, internet files of enormous diversity have been consulted, and copies of authentic documents have also been studied.

Initially the writing of this book seemed relatively easy, because in the post-Soviet era so many books and memoirs have been published by former officers of the KGB, and so many previously secret documents have been made available. Indeed, one might doubt whether a reciprocal amount of information will ever be published about the CIA or FBI, or their equivalents in other countries, in the decades to come. Nevertheless, it was still a difficult task compiling this work, as a great many documents of paramount importance in the USSR were destroyed in the 1920s, 1930s and 1950s, and were often replaced by false ones.

Thousands of fake documents have been circulating in Russia and elsewhere since the beginning of *perestroika* (literally "reconstruction", the policy of restructuring the Soviet state under the leadership of Mikhail Gorbachev). Dates, figures, names, events – everything has been manipulated in Russia for political reasons for such a long time that digging up Russian history really is hard labour.

But there is always a great reward: the truth.

CHAPTER 1

CHEKA: THE RED TERROR

Felix Dzerzhinsky and his *Cheka* used murder and terror to consolidate Bolshevik rule in Russia in the early 1920s.

Vladimir Ilyich Lenin and other leading Bolsheviks (Russian Communists) admitted on a number of occasions that they did not take power in Russia in October 1917, but rather "picked it up". The inability of the Provisional Government, set up in February 1917, to control the situation and the fierce opposition to all its actions from leftist parties, of which the Bolsheviks were far from being the largest or indeed most popular, meant there was no authority in Petrograd (now St Petersburg, formally Leningrad) or the country at all. The Provisional Government was headed by the Socialist Alexander Kerensky. Soviets – revolutionary councils – were formed in October 1917 throughout Russia to end the country's participation in World War I and establish citizen-run industries and farms. The Bolshevik Leon Trotsky assumed command of the military revolutionary committee at Petrograd, and soon had control of the city. Lenin became president of a Council of People's Commissars, and within a month had control of the whole country. The power vacuum allowed the Bolsheviks and their sympathizers to seize the capital of Russia without any significant resistance.

The most effective slogan Lenin, Trotsky and their associates used to ensure the victory of their party was "Expropriation of the

■ *Left: Cheka* **chief Felix Dzerzhinsky (second from left), photographed with his senior commanders in 1919.**

9

■ *Above:* Leon Trotsky arrives in Petrograd in September 1917. He was shortly after elected chairman of the Petrograd Soviet of Workers' and Soldiers' Deputies.

expropriators" – in Lenin's simplified version: "Rob the robbers!" Plundering, the burning of landowners' houses, robberies, rapes and murders immediately followed, just as the Bolshevik leaders expected.

First and foremost, the Bolsheviks were unleashing forces that would not accept law and order at all, except when it came from the barrel of a gun. In January 1918, they used their own supporters and their allies in the leftist parties to forcefully dissolve the Constituent Assembly that was meant to establish a democratic regime (the Provisional Government had proposed a Constituent Assembly in May 1917, the elections for which took place in November; in more or less free parliamentary election the Bolsheviks won only 25 percent of the votes cast). And then they launched the terror against any opposition, be it the instinctive resistance of the monarchists and bourgeoisie (middle class), or that generated by the pervading lawlessness and chaos. It was a terminal terrorizing of bourgeoisie and intellectuals that Lenin and Trotsky wished to achieve, and "the mob" seemed to be an ideal instrument for that purpose. But the result was far from the one expected. Faced with the anarchy that jeopardized the very existence of their regime, as well as the growth of organized opposition, Lenin and his supporters created a body that would ensure the continuance of Bolshevik rule.

The Council of People's Commissars (essentially the Bolshevik government) readily accepted the recommendation of Felix Dzerzhinsky, one of the most ruthless Bolsheviks, to establish a body to fight counter-revolution, speculation and sabotage – the *Cheka* (All-Russian Extraordinary Commission to Combat Counter-Revolution). Political repression was to be the top priority of the *Cheka*. Dzerzhinsky stated that the arrest and execution of opponents to the new regime could not be random and unsystematic – "that work must be properly organized". The commissars agreed.

Dzerzhinsky reserved for himself the position of chief of the first secret service in the Bolshevik state, a task he undertook for eight years. Lenin called him a "Thunderbolt against the Bourgeoisie" and "Iron-Clad" Felix. Russian émigré nationalists hated him and called him "a Polish nationalist agent assigned to undermine Russian influence in Eastern Europe", but his record was simply that of a Bolshevik fanatic who had spent half his life in prison and exile for political reasons.

"Iron-Clad" Felix

Felix Dzerzhinsky was born in 1877 on the Dzerzhinovo estate in Vilno province into a provincial noble family. He succeeded in graduating from only seven forms of the Vilno 10-year classic school, where he was known for his disobedience and mutinous nature. In 1895 he joined the Russian Social Democratic Workers' Party. Four years later he was arrested and sent to Kovno prison, and then exiled for three years to Viatka province. He fled by boat down the River Kama, and in Warsaw soon created a party for the Polish proletariat (working class): the Social Democratic Party of Poland and Lithuania. As the creator of an opposition party, he would have risked the firing squad in Bolshevik Russia, but the government of Tsar Nicholas II (1868–1918) was more liberal. Dzerzhinsky was arrested and sent to Siberia, but he escaped again and went abroad. He was re-arrested in 1906 on his return but escaped once more and lived abroad illegally. He was arrested for the last time in 1912, and placed in Warsaw prison, later in the Orel central prison and finally in the ill-famed Butyrka prison in Moscow. After the February Revolution of 1917 (a spontaneous outbreak of strikes and riots in Petrograd, caused by war defeats, low wages and shortages, which led to the establishment of a soviet of workers and soldiers in the city and the abdication of Tsar Nicholas II) he was one of the main organizers of the Bolsheviks' seizure of power.

Lenin had always dreamt that his secret service would be supervised by "a true proletarian Jacobin" (extreme political radical). Dzerzhinsky, certainly Jacobin if not proletarian, was the embodiment of the Bolshevik ideal: a man who knew no pity for the enemies of the revolution. He truly believed, as did Lenin and Trotsky, that in the interests of a bright Communist future one could sacrifice hundreds of thousands of political opponents, or even totally innocent people who had the misfortune to be descendants or relatives of political

opponents. He chaired the board of 15 battle-hardened Bolsheviks that were furnished with much greater powers than any other security officers in the entire history of Russia.

In March 1918, Lenin and his commissars moved from tormented Petrograd to Moscow, which became the country's capital. The reason for the move was twofold: they wanted to hide behind the walls of the Kremlin fortress, and be far from the main centre of the opposition to their regime. It was here, in Moscow, that the Bolsheviks appreciated how far lawlessness had spread. In January 1919, for example, Lenin's automobile was stopped by gangsters in the Sokolniki Road. Lenin and other passengers were thrown out, the gangsters took his Browning handgun and papers, and then drove away. They later returned after looking through the papers and discovering they had robbed the Bolshevik leader. They wanted to take him hostage and ask for a ransom, but it was too late. This episode resulted in a massive manhunt, and substantially increased the number of *Cheka* units investigating

■ *Below:* Members of the Bolshevik power base in Petrograd: soldiers, sailors and workers. The Bolshevik programme of "peace, land and bread" was crucial for winning support among the hungry urban workers and military personnel.

organized crime in Moscow and elsewhere. However, the main focus of *Cheka* operations throughout its existence was political opposition.

Investigations, both those initiated by the *Cheka* itself and those provoked by denunciations, began running at full speed. Breslav, the vice-chairman of the Moscow *Cheka*, happily boasted that his unit completed at least 50 cases a day. Initially about half of all the investigated cases were criminal, but by 1920 homicide units and local police forces had been substantially strengthened, and the proportion of criminal cases the *Cheka* was investigating fell to between 10 and 15 percent. The rest were mainly political.

In 1918 some *Cheka* operatives and special detachments were not Bolshevik, but Socialist Revolutionaries (essentially agrarian Socialists who wished to mobilize the peasantry), a popular party in Russia, and Anarchists. These people were as ruthless as the Bolsheviks in dissolving the former regime. When that work was done, however, the Bolsheviks also destroyed them. Using as a pretext the assassination of the German ambassador, Wilhelm von Mirbach-Harff, by Yakov Blyumkin, a Left-Socialist Revolutionary (in October 1917 the left-wingers among the Socialist Revolutionaries broke

entirely from their party and formed a separate organization), they imprisoned the leaders of both parties and disbanded them. It now appears that this assassination was a pre-arranged provocation, as Blyumkin was Dzerzhinsky's deputy, and was not only "forgiven" by the chairman but even returned to the force. He was to be executed in the 1930s, his crime being collaboration with Trotsky.

The murder of the Romanovs

In July 1918, a special team of *Cheka* commissars, reinforced with Lettish and Austrian mercenaries, was sent to Ekaterinburg on Lenin's orders to exterminate the family of Russia's last tsar, Nicholas II. No collective decision was taken; Lenin simply instructed Dzerzhinsky and the government chairman, Jacob Sverdlov, to do it immediately in order to undermine the morale of the attacking White Guards (anti-Bolshevik forces). The tsar, tsarina and their children, as well as some of their attendants and servants, were brutally killed in the cellar of an old merchant house in a hail of gunfire. Those who survived the bullets were finished off with bayonets. The bodies were then buried secretly to prevent the execution site becoming a monarchist shrine. The man who led the execution, Yankel Yurovsky, was selected for the job because he was fully trusted by both Lenin and Dzerzhinsky, and was later promoted to one of the top *Cheka* posts in the country. The rest of the executioners reportedly went unrewarded. Yurovsky ordered those who had volunteered to take part in the execution to hand over all the jewellery they had collected from the slaughtered royals, and reluctantly they had to obey.

Cheka executions were the fate of hundreds of former imperial army and gendarme officers and *Okhrana* detectives who failed to realize the essence of the new regime (the *Okhrana* was the old imperial secret police). In January 1919, the Bolsheviks formed the Byelorussian Soviet Socialist Republic, and three days later

■ *Below:* Lenin rallies his supporters in Moscow during the Civil War (1918–20). He formed the *Cheka* to weed out criminals, political opponents and "counter-revolutionary" agitators.

established their power in Latvia. In Riga alone, 57 people were executed in the first few days after the Red invasion. In February 1919, Bolsheviks seized power in Estonia and started rounding up nationalists there – the terror lasted for about two months. In the North Caucasus thousands of people were killed in just seven days.

But the punitive forces were already overstretched, especially in the view of the new tasks they were facing. On 11 January 1919 the government, unable to end the famine in many areas, introduced the *prodrazverstka*, the surplus grain confiscation law. Grain that was not needed in the household had to be handed over to the government. There were no criteria, just

■ *Above:* Lubianka Square in tsarist times. The Bolsheviks later destroyed the old walls and made their headquarters in the buildings in the square.

■ *Left: Cheka* chief "Iron-Clad" Felix Dzerzhinsky. A rabid Communist, he organized the first concentration camps in Russia.

13

■ Above: Tsar Nicholas II, Tsarina Alexandra and their children, who were all murdered by the Bolsheviks during the night of 16/17 July 1918 when "White" Russian forces approached the area in which they were being held.

working class". Under this pretext there was a massive confiscation of precious objects, furniture and paintings, not merely from the nobility and merchants, but also from teachers of the best tsarist schools, engineers who worked at military plants, postal employees and even local veterinarians. It is safe to assume that only a part of the confiscated treasures ended up in government safes.

Anatoly Lunacharsky, the People's Commissar of Education and Culture, was also plundering private collections and museums, and almost every week trucks filled with antique furniture and paintings arrived at his villa in Moscow. He decorated the houses of his friends as well, and his young wife received gifts that came from unknown sources. But, with somewhat poetic justice, most of the commissars parted with such plundered property about 20 years later. After the Great Purge in the 1930s, the furniture from the flats and houses of the "repressed" party and government bureaucrats was auctioned off at rock-bottom prices to NKVD officers.

Cheka atrocities

The Russian Civil War frontlines saw unprecedented Bolshevik (Red Army) and White Army cruelty, especially in the summer of 1919. One Bashkirov, a former squadron leader of a special detachment, confessed almost 50 years later to his grandchildren that his troops had raped and then murdered with their swords the nurses from the White hospital they had captured. And when the units of the White general Anton Denikin retook Tsaritsin, Kiev and Kursk, and launched an offensive towards Moscow, Lenin issued a secret order to local and frontline *Cheka* units to exterminate all White officers from staff captain upwards. That was his idea of handling prisoners.

The first *Cheka* units set up in every city or town were engaged, first and foremost, in the extermination of tsarist bureaucrats, gendarmes and high-ranking officers, the families of White Guards, and all citizens whose property was valued at 10,000

recommendations that might or might not be followed. Those who tried to defend their harvest ended in prison or were shot *in situ*. By now the number of people imprisoned and temporarily detained was so massive that all the prisons were overcrowded. This led to the forming of correction and labour camps. The date 15 April 1919 can thus be considered the birth date of the Gulag system, which then grew at an enormous pace.

The Bolsheviks also wanted to force the recovery of Russian industry, transport and agriculture. Trotsky saw the solution in the creation of labour armies, which would have made Russia a land of militarized slave labour. This idea did not find support among Trotsky's associates, however. Nevertheless, the notion was not totally wasted – there was wide-scale use of prison labour in later years.

The *Cheka* was also involved in state-organized plundering: taking from well-to-do families everything that had a high value. The government wanted to get gold and jewellery from the "former lackeys of the tsarist regime and exploiters of the roubles or more. There were thousands of scientists and engineers who were killed as "exploiters", and about half of the country's doctors were either killed or forced to emigrate. People were murdered at home, in the streets, and in the cellars of the *Cheka* headquarters irrespective of their age. In Kiev, Odessa and Nikolaev even small babies were sometimes bayoneted in reprisal for their fathers volunteering for service with the White Army or with local nationalists. For about two years *Cheka* commissars not only allowed drunken soldiers and sailors to maraud and rape in Petrograd, but sometimes facilitated such acts.

When volunteers of the White Army entered Kharkov after Red forces had retreated (June 1919), they discovered from remains at the local *Cheka* headquarters that captured officers and their wives and daughters had been methodically cut to pieces. In Petrograd, the *Cheka* shot about 6000 White officers without any trial, but

at least they had not been tortured. In Moscow a *Cheka* sadist called Orlov shot hundreds of small boys in the street. In Kiev, the *Cheka* was led by another "romantic sadist", Laczis, a Lett who enjoyed Trotsky's full support. His executioners were young women, former prostitutes, led by the ill-famed Roza Shvarts. She personally killed about 200 people in the *Cheka* cellar. She and her colleagues tortured both officers and their loved ones publicly. Six months of Bolshevik rule in Kiev witnessed more than 100,000 people killed and tortured to death.

But there were even more bloodthirsty executioners. Deitch and Vikhman of the Odessa *Cheka*, for example, instructed their henchmen to roast captured officers and nobles against the sides of ships' furnaces or break their bones. In Voronezh officers and nobles, irrespective of their age, were put in barrels into which nails had been hammered, and then rolled down hills. In Nikolaev, a sophisticated *Chekist* named

■ *Below:* The room where Tsar Nicholas and his family were murdered. Their deaths were but the first in what became known as the "Red Terror", when the *Cheka* arbitrarily executed real and alleged enemies of the Soviet state.

Bogbender killed "class enemies" by walling them up. In Alupka, the local *Cheka* commissars shot all the wounded officers in the hospitals. Bela Kun, Lenin's favourite "internationalist" from Hungary, and local *Cheka* vampires executed at least 40,000 in the Crimea, including 12,000 captured officers, and in Piatigorsk the *Cheka* killed several thousand hostages. Who can believe that Lenin and Trotsky were not aware of what was going on in the whole country in the name of Communism?

The total lack of principles typical of Lenin, Trotsky and their supporters was shown clearly when the garrison of Kronstadt, the major Russian Baltic naval base, began an uprising against Communist rule in March 1921. The sailors had been angered by the Bolshevik failure to distribute food to Russian cities, the general restriction of freedom and the harsh labour laws. They demanded an end to Communist dictatorship and greater political freedom. The very same sailors who had helped the Bolsheviks seize power; and rout the forces of the Provisional Government, and even guarded Lenin in the critical hours of the Bolshevik coup, were first the targets of false propaganda and then of a massive

assault. The Kronstadt base had a limited amount of ammunition and even less food. Some 500 Communists in the naval fortress, including some commissars, were detained, but none were executed. When Trotsky's forces took Kronstadt after a lengthy bombardment and a bloody assault, he ordered 1800 sailors to be shot. Fewer than 10 percent of them were executed by the *Cheka*; the rest were shot by the army, commanded by Trotsky and Tukhachevsky. Two decades later Trotsky tried to switch the responsibility for the executions to Dzerzhinsky and Tukhachevsky. However, in this period the military tribunals were not subordinate to either the head of the *Cheka* or army commanders; they followed the orders of Trotsky, the People's Commissar of War.

The *Cheka* out of control

Throughout the country, the *Cheka* had its own tribunals, the so-called *troikas* (three-man panels), that were outside of any legal control. The more moderate Communists, knowing the excessive use of force and punishment that was typical of the *Cheka* in this period, and aware of numerous cases where innocent people were arrested and even executed, demanded that the *Cheka* be controlled by judicial authorities. But Dzerzhinsky energetically resisted such a move, and received Lenin's full support. As a result, between 1918 and 1921 the *Cheka* was practically uncontrollable: there were neither laws that regulated its activities nor a legal body that could at least question the legitimacy of its operations. It was thus an agency of Communist Party-controlled terror, which suited both Lenin and Trotsky.

At the beginning *Cheka* operative staff consisted of all types of individuals, most of them recruited only on the grounds of being anti-capitalist and anti-monarchist. It is now known that some were sadists and murderers, and many were former criminals. But the majority of *Chekists* were sailors from Baltic and Black Sea naval units, revolutionary soldiers from the

■ *Below:* Moses (Moissey) Solomonovich Ooritski, the head of the Petrograd *Cheka*. He revelled in his position, sometimes signing hundreds of death warrants a day. He was assassinated in 1918.

Russian Army, young Bolsheviks from provincial universities and mature workers from large industrial enterprises. Juvenile delinquents already had some experience in street fighting and robberies, and thus were ideal material for the flying squads. A number of "radical *Chekists*" were just teenagers as young as 17. In most cases they were to spend their lives in the secret service. For example, there was Boris Gudz, a 14-year-old radical, who stormed into the apartment of General von Wolsky, head of the Tula Gendarme Directorate in 1917, without a warrant and cried in a falsetto voice: "In the name of the Revolution, you are arrested!" He later became an officer of the counter-intelligence department, and after that was an OGPU agent in Japan.

The top echelons of the *Cheka* consisted mainly of true believers in Red

■ *Left:* General Anton Ivanovich Denikin led White forces in southern Russia during the Civil War. He was unaware that Communists operated in the schools he financed during the war.

■ *Below:* Red Army units in Moscow. Compulsory military training for workers and peasants was introduced on 22 April 1918.

Terror. Their mentality is amply illustrated by *Cheka* vice-chairman Peters' statement after the attempt on the life of Lenin in Moscow: "Let the enemies of the working class remember that any person who is arrested with a gun in his hands, without the corresponding permission and identification, is subject to immediate execution, and any person who dares to talk against the Soviet power will be immediately arrested and put in a concentration camp. The members of the bourgeoisie must feel the heavy hand of the working class. All capitalist robbers, all marauders and speculators will be sent to compulsory public works, their property will be confiscated, and persons involved in counter-revolutionary plots will be destroyed and smashed by the heavy hammer of the revolutionary proletariat."

In 1920 the investigation section of the Odessa *Cheka* was in the hands of a former lawyer, Galperin, but he sent people to their deaths with the same ease as his colleagues in Yalta, who were mainly petty shop-keepers and fishermen. Mass executions were recurrent in many regions. "I was an excellent swimmer," remembered Evgenia Krichuk, a woman who lived in Odessa in 1920. "Sometimes I swam as far as the port's distant moorings. Once, swimming far out, I looked down and almost fainted. There was a forest of naked figures below me, on the seabed. Their hands were moving, as if they were waving. These people were executed by the local *Cheka*. The executioners tied ship deck grates to their feet and threw them into the sea."

By 1920 the sadists and murderers were gradually replaced by "steadier" people in order to pacify local populations. But the Extraordinary Commission existed for another two years, until 1922, and during its lifetime there was no man and no family in the country, except for the really dispossessed, who felt safe. Almost all educated people in the country were, one way or another, involved in public life or private enterprise before the revolution, which made them liable to all sorts of intimidation, humiliation and confiscation. It would not be easy to find many families in Russia today whose forebears survived the first years of mass terror unscathed, and who did not suffer from the *Cheka* later.

Clearing out the ranks

Thanks to the destruction of the tsarist crime archives in many cities, former criminals could enroll in the *Cheka*, then invade houses and simply rob people and sometimes kill them for their valuables. Colonel Chernov wrote: "I joined the *Cheka* in 1921 in North Caucasus as a veteran member of the underground Communist youth organization. Most of the *Cheka* squad were workers, and these people were disciplined and honest. But, as we expanded, some other people joined. Two of them were later revealed as tsarist army deserters who had lived for almost four years solely by stealing and racketeering. They were shot according to the wartime regulations, but I am sure there were other suspicious characters in the force. No one could be properly checked in those days.

"We were truly committed to fighting sabotage, the black market, bandits and thieves, and we were successful in many areas, especially in catching bandits who attacked people in their homes. We had informers in many villages who reported the movements of armed gangs as soon as they

■ Right: A young Tukhachevsky in Red Army uniform. In 1918 he organized the defence of Moscow. On Trotsky's instructions he ruthlessly and methodically exterminated peasants who opposed the Bolshevik regime.

saw them, and we immediately sent our operatives to catch them. But on a couple of occasions we walked into a trap set for us by the bandits. For instance, in the Piatigorsk area our forces were once intercepted by bandits when they were called to catch a thief, and all the *Cheka* officers were shot in cold blood. Obviously it was done to warn us that we must stay away. We learnt later that the killers were professional criminals, and we finally got them all in crossfire near another city, Vladikavkaz. To our surprise, we found authentic *Cheka* papers on them which had been issued by a *Cheka* unit in southern Siberia. Unfortunately, due to the Civil War conditions we were unable to ascertain whether the criminals stole the papers from dead *Cheka* operatives, or somehow got them lawfully in order to commit crimes under the protection of the *Cheka* documents."

Some educated men did enroll in the force, mainly because there was prestige attached to the jobs; and besides, in a period of chronic food shortages *Cheka* members received food rations. Fancy leather jackets, brand new Mauser hand-guns, respect, adventures, hot pursuits and cars (rarities in those times); all these had a magnetic attraction for able young men. The *Cheka* was also exempt from the army draft, and the Red Army was definitely not a healthy place to be in those turbulent times. The *Cheka* also provided professional training and evening classes. It was a good school, and many professional spy-catchers and intelligence officers of the 1930s and 1940s started as minor *Cheka* operatives.

"Although there were people of all ages in the *Cheka*, the majority were very young, especially rank-and-file operatives," Colonel Gorlin wrote. "I was 17 when I joined in 1919, and there were five or six people about my age in our squad. We worked from 14 to 16 hours every day, and our job was, in addition to patrolling certain areas,

■ *Above:* Anatoly Lunacharsky, the People's Commissar of Education and Culture, who plundered private collections and museums for his own gain.

visiting markets, restaurants, public parks and hostels. We took part in arresting known criminals, black market traders, smugglers and enemies of Soviet power. That was done on instructions from headquarters or local Soviets (councils).

"I lost my left eye when we were arresting a raider who robbed houses in the city of Batumi and killed witnesses. He was, we found later, a mentally deranged former army officer. When we surrounded the house he started shooting and throwing grenades, and I was hit by some fragments. There were also two bad wounds in my left foot. Thus I had blood ties with the *Cheka*, and stayed in the secret service for 36 years."

Although Dzerzhinsky tried to set up his units in every populated area of the country, Petrograd was of special concern because the greater part of the city's inhabitants were linked to the overthrown tsarist regime. The man who headed the Petrograd *Cheka* in 1918 and simultaneously performed the functions of the interior and

foreign minister of the Bolshevik government in the whole of north Russia, was Moses (Moissey) Solomonovich Ooritski. Born in 1873, he was a timber broker in the small provincial town of Cherkassy before becoming a politician. He began as a social democrat, and from 1903 was a Menshevik (a member of the moderate wing of the Social Democratic Workers' Party). Dull and insignificant, the tsarist *Okhrana* never took him seriously, letting him emigrate to Germany in 1906 instead of sending him into exile in Siberia. When World War I started he moved to Stockholm, and then to Copenhagen. He was a minor figure in the Social Democratic movement until Trotsky made him his proxy. After the October 1917 coup he was commissar in charge of convening the Constituent Assembly. Later he took – or was offered by Trotsky – the ministry of interior affairs. Soon, Russian literary figures were asking his permission to leave the city, noblewomen were kneeling before him begging for clemency

■ *Below:* Felix Dzerzhinsky (front row, third from left) with other top commissars during the Civil War. By 1920 his *Cheka* had become a very powerful organization, with jurisdiction to hunt down all enemies of Bolshevism, including the bourgeoisie, the former nobility and the clergy.

for their relatives, and the prisons were full of princes and celebrities. Ooritski enjoyed his position immensely. For example, at times he signed hundreds of death warrants a day, drinking much wine to support himself in this tiring job.

Leonid Kanegisser

Ooritski was assassinated in 1918. The man who shot him, Leonid Kanegisser, was a romantic poet and idealist who had tried to volunteer for the army and fight against Germany. The 1917 February Revolution moved him to become a leading member of the Socialist-leaning cadets, but then the events in 1918 and the signing of the Brest-Litovsk peace agreement with Germany by the Bolsheviks changed him entirely (by this treaty Russia lost one-third of her population to the Germans, a quarter of her territories and over half her industries). He now hated the Bolshevik leaders and their regime, and especially the people who executed his friends – young officers and cadets who formed a secret circle to fight Bolshevism. They did not know what they were really facing, inexperienced and naïve as they were, and their cause was doomed from the very beginning. They were soon betrayed and arrested; most of them were shot immediately, including Pereltzveig, Kanegisser's closest friend of 10 years. Two weeks later Kanegisser assassinated Ooritski.

Grigori Zinoviev, the party boss in North Russia, wrote an article in *Izvestia* in which he stated that the assassin, "as could be expected, is a Right-Wing Socialist Revolutionary". That was a lie, as Zinoviev knew perfectly well, but only one thing was important at that moment: the ending of any political competition. The conclusion of the article was predictable: "The workers' revolution will respond to the counter-revolutionary terror against individuals by the terror of the proletarian masses directed against all the bourgeoisie and its lackeys." In the Petrograd Commune, controlled by Zinoviev, 500 innocent people were shot in one night as a reprisal.

■ *Above:* Lenin (seated immediately behind the driver) takes a drive with his *Cheka* bodyguards in the early 1920s.

This was not the first time reprisals were used. The Bolshevik leaders made clear that the execution of any assassin caught would be followed by the arrest and execution of his relatives. So the radical opponents of the regime would not only sacrifice their own lives for the cause they considered noble, they would also sacrifice their families and maybe dozens of friends as well. And the terror went beyond that. Decimation or, indeed, the shooting of all hostages, often with no family ties or political connections with the person who had committed the particular act of resistance to Bolshevism, was acceptable to Lenin and Trotsky as well as to most of their supporters.

The first concentration camps

Ooritski was immediately replaced by one Bokiy, a member of the *Cheka* from the very outset and a young sadist who was steeped in blood. It was Bokiy who advanced the idea of creating the first Russian concentration camp, becoming its its first supervisor. Bokiy's own son-in-law, the writer Razgon, conceded that it would have been impossible to count the number of innocent victims he murdered. In Moscow the *Cheka* commanders were no less fanatical and bloodthirsty. The man in charge of the regional units of the Moscow

■ *Above:* Lenin (left) photographed with the leader of the Left-Socialist Revolutionaries, Maria Spiridonova, during the Civil War. The Bolsheviks initially worked with the Left-Socialist Revolutionaries, but ditched them once they had gained power. Maria herself was shot in 1940.

Cheka was none other than Yurovsky, who organized the killing of Tsar Nicholas II and his family in Ekaterinburg.

For decades teachers at Soviet schools taught their pupils that the woman, one Fania Kaplan, who tried to assassinate Lenin in 1918, firing two shots point-blank at him as he was leaving a factory in Moscow, was pardoned by Russia's humane leader. This is totally false. Kaplan, a myopic and unhealthy Socialist Revolutionary terrorist, always sure that she was in the right, was executed by a *Cheka* officer on Lenin's orders, as were most of her family; some of her distant relatives were even imprisoned until after 1945. In addition, immediately after the attempt on Lenin's life more than 300 people were shot in reprisal on the order of Dzerzhinsky and his deputy, Peters. Those executed had mostly been imprisoned by the Bolsheviks since 1917, including the tsarist ministers Shcheglovitov, Beletsky and Khvostov, and several groups of generals, admirals and nobles. They were followed by many more; the cream of the nation reduced to dust for the sake of the "bright Communist future".

Felix Dzerzhinsky and his close associates believed that opposition to

Bolshevik rule could only be stopped by mass extermination, in conjunction with the use of *agents provocateurs*. They did not see anything reprehensible in their behaviour. After all, everything was done in the interests of the Communist cause, and thus was above any blame or remorse.

Following anarchist manifestations in Petrograd and in the Baltic Fleet, the Bolsheviks started to disarm and arrest suspects there. In 1919, a bomb was thrown into the office of the local party committee in Moscow. Then a letter was found on an Anarchist that read: "Moscow is on the alert now. A couple of days ago the local committee of Bolsheviks was blown up by a bomb, and more than 10 people died. That seemed to be a deed of the underground anarchists, with whom I have nothing in common." A few days later a statement appeared, presumably issued by the organizers of this terrorist act, in which Anarchists claimed responsibility. The Moscow authorities and the *Cheka* immediately accused Anarchist groups, "which were obviously guided by the hand of the White Guards provocateurs", of terror against the working class. The hunt for Anarchists became the main occupation of the Moscow *Cheka*. Hundreds of people were arrested or shot during raids on Anarchist flats and houses if they tried to defend themselves, but their force was negligible compared to the *Cheka*. On the eve of the second anniversary of the October rising, the *Cheka* surrounded and blew up a suburban house where the Anarchists had their printing press and other equipment, killing all its occupants. That was the end of the Anarchist Party.

Fighting the Socialist Revolutionaries

The Socialist Revolutionaries were far more serious adversaries for the *Cheka*, especially in the view of the support they could get from the well-to-do peasantry. The Left-Socialist Revolutionaries were quite as extreme as the Bolsheviks in their hatred of capitalism and imperialism, but unlike the

Bolsheviks were not prepared to go to any lengths in their desire for peace, and rejected Bolshevik dominance in the coalition government of which they were a part. An unsuccessful revolt of the Left-Socialist Revolutionaries in 1918 was crushed by troops and *Chekists* and, after the execution of about 20 people, the rebels laid down their arms. The Right-Socialist Revolutionaries were, however, maintaining useful contacts with foreign intelligence services in Moscow and Vladivostok. In 1918 the *Cheka* disclosed that the US, British and French missions in the Far East were involved in the attempt of a Socialist Revolutionary named Derber to form an independent "Siberian Government" at Tomsk. The *Cheka* demanded that the Allies recall their diplomatic representatives at Vladivostok. Soon after this incident the *Cheka* uncovered the so-called Diplomatic Conspiracy (also called the Conspiracy of Ambassadors in Russia). Robert Bruce Lockhart, head of the British special mission in Russia, and his assistant Sidney Reilly were involved, plus the French consul-general Grenard and former US consul-general Kolomatiano. They were accused of using their positions and

connections to set up a counter-revolutionary organization in violation of international law. Its alleged aim was to destroy railway bridges and transport routes, which in turn would cause an unavoidable famine, and to overthrow the workers' and peasants' government using corrupted Lettish riflemen.

The story of the conspiracy became the basis for hundreds of books and films in the USSR, and has been used for many decades to demonstrate the subversive activity of foreign diplomatic services. In essence, the story was truthful, in that Lockhart and other characters in this drama were trying, to the best of their abilities, to promote anti-Bolshevik efforts in Moscow and Petrograd, especially Right-Socialist Revolutionaries, and to encourage them to take decisive action. Lockhart met Berzin, commander of the Light Artillery Battalion of the Lettish Rifle Brigade stationed in Moscow, and tried to talk him into rising against the Soviets and overthrowing them. Berzin, a long-time informer, reported this to the *Cheka*, and Lockhart was arrested at the next meeting. He was later released by Peters and left the country. But Dzerzhinsky and his

■ *Below:* **Rosa Schwartz (holding the bouquet of flowers), the dreadful *Cheka* killer of several hundred Russian officers, is warmly received by "the builders of the new world". After her job was completed, she toured various regions of Russia attired in a white lace dress and red head-scarf, posing as a goddess of justice and freedom. For her bloody work she was appropriately named "Red Rosa".**

■ *Above:* Bagmen – mostly army deserters – who speculated in bread, salt and sugar, were hunted by *Cheka* teams.

colleagues made the whole affair a political *cause célèbre*.

In August 1918 the *Cheka* stormed into the British Embassy in Petrograd, whereupon its administrator Francis Cromie opened fire, killing one intruder and wounding two others, until he was shot dead. All the embassy staff were arrested and imprisoned in the Saint Peter and Paul Fortress, and the Russian personnel of the embassy were tortured. The Soviet newspapers stated that about 40 White Guards officers were seized at the embassy, but that was clearly done to pacify the nervous diplomatic community.

Simultaneously, about 50 people were arrested and accused of gathering intelligence information as well as sponsoring terrorist activity, although the information they provided was purely commercial and mostly non-confidential. To support its theory of a large-scale conspiracy, the *Cheka* published a letter from one René Marchant, a member of the French mission and most probably a French Communist, to the

French President Raymond Poincaré, in which he warned the president that French and British diplomats had been fomenting class struggle in Russia and thus would aggravate the suffering and famine. Kolomatiano, who seemed to be an American agent and had a false passport, and a former Russian lieutenant-colonel named Fride, were sentenced to death and shot. Reilly, who played an important role in British intelligence plans, was sentenced to death *in absentia*. Although some of the arrested were acquitted, 10 to 15 people, including military officers, students, journalists and teachers, were secretly executed after the trial.

The trials and arrests in Petrograd and Moscow showed clearly that the main targets of *Cheka* repression, besides the active opposition, were nationalists, intellectuals and clergy. The first could never adopt the defeatism of the Bolsheviks in the face of Germany, or accept the destruction of the empire's assets; intellectuals were a threat because their mental potential exceeded that of the Bolshevik leaders, and it was natural for the *Cheka* to persecute the luminaries and celebrities of Russian culture. The poet Nikolai Gumilev, one of the greatest Russian talents, and 19-year-old Prince Palei, who was thought to be the hope of Russian literature, were executed, along with many others. Writers like Tolstoy, Bunin and Kuprin, the chess player Alekhin, and many engineers, ballerinas, film directors and painters emigrated to forget about the nightmares of *Cheka* interrogations.

The church became the target of Bolshevik hostility from the very beginning. Resistance to the confiscation of church properties, especially silver and gold items, was especially fierce. It became evident that the Bolshevik government intended to rob the churches and monasteries to acquire financial resources for the areas struck by famine. For their part, religious leaders had previously accused the Bolsheviks of being directly responsible for the famine. They claimed that Lenin and his henchmen had not only no consistent economic policy but also intentionally deprived some areas of food supplies, especially those where support for the Bolsheviks was far from that desired in the Kremlin. Now priests in some areas openly called on their parishes to resist confiscation, accusing the authorities of pocketing most of the proceeds. In some areas – in the old town of Shuia, for instance

– clashes between the local population and Bolshevik marauders took place.

The results were disastrous for priests and monks alike. Lenin presented his plan to deal with the problem to the Political Bureau of the Bolshevik Party on 19 March 1922. "The greater number of the representatives of the reactionary clergy we execute by firing squad the better. We need to teach these people such a lesson that they will not even think of any resistance for several decades." Realizing the incriminating nature of this, he suggested that no members of the Political Bureau take down notes of his plan (the conference secretaries did). His instructions were obeyed, and the *Chekists* actually did more than he expected. According to the memoirs of Colonel Gorlin, in some regions in southwest Russia

■ *Above:* Colonel Ivan Gorlin, a *Cheka* officer whose adventures are described in this chapter. He lost his left eye during one operation.

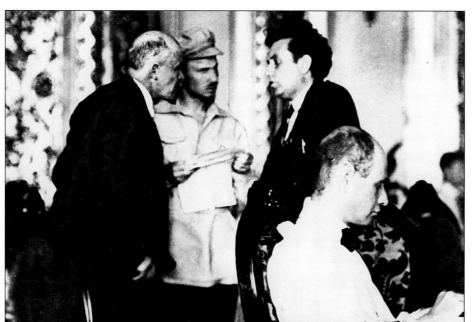

■ *Left:* Eager participants in the Red Terror: (from left to right) Lenin, Bukharin, Comintern executive committee member, and Comintern Chairman Grigori Zinoviev, who advocated "the terror of the proletarian masses".

all the monks and about 90 percent of all priests were rounded up and sorted into two groups: "reactionaries" and "neutrals". The latter, a minority, were released while the rest were sent to the concentration camps and prisons. Very few survived: they were targets for the hardened criminals and perverts in prison.

It was much more difficult for the *Cheka* to cope with the banditry that plagued the whole country, and the big cities in particular, since in many localities not only homicide squads of the people's militia but also some *Cheka* officers were corrupt and collaborating with gangsters. A typical incident happened on 1 May 1919, when the citizens of Moscow were witnesses to – or victims of – an outstanding robbery. A car drove slowly towards the Kremlin on Vozdviszenka Street, while five gangsters were walking on both sides of the street, robbing all the respectable pedestrians of their clothes and valuables, which were thrown into the car. Reaching the end of the street, they killed three police officers sent to intercept them, and drove away. The infamous bandit Safonov, whose codename was Saban, had a gang of 34 highly

skilled criminals. On 24 January 1919 this gang, cruising in the centre of Moscow, killed 16 city policemen (*militsia*) without provocation. They called a policeman over to the car, asked for directions, and then shot him in the head. Policemen then refused to patrol the street alone, and special groups had to be formed. Koshelkov, the man who had stopped and hijacked Lenin's car, had a gang of 18 gangsters armed with automatic weapons and grenades. When the gangsters raided a home, they frequently killed the whole family so as not to let any potential witnesses escape.

What troubled the *Cheka* most was that the gangsters increasingly targeted its officers. *Cheka* commissars in surveillance jobs were attacked and their throats cut. When Koshelkov learnt that one Vedernikov, an officer of the *Cheka* homicide unit, was assigned to catch him, he came to his home and killed him in cold blood in front of his family. Many top officers of the *Cheka* flying squads were killed by gangsters during the raids on their safe houses and restaurants, or fell into traps by following up false reports. The cruelty of the

■ Below: Cheka terror and the ravages of civil war ensured that much of the rural poor starved, their lands laid waste during the early 1920s.

criminals set free by the revolution was unheard of: there were cases when all the members of a family were axed to death one by one after a robbery.

About 200 professional gangsters were either killed during interception operations or later executed by the *Cheka* in Moscow in 1920. Not until the end of 1921, however, did the *Cheka* reduce criminal activities in Moscow, so that they could turn their efforts to Petrograd. Experienced officers spent four months there dealing with the five most dangerous gangs, numbering more than 150 "career criminals". Some 63 of the arrested were shot on the instructions of the Petrograd *Cheka*. The period of criminal terror was over – at least in the major cities.

The first Bolshevik spies

The Russo-Polish War of 1919–20 was intended to be a demonstration of Bolshevik power: to prove that the Red Army had enough strength to defend the new regime. There was also speculation that German agents within the Bolshevik government had received orders from Berlin to try to weaken the nationalist government in the newly independent Poland as much as they could. The advance of the First Cavalry Army was extremely successful in the beginning, but as the Red Army approached Warsaw and its lines of communication lengthened, its vanguard was almost totally destroyed and the war was lost.

The Bolshevik government drew the conclusion that its armed forces had no idea about the strength and location of the enemy and its battle plans. So Order No. 169 was issued on 20 December 1920 by the Chairman of the All-Russia Extraordinary Commission to create a political intelligence unit, called the Foreign Department (INO). At Dzerzhinsky's request, one Davidov (real name Davtian), a department chief in the People's Commissariat for Foreign Affairs, was appointed to head the INO.

This was a predictable appointment. An experienced conspirator with worldwide

■ *Left:* Patriarch Tikhon urged his followers to resist Bolshevik efforts to seize church property. Such "subversive" words could have but one result: he was shot by the *Cheka*. Many of his clergymen followed him to the grave.

contacts, Davtian was able to set up a sizeable international operation in a very short time. He also knew the weaknesses of the Russian émigrés: they cared about their relatives and friends living in Russia. Thus as many of the latter as possible were made hostages, especially if they had links to the top figures in the émigré communities in France and Germany. Most of the Russians in these countries were from the upper strata of society, accustomed to luxury, and so were looking for a sizeable income. Davtian could play on this, too. His friends abroad earmarked some figures who could be recruited to his cause.

Philippov, a journalist, was one of them. His area of coverage was Finland and Sweden. As there were thousands of Russian ex-officers in these states conspiring against the Bolshevik regime, his information was extremely valuable. Dzerzhinsky was so interested that he switched control of this contact to his personal office. Another agent operated in Constantinople: he was a Russian émigré priest with a paedophile past whom the INO blackmailed.

The two years following the October Revolution had been turbulent for Europe. In Berlin the Communist Spartacist rebellion was suppressed, and its leaders

Karl Liebknecht and Rosa Luxemburg were arrested and shot in early 1919. In Hungary a Soviet government was formed that year, headed by Lenin's friend Bela Kun, but was suppressed by Romanian troops and nationalists in the summer. In Bavaria a "Red Republic" was formed in March 1919, but survived only two months. Many of the participants fled to Russia, and soon swelled the ranks of Bolshevik agents.

March 1919 saw another important event: in Moscow the Constituent Congress of the Comintern (Communist International) took place. There were 52 delegates from 30 countries present, and Grigori Zinoviev was elected its chairman. From now on Bolshevik intelligence had a powerful tool to help its operations, recruitment and political influence. For at least three decades almost all assassinations, kidnappings and covert operations in Western Europe would be effected with the efficient help and support of local Communist agents.

One of the first Comintern agents active in the USA was Saul Saltman (Zaltsman). A young Communist from an educated Russian émigré family and an extremely eloquent speaker, he was instructed by a Comintern agent to assassinate one Boris Brasol, an infamously violent and prolific anti-Semitic propagandist in America. A former tsarist officer, Brasol played an important role in the notorious case of Mendel Beilis who allegedly killed a Christian boy in Kiev in 1911. This case was fabricated by the tsarist secret service to prove that Jews were still practising ritual murder. Later Brasol formed anti-Semitic and anti-Communist groups in the USA and had the book *The Protocols of the Elders of Zion*, a tsarist police forgery designed to incite pogroms, translated into English and widely distributed. Brasol's own book, *The World at the Crossroads*, which was circulated in factories and railway stations, asserted that the revolution in Russia was financed and led by Jews. As Brasol and his sympathizers were getting substantial financial support from industrialists, including Henry Ford himself, *Cheka* emissaries in the USA thought it imperative to terminate him. Saltman tried to intercept and shoot Brasol in Boston when he was talking to journalists, but did not open fire because of the risk of harming other people around him.

Famine relief in Russia

In pursuit of the Comintern's target of worldwide revolution, many outstanding cultural figures would later collaborate with Soviet Russia and its secret service. But by the time this collaboration started to gain momentum, entirely different priorities were on the Communist agenda. The ill-conceived economic measures of the Bolshevik leadership in combination with acute drought resulted in a great famine. From 24 to 28 million people in the Volga region, Urals, southern Russia and Ukraine were starving by the end of 1921, and it is estimated that at least seven million people died of hunger. Cannibalism and epidemics aggravated the situation. Aid was urgently needed, and so Communists and Social Democrats made worldwide appeals to their colleagues and charitable organizations to assist Russia.

The French writer Anatole France gave his Nobel Prize, the Norwegian polar explorer Fridtjof Nansen appealed to all the world and received an unexpectedly

■ *Right:* The American industrialist Henry Ford gave financial aid to Boris Brasol, a former tsarist officer and anti-Semitic propagandist whose writings asserted that the Russian Revolution had been financed and led by Jews.

VIVE LA IIIme JN

LONG LIVE THE IIIrd

generous response, and some Russian émigrés even volunteered to help. Christian churches also helped, responding to the appeal of the Russian Patriarch. The Comintern set up the so-called International Workers Aid for the Starving, and workers in Germany, France and even Finland donated money to the fund. About 318,180kg (700,000lb) of foodstuffs was delivered to Russia. But it was the United States which was most effective, via the American Relief Administration (ARA). In association with the Young Men's Christian Association (YMCA), it started a programme for the relief of hungry children in Russia as early as 1919, and in 1921 an agreement was signed by Russia and the ARA for an intensified programme for the famine areas, where it helped to save about three-quarters of the population. By the autumn of 1922 it had delivered about 13.63 million kg (30 million lb) of food, medicines and clothing. But the Bolshevik leaders, and especially the *Cheka*

hierarchy, were convinced that the ARA was an enemy of Soviet power. Booklets distributed among the officers of the *Cheka* who were dealing with ARA operations and personnel stated that "the organizers of the ARA are pursuing certain economic and political goals", and should be closely monitored and arrested if necessary. As a result, a number of ARA employees were accused of counter-revolutionary activities and harmful propaganda, and later arrested by the Bolshevik secret service. Russian ARA personnel were spied on and intimidated, and as soon as the ARA operations in Russia were discontinued many were interrogated and exiled. Later, some were branded as traitors during the Great Purge of the 1930s and imprisoned on the grounds of having been "corrupted by counter-revolutionary propaganda". Those few not persecuted were *Cheka* operatives planted in the ARA for surveillance, who would soon be used in secret service operations in other countries.

■ *Above:* Lenin at the Third International, also known as the Comintern, in 1920. Its aim was to promote world revolution on the Russian Communist model. Zinoviev is seated to Lenin's left.

CHAPTER 2

THE TIME OF OGPU

The Bolshevik victory in the Civil War allowed Moscow to reorganize the secret service. The *Cheka* gave way to the more effective OGPU.

In the early 1920s, realizing that the economy of Bolshevik Russia could only be rescued if it was radically reformed, Lenin proclaimed his New Economic Policy (NEP). It allowed a measure of private enterprise, and the boost to the economy was almost immediately evident. The disastrous famine of 1921–22 was forgotten, farmers and peasants were eager to resume work, and "nepmen", the new entrepreneurs created by the NEP, were instrumental in restoring many small and medium-size enterprises, mostly in food processing and textile production. In 1923–24 the new bourgeoisie was responsible for about a quarter of all industrial output and controlled two-thirds of urban trading.

However important their economic contribution, though, private entrepreneurs were, along with the nobles, former police officers, the clergy, the mentally deranged and people convicted of infamous crimes, constitutionally deprived of all political rights, including the right to vote. The numbers of members of the deprived categories varied greatly from locality to locality. In Penza Province in 1922, for instance, the "deprived" were about 1 percent of the total population, while in Kiev, Moscow and Petrograd they were as high as 10 percent. Even in 1934 over two million people were disenfranchised, at least half of them on political grounds.

■ *Left:* A *Chon* detachment during the early 1920s. *Chon* units were better trained and equipped than their Red Army equivalents.

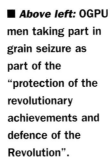

■ *Above left:* OGPU men taking part in grain seizure as part of the "protection of the revolutionary achievements and defence of the Revolution".

■ *Above right:* Less than happy *kulaks* transport their produce to surrender to the Soviet authorities. The *kulaks* were perceived as a threat by the Communists.

The new dispensation required a reorganization of the secret service. The *Cheka* was replaced by the State Political Administration (in Russian, GPU) within the People's Commissariat of Internal Affairs. This was meant to show to the world that the Extraordinary Commission (*Cheka*), as well as the extraordinary measures it employed, were not needed any more. But the core of the previous body – and its chief Felix Dzerzhinsky – remained unchanged. A year later the secret service, now called the Unified State Political Administration (OGPU) of all Russia, became independent of the People's Commissariat of Internal Affairs, which meant the OGPU was going to be "a state within a state".

As the country's economy improved, so too did the economic situation of the OGPU. The money raised from taxing and fining nepmen made it extremely well-funded. Its personnel also changed. Instead of small teams of poorly equipped and underfed hardcore Bolsheviks, or random adventurers engaged in arrests and confiscations, as was the case after the October 1917 Revolution, it acquired a legion of well-trained officers in clean-cut uniforms. They were feared, invoking an involuntary shudder in almost every citizen in the country, and even in those few foreigners who dared to work in Russia.

In addition to operatives, agents and investigators located in every corner of Russia, the OGPU now had special detachments. The officers and soldiers of these units also wore a special uniform with the initials "OGPU" on it, were accommodated in better barracks than those housing regular troops, and were better fed and received higher salaries. Along with Red Army troops, the OGPU special units took part in routing about 300 detachments of former White Guards and nationalists making incursions through the western frontiers, as well as some 70 detachments of local nationalists and ethnic insurgents in Central Asia, operating primarily from bases in Afghanistan and Iran. The Bolshevik regime was thus consolidated in almost all the territories of the former Russian Empire.

Meanwhile, the process of creating a one-party police state started by Lenin and Trotsky was effectively continued during the 1920s. In 1922 the trials of the leaders of the Right-Socialist Revolutionaries began: 34 prominent figures in the party, including 11 members of its Central Committee, were accused of counter-revolutionary activities. The *Cheka*/OGPU supplied evidence of such dubious quality that even Bolshevik prosecutors were sometimes at a loss about how to handle it during the trials. The Socialist Revolutionaries represented mainly the well-to-do farmers, the *kulaks* (*kulak* means "clenched fist" in Russian), and the shooting of the party leaders spelled their future fate. Sure enough, about a year later another trial took place in Siberia, this time of over 300 people accused of conspiratorial activity on the Socialist Revolutionaries' platform, including an attempt at mutiny. Only a small number of them were former tsarist officers (21) and clergy (6 priests and 2 deans), while the rest were farmers and intellectuals. Executions and deportations again followed.

The OGPU's brief was the "protection of the revolutionary achievements and defence of the Revolution, and putting an end to counter-revolutionary activities". These last included, in addition to betrayal and espionage for a foreign country, "any coup or participation in a coup of the enemy of the Soviets or failure to report such a coup". That allowed a whole range of reprisals against any person or group of persons who showed any discontent with the regime, and against people who, even in the distant past, had been connected with ideological or political enemies of the regime, such as Constitutional Democrats, Mensheviks and Socialist Revolutionaries. It did not matter whether the accused had been prominent figures or so-called "passive" low-level members of political

■ *Left:* The singer Theodore Tetov photographed in his White Guards uniform. He was imprisoned for 25 years for being a member of the Whites. His arrest is described in this chapter.

parties. Even after many years these people were considered enemies of the state.

People who had once fought in the White Army were also subject to immediate arrest, irrespective of whether they had enrolled voluntarily or happened to be part of it due to various other circumstances, including forced conscription. Sometimes they were not even tried, but were simply exiled to Siberia to be constantly monitored by the local officers of the OGPU. Such measures made it possible to claim that the mistakes of the past would not necessarily lead to conviction.

Theodore Tetov (Terdat Ter-Minasian), a son of a priest, had a beautiful baritone voice and, after training as an opera singer,

■ *Below:* Members of an OGPU detachment photographed during a raid to seize "illegal" grain, i.e. privately owned.

became a cabaret star before the revolution. He told the story of his life to his grandchild shortly before he died. "I joined the White Army when I saw endless executions and marauding in the north Caucasus. After a short period of training I became a *podporuchik* (lieutenant) and joined an artillery battery. When our troops were routed by the Red Army we were disbanded, and I went to Tiflis to study. I was not a bad draughtsman, and wanted to be an architect. I was successful, building motels and roadside centres. But in the mid-1930s, walking in the street, I met a familiar face. I tried to recall the name but I could not. Later I learnt that the man was a soldier from the White Army. Fearing that I would report him, he reported me. The secret service searched my apartment and found some epigrams which I had written about my acquaintances, which they said were 'politically damaging'. In combination with my record in the White Army that led to a 25-year sentence. I was sent to a camp in the coldest place in Russia: Krasnoyarsk. I survived only because the camp commanders needed me to conduct the choir of inmates and draw posters in the camp. Most of the ex-officers of the White Army in the camp died long before I got there."

Contacts with émigrés

Another crime severely punishable in Russia was communication between Soviet citizens and their émigré relatives. Even if the letters did not contain any information that could be considered damaging to the regime, even if a letter was only three or four lines telling about one's health and whereabouts, the OGPU officers could either demand that the correspondence cease or start permanent surveillance of the writer, who was considered "disloyal" because he or she communicated with an enemy of the people. In most cases such decisions were arbitrary and depended entirely on the attitude of the OGPU "curators".

The OGPU was extremely active in the economic sector. Colonel Gorlin wrote in his memoirs: "By 1926 the OGPU was almost omnipotent. An officer of the OGPU who oversaw and inspected an industrial enterprise had a right to arrest any worker, and in exceptional cases even a group of workers, on suspicion of intentional or involuntary sabotage. And there were cases of sabotage, sometimes strange ones. I once came to Gorlovka in the Ukraine at the end of the 1920s and was greeted at the railway station by an officer of the OGPU – we called him Timofey – who had just been promoted. I had known him for quite some time, and it was not a secret to me that he was uneducated and poorly brought up, but he was tough with his subordinates and obedient to his superiors. He told me how he was promoted. There was an old engineer at a metal works who was in charge of repairing lifts. Somebody was reckless and irresponsible in the repair team, and that led to a bad accident in the mine in which seven people died. The old engineer was immediately arrested and taken to the local OGPU headquarters. About 20 minutes later there was a telephone call from the local party leader who insisted on having the old man immediately imprisoned and tried.

"After the spilling of oceans of blood"

"Timofey, however, took him back to the works and instructed him to keep his mouth shut and inform the team about the arrival of a new member. Timofey then dressed as a worker and pretended he was a peasant returned from exile when he joined the team. After some hours of working together one of the team told him in a conspiratorial tone that they wanted to get rid of 'the old timer', who was too demanding, and were even prepared to cause another accident for this purpose. All 11 people of the team were arrested, and Timofey got a promotion. Such cases were not unique. In the 1920s, after the spilling of oceans of blood, very few people cared about human life."

The black market and shadow economy were enormous in the Soviet Union, and

■ *Above:* An ailing Lenin. Between 1922 and his death in January 1924 the Soviet leader suffered three strokes. His condition gave Stalin the opportunity to seize power.

this period were more modest. In the small town of Kineshma one Khalfin, for example, a successful producer of tarred felt used in roofing, was arrested for accusing trade union workers of stealing, and was immediately sentenced to six years in prison and a fine of 25,000 gold roubles. In a six-month period in 1923 alone, the Moscow Directorate of the OGPU provided the courts with evidence for 650 cases, and nepmen paid about 100,000 gold roubles in fines and penalties as a result.

The spread of corruption

The bureaucratic apparatus of Soviet Russia was getting increasingly corrupt, and bribes became widespread. Nepmen claimed very little could be done without a bribe to government officials, and the years 1923–26 witnessed the arrests of thousands of people taking or offering them. The most publicized case of this type was in 1923, when a group of court and judicial employees was arrested along with 17 nepmen; it was typical that the employees were sent to jail while all 17 entrepreneurs faced the firing squad for "making the government officials corrupt", and thus undermining the state.

The main feature of the OGPU that made it different from the secret services of almost all other countries in the world was that up to the mid-1930s it was not only in charge of spying on all the population and the arrest of those it singled out, but it also suggested the type of punishment, and then organized it. Given that the fate of the accused was decided well before his arrival in court, the punitive mechanism was thus universal and self-contained; it was truly an archipelago of centres of persecution and repression. Yet the OGPU repression machine was actually driven by the party apparatus. The apparatchiks demanded more arrests and more trials so they could report to their superiors about the successful eradication of political opposition.

Felix Dzerzhinsky remained the chief of the OGPU till the last days of his life (he

growing rapidly. The newly created Economic Department of the OGPU was supposed not only to investigate economic crimes committed by the nepmen and corrupt officials, but also, as People's Commissar of Justice Kursky openly declared, to wage in 1922–23 an "assault on private capital". The new capitalist stratum in Russia, well aware of the chaos in accounting and law enforcement, did its best to evade all forms of taxation. The OGPU had a free hand in dealing with any nepmen involved.

As early as 1922, the OGPU arrested a former manager of a state tobacco factory in Moscow, Cherkes by name. He had been channelling about 90 percent of the whole production of the factory to his contacts, wholesale traders called Shemshurin and Zagriazkin, and the trio quickly made a fortune. But most of the OGPU catches in died in 1926). Although his main job from 1924 was the supervision of the All-Russia Council of the State Economy (VSNKh), he did not leave his creation unattended and frequently reminded his colleagues that the regime would not survive without a well-oiled security system. "He died because of a heart paralysis," remembered OGPU officer Victor Chernov. "But I thought his death was not an accident. Talking to an archives officer in about 1935, I heard him saying that some documents pertaining to Dzerzhinsky's collapse were destroyed in the late 1920s. He was an ill man, with lung and kidney illnesses, but he reportedly never complained of heart problems. If he was murdered, I don't think Stalin was responsible. Most probably, somebody else was. But we shall never know the truth."

Viacheslav Menzhinsky

Dzerzhinsky was succeeded by Viacheslav (Valdemar) Menzhinsky, another Polish aristocrat. Born in 1874 into the family of a history teacher in St Petersburg, he graduated from the St Petersburg University with a degree in law. In 1902 he joined the Russian Socialist Workers' Party and was practising law in the interests of the Social Democrats while secretly creating underground party cells. Menzhinsky joined the All-Russia Extraordinary Commission as early as 1919, and soon became Dzerzhinsky's confidant and personal advisor. In 1923 he became vice-chairman of the OGPU, and in July 1926 the chief of the secret service.

Some historians have recently tried to whiten him, portraying him as a devoted revolutionary with liberal views and clean hands. But it is a difficult job to do. To organize the network of overseas informers Menzhinsky made the relatives of important émigrés hostages of the regime. During his time as chairman, a new body was created within the OGPU: the 9th Directorate. It was engaged in political assassinations in Russia and abroad, using

all sorts of weapons including poison, and the head of the 9th Directorate was Genrikh Yagoda, future chief of the OGPU/NKVD.

Menzhinsky died in May 1934. He was a sick man and was said to have died of natural causes, but there are other versions. Stalin thought Menzhinsky, as the enemy of the Trotskyites, had been assassinated by them. During the 1936–38 Great Purge trials some witnesses claimed that he was killed by the secretary of his successor, Yagoda, who administered poison to him instead of medicine. If true, it was poetic justice since Menzhinsky was the man who advocated the use of poison for political killings.

Dzerzhinsky, Menzhinsky and their close associates were all professional conspirators, with a lengthy record of underground operations before they came to power. They also knew the modus

■ *Above:* Rural labourers on their way to work the land during collectivization, the effort to industrialize and modernize the Soviet Union.

■ *Right:* Peasants vote for collectivization in a staged ceremony. Many who did not cooperate were arrested, shot, exiled or sent to the Gulag. In addition, their lands were seized.

operandi of the Russian, French, Italian, Austrian and German counter-intelligence services, and made good use of the best features they found in each. The people who created the system of surveillance and informers for them in the early 1920s took over as leaders of the secret service until the mid-1930s, when inevitably they were executed during the Great Purge. They were vice-chairman of the GPU Genrikh Yagoda (People's Commissar of Internal Affairs from 1934 to 1936) and chief of the GPU secret operative department Artur Artusov (later chief of the foreign intelligence department and then deputy head of military intelligence). Under them the backbone of the system were the young operatives, well trained and hard working.

"My working day started at 10 am and ended at 6 pm, with a short lunch break," wrote General of State Security Sudoplatov in his book *Special Operations: Lubianka and Kremlin 1930s–1950s.* "After that the meetings with informers at safe flats would begin. These meetings lasted from 7.30 pm till 11.00 pm. Then I walked back to my office to report to my superiors about the

operative information acquired." A similar schedule was adopted in all OGPU outfits, and this was explained by two facts. The first was that Stalin normally worked until very late into the night, and almost all organizations in the state followed suit. Secondly, Stalin, basing his thinking on his experience in clandestine operations before the revolution, forbad meetings with informers in the daytime.

"Some of my informers lived many kilometres away from the city of Batum where our local headquarters were located," wrote Colonel Gorlin in his memoirs. "The car was not always available. There were days when I hitch-hiked on a horse-drawn or donkey-drawn carriage to get closer to the Turkish border, and then walked for an hour or so to meet my informer, who described to me the situation in the villages along the border. I seldom came home earlier than 1 am after such trips. It was a tiring job but I liked it. It was something I lived for. I was very idealistic and truly believed that life would soon be fine."

The *Chon*

In addition to the OGPU, the system of total espionage included intelligence elements of the so-called *Chon* (Special Purpose Units). They were created as punitive squads from units of the People's Commissariat of Interior Affairs and the Red Army, and staffed with Communists and sympathizers to counter the remains of White forces, local resistance and anarchist bands, and if necessary to smother popular unrest. The *Chon* were élite units, better fed and equipped than the regular army and led by commanders who were among the best educated, as well as being absolutely loyal to the regime. They would later become NKVD troops.

In December 1922, Genrikh Yagoda issued Order No. 143 for the creation of yet another informers' network. All the local *Chon* commanders had to establish, without any additional funding, a vast chain of informers in the area they were

responsible for. The text of the order is unclear, but its underlying message cannot be missed: peasants were hostile to the regime, as were many workers. Artusov, much better educated than his superior Yagoda, explained the tasks of the *Chon* informers in the regulations he issued: they were to set up informers' networks in every population centre (however insignificant), in military units, headquarters and schools, main state and local government organizations, at industrial enterprises and, whenever possible, in diplomatic and trade missions, and even famine aid missions where foreign nationals worked alongside local employees.

Mixed results

The *Chon* informers' network was a failure, though. The soldiers did not have any training for the job, did not understand their mission properly, and in most cases reported on drunkards and gamblers rather than political opponents. Local populations were reluctant to collaborate with *Chon* forces. The informers' network in big cities, where the local housing managers reported on their tenants and visitors, was much more successful. Spying on the ordinary population was organized in every locality by both the low-level OGPU officers and the people's militia (police). As most apartments now became communal flats, the "deprived" and members of the working class now lived together, and the latter were instructed by the OGPU to report any anti-government sentiments. Sometimes kitchen disputes resulted in one family reporting another, accusing them of anti-Soviet views, and the OGPU duly made a note of this. In many cases the accused were summoned to the local OGPU headquarters and given a stern warning, some accusations led to a formal investigation.

Many of the scientists, teachers and engineers from tsarist times remained after the revolution in quiet and obscure poverty, as they did not wish to serve a repressive regime. Later, though, when the NEP was

■ *Left:* Genrikh Yagoda, head of the OGPU between 1934 and 1936. Responsible for many arrests and executions, he too was eventually shot on 13 March 1938 during the Great Purge.

adopted, they became either experts in government organizations or in private enterprises. These were the people the OGPU was now taking an interest in besides the active opponents of the regime. The so-called *spetsy* (specialists) were always under suspicion. OGPU and police officers went on a round in their assigned area almost every day, talking to the inhabitants of the communal flats and even yard keepers, taking notes of who visited the "old timers" and how much time they spent together.

The OGPU was also meticulously and systematically creating a vast network of informers that were later called *seksoty* (acronym of the Russian *sekretny sotrudnik* – secret associate). They were assigned regular jobs in various organizations but their main mission was to constantly monitor their surroundings. Millions of people were under the permanent surveillance of informers, and the latter were instructed to report on the minutest deviations in the attitude of the local population to the authorities. It goes without saying that the people who agreed to report on their friends and colleagues were for the most part covetous and greedy (the OGPU sometimes paid them extra or eased their life in other ways), and envious of the achievements of their successful and talented colleagues. As a result, they often reported non-existent political deviations, and thousands of able and industrious men and women were imprisoned or lost important jobs in government enterprises for no apparent reason.

As far as the rural areas were concerned, in addition to *Chon* information networks, the OGPU largely relied on the so-called *selkory* (village correspondents). In 1925 these totalled 116,000. The village correspondents reported to the local and central newspapers on the deficiencies in cooperative enterprises and local Soviets (councils), but many of them also wrote about the *kulaks*, accusing them of bullying poor peasants and labourers and of collaborating with the enemies of the regime. This information, only some of which got into print, was extensively used by the OGPU and *Chon* for their investigations and arrests in rural areas. This resulted in instant repercussions from the *kulaks*, and in 1924–25 about 140 village correspondents were attacked and 25 killed. This, in turn, led to reprisals.

Rural revolts

The 1920s witnessed a rapid rising of tension in rural areas. At the end of 1923, for example, a mutiny started in a Cossack village 50km (31.25 miles) from the city of Piatigorsk. More than 700 people took part in it, not only *kulaks* but poorer peasants too. Similar mutinies happened elsewhere as the agricultural policy of the government was disputed. *Chon* and OGPU teams made thousands of arrests. The most dangerous threat to the regime, from its scale and goals, was an armed rebellion in August 1924 in predominantly peasant Georgia, which had been forcefully attached to the Bolshevik empire in 1921. Organized by Georgian émigrés in France and local anti-Soviet forces, its goal was to restore the country's independence and capitalist economy.

Armed risings started in many localities at the same time, and the Provisional Government of the Georgian Republic was formed. However, the rebellion was soon suppressed by the Red Army and OGPU. Special teams of OGPU officers travelled to Georgia by aircraft from Moscow and the north Caucasus to carry out arrests and interrogations, since the OGPU hierarchy was not confident that their local colleagues would be tough enough in dealing with their compatriots. Since Stalin and Sergo Ordzhonikidze, another leading Bolshevik, were ethnic Georgians, the restoring of Soviet rule in Georgia was considered especially important, and the OGPU was ruthless and methodical in its reprisals. The number of victims in this small country was enormous, although the real figure has never been published.

"Rebellion in Georgia was very risky because there was quite a substantial Red Army and OGPU force in the Republic," wrote Colonel Gorlin in his memoirs. "The rebellion involved not only the former nobility, landowners and shopkeepers but also some of the poorest peasants, especially in the region of Guria. They were starving because the government was buying their corn and other produce at ridiculously low standard prices, below what they needed to subsist, while not allowing them to sell corn in the market place."

Cracking down on the opposition

In the cities, the OGPU was much preoccupied with the activity of the opposition inside the Communist Party itself. By 1926 opposition leaders were organizing unauthorized meetings and even demonstrations, and forming illegal committees and groups – in short, everything that could be considered an embryonic opposition party. This in-party opposition was not numerous, though, and in 1926 only about 500 people, i.e. 0.6 percent of party members who attended the local conferences, voted for the opposition.

The dissident groups had differing platforms, but the ruling bloc labelled them all "Trotskyite-Zinoviev Opposition"

(Zinoviev was expelled from the party in 1927; Trotsky had been exiled to Central Asia in the same year) and called for their expulsion from the Communist Party. When some dissident leaders applied to the Social Democratic movement in Europe and to left-leaning intellectuals in Russia for support, the OGPU came in on the instructions of Stalin and his supporters. Some were arrested, and others were exiled. The OGPU now had a long list of people considered "politically unreliable". If they were not repressed in the late 1920s, their turn would come during the Great Purge.

The OGPU was not only a repressive machine, it was also a rumour factory. Its secret agents circulated tales of the sophisticated tortures used both in the interrogation chambers and in places of detention. OGPU bosses considered these rumours a deterrent, and also as a lever to bring psychological pressure to bear on witnesses and suspects. This pressure began with the arrest made in the dead of night by stone-faced and coldly polite officers, and ended with a matter-of-fact notice in newspapers reporting that the sentence of death by shooting had been carried out by the OGPU. The shooting was not by firing-squad. Normally the doomed person was shot in the back of the neck as he walked between two guards along a corridor. Sometimes, however, if the victim was a highly qualified professional, he was secretly transported to work hard on a super-secret government project in some desolate location. Only one in five people who were sent to such projects had a chance of living more than two or three years, although there were exceptional cases when a person sentenced to death was released and returned to normal life.

The death sentences were, of course, a small fragment of the overall picture of repression. The great majority of the people arrested by the OGPU were channelled through regular regional courts to be tried as if common criminals, and then sent to camps to live and work with such criminals. That was an additional penalty they had to bear because thieves and muggers hated "that political trash", and treated it accordingly. Only a few were set free, with a strong warning to stay away from politics and live the life of a vegetable; others were ordered to reside outside the seven most important cities in the country. The Gulag system was not yet in full swing; the untruth-worthy were instructed to live in Siberia or close to the Arctic Circle, while *kulaks* were sent to labour camps and industrial centres where they worked from dawn till sunset for a bowl of soup. Prisons were still mainly on the shores and islands of the North Sea, not far from the cradle of the revolution. The biggest was the one created by the *Cheka* in an ancient monastery on the Solovky Islands.

The Gulag camp commanders

Most of the *Cheka*/OGPU officers recruited in that period purely on a class basis or because of their revolutionary services, had never been interviewed before selection by psychologists and psychiatrists. Some were very sick, or had contracted psychiatric disorders as a result of the cruelties and privations of the Civil War. Finkelstein, an OGPU officer in the Solovky prison, once ordered 34 prisoners to stand on the ice of the White Sea the whole night, in a temperature of minus 30 degrees Centigrade (−22°F), as a punishment for not

■ *Below:* A political prisoner in one of the Soviet camps in the Arctic Circle.

■ *Above: Kulaks* at
work in a labour
camp. Many of
these camps were
run by sadists and
mentally disturbed
individuals, and life
expectancy among
inmates was low.

fulfilling their wood-cutting quota. All had to have their frozen legs amputated at the local medical station, and most of them died. Only then was Finkelstein inspected by doctors and found to be deeply psycho-neurotic. In 1929, 10 highly qualified former tsarist railroad engineers were sent to Solovky. These elderly people, who had served their country so well in the past, were ordered to pull carts loaded with snow. One of them, Professor Pravosudovich, was considered lucky since he was soon executed. Professor Minut, a very ill man, was kept in the hospital for a while but was then thrown out despite his swollen legs. He died of a heart attack the same day. In addition to the brutality of the jailers, the inmates suffered from the harsh climate and shortage of food. Most of the skilled engineers were, however, gradually separated from the rest of the prisoners and transferred to *spetslag* – special camps – where they worked on new military equipment, industrial machinery, chemicals and even bacteriological weapons and gases. These camps were later to be the backbone of the Gulag system.

By the end of the 1920s, the OGPU was deeply concerned about the growing activity of some radical émigré organizations trying once more, in most cases in vain, to perform acts of terror against Bolshevik dignitaries. There were also attacks on Communist Party clubs and local offices. In June 1927 a White Guards officer killed Voikov, the Russian plenipotentiary in Poland. The OGPU reacted with reprisals in the same way as in 1917–18, sentencing 20 people to death by firing-squad. They were Prince Pavel Dolgorukiy and other nobles, former senior officers of the tsarist army (some of them pensioners), famous industrialists and landowners, none of them in any way connected with acts of terrorism and sabotage. The message of the OGPU was clear: the death of any prominent Bolshevik would result in dozens of death sentences applied indiscriminately.

It is interesting to note that Artur Artusov, Yagoda's deputy mentioned above, whom some Russian historians endeavour to portray as an honest and blameless idealist and an innocent victim of the Stalinist regime (he was shot in 1937), was a member of the OGPU Collegium that was so efficient in killing these innocent people.

Wreckers and saboteurs

Opposition to the ruling party and the regime took various forms in the 1920s. Besides the political struggle inside the party and within local soviets (councils), there was collaboration with émigré White forces and cooperation with foreign intelligence services. In addition, sections of the country's population regarded the Bolsheviks as having carried out a hostile and cruel occupation of their land, and so resorted to acts of sabotage and the wrecking of industrial and transport equipment. From 1928 onwards there were numerous acts of this kind in almost all areas of Russia. Some modern authors say that wrecking and sabotage were only in the minds of those who invented them in order to acquire commendations and rewards from their superiors. But American and British technical specialists who worked at the end of the 1920s in gold mines and at metallurgical plants in Russia stated later that wrecking of equipment took place, and was epidemic. John Littelpage, for example, a British engineer, wrote in his book *In Search of Soviet Gold* (1939): "Such petty industrial sabotage was – and still is – so common in all branches of Soviet industry that Russian engineers can do little about it, and were surprised at my own concern when I first encountered it. The authorities in Russia have been – and still are – fighting a whole series of open or disguised civil wars. In the beginning they fought and dispossessed the aristocracy, the bankers and landowners and merchants of the tsarist regime. They later fought and dispossessed the little independent farmers and the little retail merchants and the nomad herders in Asia. From these groups have come a considerable number of disgruntled workers who dislike Communists so much that they would gladly damage any of their enterprises if they could."

Some bureaucrats expressed their solidarity with the saboteurs by covering up for them, and sometimes even encouraged the people who poured sand into engines or drained oil from turbines. In 1928 the OGPU uncovered a major wreckers' organization in the Donets coal-mining area. It was a huge sabotage operation, plaguing 11 mining directorates out of 28, and about 20 percent of all engineers and technicians working in these 11 directorates were saboteurs. Types of sabotage were diverse: intentionally wrong planning, the purchase of unusable equipment, the wrecking of usable equipment and so on. Although the wreckers had moral support from overseas centres set up by former mine owners, they did not have any political platform. But they were sure, judging by the court reports, that the "proletarian dictatorship" was doomed, and hoped for the establishment of a truly democratic society with capitalist elements in the economy. Some 53 saboteurs were tried in Moscow, and most sentenced either to death or imprisonment; only a small number of the accused were found not guilty.

The Industrial Party

Similar trials took place of wreckers in transport, the petroleum industry, and the food-processing sector. But the biggest and most publicized trial was that of the Industrial Party (*Prompartia*). This is a unique case in the history of post-imperial Russia, when an organization of technocrats was created in order to derail Communist plans and return the country to the democratic and capitalist path. The Industrial Party was led by professors, top managers and high-class engineers, and

numbered more than 2000 engineers and technicians, all prepared to act in conjunction with foreign intervention or even armed anti-Communist opposition. Most of the leaders of the Industrial Party favoured the establishment of a temporary military dictatorship under the tsarist General Lukomsky.

The leaders of the Industrial Party were tried in 1930; six were sentenced to death, and two to two years' incarceration. Professor Ramzin, who had reportedly been the brains of the party, survived and even received a Stalin's Prize for his inventions in the years to come. But most of the Industrial Party members were not so lucky. This trial inaugurated a reign of terror against intellectuals. No engineer could now regard himself as beyond suspicion and immune from arrest. Thousands were sent into administrative exile in distant areas of the country, and the jails were filled.

The lack of engineers and managers in industry was appalling, prompting the Supreme Economic Council to complain that the OGPU was interfering with the process of industrialization. In June 1931 the secret service backed off on Stalin's instructions: none of the condemned engineers were executed, and terms were reduced for those who had been imprisoned. But the harm had already been done. The OGPU, headed by the "humane" leader Viacheslav Menzhinsky, used the chance to the full to inflict irreparable losses on liberal intellectuals and to show that nobody in the country was immune from persecution and accusations of any kind. As late as 1934 Deputy State Prosecutor Vyshinsky had to issue an order to local prosecutors to stop making engineers and factory managers scapegoats for production failures.

The OGPU was also extremely active in this period fighting incipient nationalism

■ *Above:* The façade of the happy Soviet state: the 1928 May Day parade in Moscow. Behind the scenes the OGPU maintained an iron grip on the "workers' paradise".

within the USSR. In 1925 Yagoda and Artusov organized the first massacre in Chechenia after the OGPU and *Chon* had encountered resistance in collecting weaponry from the local population. In 1926 a similar bloodbath happened in neighbouring Daghestan. In 1930, OGPU operatives arrested the members of the Ukraine Liberation Union. As this organization largely depended on and cooperated with church leaders, both Russian Orthodox and Catholic, it was particularly hated and persecuted by the OGPU. Most of those who were arrested and executed were former tsarist officers.

The trial of the Menshevik professors was yet another charade elaborately staged by OGPU and party officials in 1931. Fourteen professors and state officials were in the dock, including member of the State Planning Committee Presidium Groman, member of the State Bank Board Sher, and All-Russia Economy Council officials Ginzburg and Shtern. They were accused of "counter-revolutionary activities" in conspiracy with Mensheviks in the USSR and their colleagues in Europe. The Menshevik Wreckers, as they were called, were, according to prosecutors, undermining the state economy by rejecting collectiviz-ation, retarding industry, creating problems in the financial sector and in supplies, and causing popular discontent. All 14 were sentenced to long prison terms. But it was not difficult to recognize the real targets: members of the Russian Social Democratic Party residing abroad, who continued to constitute the Russian section of the Second International. From this point of view, the trial was an important political showcase that would be imitated later in the 1930s and thereafter.

The OGPU was also one of the main motors of collectivization, as its teams and detachments were in charge of arresting and displacing *kulaks*, and imprisoning those who resisted their actions. Collectivization was not invented by Stalin, though. As early as February 1919, when he was in relative

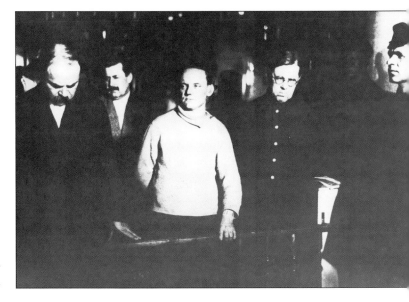

■ *Left:* Saboteurs of industry on trial in 1928. In that year the OGPU uncovered a large sabotage operation in the Donets region. Those caught were severely dealt with.

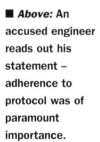

■ *Above:* An accused engineer reads out his statement – adherence to protocol was of paramount importance.

■ *Left:* More engineers on trial. Large-scale sabotage was rife in the Soviet system in the 1920s.

obscurity, the decree nationalizing all lands and announcing the transition to collective forms of land use was issued by Lenin's commissars. But it was Stalin who really pushed it through, because industry required workers, and an intensification of agricultural production was necessary to boost the country's economy. The human cost was irrelevant: Bolsheviks never talked about individuals, they talked about popular masses. But the reaction of the *kulaks*, and even other peasants with much less to lose, to the Communist assault in the villages was vigorous: thousands of clandestine organizations were formed in the country, and in 1928 alone 140 people were killed in rural areas, most of them Communists and *Komsomol* (Young Communist) members.

By 1930 the OGPU had ruthlessly swept away all opposition to collectivization. It had also destroyed religious sects that lived in seclusion, on the grounds that some of the sect members were former tsarist soldiers. In the Moscow region the OGPU boasted of arresting 206 underground groups of *kulaks*, but the harvest was greater in the areas where there were fewer checks by the headquarters and the OGPU enjoyed a really free hand. It took only a year-and-a-half to round up 32 opposition groups and 190 *kulak* assemblies in the Lower Volga region alone,

imprisoning over 3000 people. Before collectivization in the mid-1920s, there were 876,000 *kulak* families in the Soviet Union – 4.5 million people in all. By 1934 the total number of people in all *kulak* families numbered only 150,000, i.e. 30 times fewer.

The Foreign Department

During this period there was also an expansion and professionalization of the secret service abroad. In February 1922 this branch became the Foreign Department (INO) of the Chief Political Administration of the People's Commissariat of Internal Affairs, and less than two years later became the Foreign Department of the independent OGPU, subordinate to the Council of People's Commissars. Michael (Meer) Abramovich Trilisser, a battle-hardened revolutionary, became the head of the INO in 1922 and stayed in the post until 1929. He was convinced that counter-revolution could be only fought using the toughest methods, and that to achieve the triumph of the revolution all methods were acceptable.

Although the INO was a small organization, it was quite efficient. Three factors made this possible. First, the pre-1917 clandestine activity of Bolshevik conspirators in Europe had been a good school for future spies. Second, Russian relatives of émigrés in Europe, effectively hostages, could be used to get information and exert pressure on those abroad. Finally, the INO was staffed by the best people that the Bolsheviks could find for the job, including foreigners and Russian nationalists abroad willing to cooperate with the INO in the interests of the USSR. Some of them were international adventurers who later became prominent figures in the Soviet intelligence establishment.

Peter Popov is an example. A former naval officer in the Amur River Flotilla, in 1917 he was appointed head of the Kharbin section of the Chinese-Oriental Railway in Manchuria. After the October 1917 Revolution Popov stayed in Kharbin and cooperated with Western and Japanese traders. There were White Army detachments and a local headquarters in Kharbin, and the Whites considered him, an ex-officer, one of their own. But Popov, realizing the growing power of the Bolsheviks, soon became their agent. He supplied clothes for Bolshevik guerrilla forces in the Maritime Region of the Russian Far East, provided the Red Army with the personnel lists of White detachments and their locations, and even diverted 120 railway cars containing important industrial equipment to the Russian city of Chita instead of China (he forged just one letter in the bill of lading). His efforts made it possible for the Red Army to destroy the White forces in the area in only 10 hours. Later Popov became a key figure in the Russo-American negotiations on the formation of a financial and industrial syndicate to operate mines in various parts of Soviet Russia. As a result, the American-Russian Chamber of Trade was created in 1924.

In addition to the above, Popov was at times carrying out extremely risky intelligence jobs. One of them was to steal cipher codes from the Chinese Embassy. Popov was highly respected by the Chinese diplomats, and the ambassador offered him the chance to take part in the preparation of

a trade agreement between Russia and China. When Popov was at the embassy the heating system suddenly "failed", and Popov offered to repair it. Checking the radiators, he went to the cipher clerk's quarters. As soon as the clerk went to the bathroom, Popov took the cipher safe keys from the bedside table and made a mould. Everything was perfectly timed. The heating system came back to life shortly after.

Another OGPU agent, Victor Reshetov, posing as an engineer, became a confidant of the former chairman of the Russian Trade and Industry Bank. From him he learned about the preparations for an attack by White officers on the Soviet delegation going to a conference in Genoa. The delegation was to be attacked while in transit in Germany but, thanks to Reshetov, the attempt was foiled.

The INO's primary mission in the 1920s was to learn the plans of the émigré organizations and locate their contacts and branches in the Soviet state. Using its contacts in Paris, the INO was instrumental in the acquisition of émigré cipher codes in Paris and London. Communists in France and other countries sometimes actively participated in INO operations. The two main targets were the Russian All-Warrior Union (ROVS) headed by General Kutepov, and the Popular Union for the Defence of the Motherland and Freedom created in 1921 by the famous terrorist

that inspired confidence were installed as the leaders of this anti-Soviet centre: prominent intellectuals acceptable to émigré circles, or even nobles who had agreed to cooperate with the OGPU. Closely monitoring all movements of the foreign emissaries and their possible contacts in Russia, the OGPU staged a number of outstanding charades to entice its prey.

OGPU deception

Boris Savinkov, for example, a superb clandestine operator himself, fell victim to these operations first, sending a number of his agents to Moscow. A few of them were arrested and then recruited by the OGPU, while others were left alone but kept under surveillance. Savinkov wanted to believe in the massive underground movement in Russia, and so he was encouraged to believe. In August 1924, he was arrested at the Soviet border at the start of his reconnaissance trip and brought to OGPU headquarters. By the end of the month he had been sentenced to death but, in view of his widely publicized repentance, printed in all magazines and newspapers, the sentence was commuted to 10 years' imprisonment. In May 1925, however, Savinkov killed himself by jumping from the fifth floor of the OGPU's Lubianka headquarters. This calls into question his repentance. Savinkov was a staunch anti-Communist and a real fighter. He might have played with his interrogators, trying to use a confession as a method of getting a moderate sentence with the hope of escaping later, and killing himself when he discovered that he had been tricked and ultimately would be put away by his captors. Most of his associates, on the other hand, were sure that he had been thrown out of the window, and that his repentance was an OGPU fake.

Suicides were quite frequent among White officers trapped on a mission in Russia. They did not fear death; they feared arrest. They knew they would die anyway, either during torture or after the tribunal's sentence. So the outcome was the same and,

■ *Above:* In the late 1920s the biggest and most publicized trial was that of the Industrial Party (*Prompartia*).

■ *Left:* Priests on trial in Baku. Members of the clergy were always regarded with great suspicion.

Savinkov, a Socialist Revolutionary, one of the most popular figures in revolutionary Russia. Both were military organizations with substantial power bases and many trained fighters (ROVS boasted about 25,000 White Army officers in France alone).

Two classic operations, *Sindikat-2* and *Trest*, were conducted following the same pattern. In the case of *Sindikat-2*, the leaders of the émigré military organizations were informed that a powerful anti-Soviet centre had been created in Soviet Russia by secret opponents of the regime, and they were invited to cooperate with it. Figures if arrested, much greater harm to the "White Cause" would follow as a result of information extracted under torture.

The most successful OGPU operation against the émigrés was *Trest*. The existence of a so-called Monarchist Organization of Central Russia (MOCR) was fabricated, with rumours that it was a strong anti-Soviet underground force inside Russia with which all the major émigré organizations could cooperate. A well-known monarchist named Iakushev was arrested by the OGPU and agreed, under pressure, to collaborate and become the leader of the mythical MOCR. This greatly enhanced the organization's credibility. To prove that it meant business and had proper connections, OGPU agents posing as part of MOCR contacted the Estonian, Polish and Finnish intelligence services and supplied them with "information" about the Red Army which, on the one hand, inflated the strength of the army, and on the other, since it seemed truthful, supported the prestige of the invented monarchist organization.

When General Kutepov became the leader of ROVS in Paris, he immediately sent agents to Russia. They were his niece Maria Zakharchenko-Shultz, a courageous woman fighter who had a distinguished World War I record and who had lost two husbands in the space of five years, and her partner, Staff Captain Radkevich. On

■ *Below:* The OGPU sent agents abroad to further the interest of the Soviet state. This is the OGPU station in China in the 1920s.

arrival they were taken care of by a team of OGPU operatives impersonating monarchists, and soon Maria reported optimistically to Paris. The OGPU aim was total control of any movements of ROVS agents in Russia, thus minimizing the risk of any terrorist operations by its fighters.

The death of Reilly

The scale and intricacy of the *Trest* operation can be judged by the story of Sidney Reilly, once a British agent and international adventurer. Reilly, born near Odessa (his real name was Zigmund Rozenblum), had taken part in the anti-Bolshevik conspiracy within Russia in 1918 organized by foreign intelligence services and diplomats, and was sentenced to death *in absentia* after he fled abroad. Later he cooperated with Savinkov, and on several occasions met British leaders to ask them to take more decisive action against Soviet Russia. In 1924 he was persuaded by Iakushev and his associates to come to Russia for consultations with MOCR. In 1925 Reilly crossed the Russo-Finnish border through a window opened by a Russian border guard officer, Toivo Viache, an ethnic Finn. Reilly met members of the Political Council of MOCR (all were OGPU agents) and informed his friends abroad by mail that his programme was being implemented successfully. Immediately after that he was taken to the OGPU headquarters in Lubianka where he was repeatedly interrogated and informed that, in accordance with the sentence of 1918, he would be shot. Reilly refused to believe this and hoped he would be exchanged. However, he was executed by a shot in the head during a walk in the park and buried in the OGPU compound.

To conceal his execution, another theatrical performance was staged at the border. Newspapers duly reported that three people were shot while trying to cross it, one of them being British agent Sidney Reilly. They also reported that Toivo Viache had been arrested for treason, tried and shot. The latter, an OGPU informer, was in reality simply transferred to another unit, and lived long afterwards under the name of Petrov.

The death of Reilly and the inactivity of the MOCR raised the suspicions of Maria Zakharchenko-Shultz, and by the spring of 1927 she had received information that Iakushev and the rest of MOCR were all OGPU. Although she and her associates escaped to Finland, Maria and two of her friends decided to return and take revenge on the OGPU for the death of Reilly and for being made the laughing-stock of the White intelligence community. They were not successful in finding Iakushev or any of the other OGPU agents who had taken part in *Trest*, so decided to place a bomb in the OGPU building. They nearly achieved this due to a lapse in the building's security system, but, after being exposed at the last moment, the terrorists had to flee. They intended to cross the border in Belorussia, but by that time a manhunt was in full swing. Local residents reported their presence and they were killed in a crossfire.

Maria's uncle, General Kutepov, was kidnapped by the OGPU in 1930. On 26 January he was walking to church when he was trapped, pushed into a car and carried off. He was injected with morphine before the kidnappers tried to fly him from Paris to Russia. Kutepov cheated them by dying of a heart attack the same night, and he was buried in the garden of a French Communist who had taken part in the kidnapping.

This operation was organized by Jacob Serebriansky, one of the most venerated Soviet secret operatives. He was recruited into the *Cheka* in 1920 by Jacob Blyumkin, the man who had killed the German Ambassador in Russia and was then secretly pardoned by Felix Dzerzhinsky. In 1923 Serebriansky joined Blumkin in the new British mandate in Palestine, where their mission was to get information about British plans in the Middle East and the local Jewish Zionist movement. When Blumkin left in 1924, Serebriansky was given an even more serious job: setting up a

network of Moscow agents in the region, including underground Zionist groups.

After directing clandestine networks in Belgium and France, he was assigned to form a secret Special Group directly subordinate to the chief of the secret service, in effect a parallel intelligence body. From 1934 onwards, the Special Group, commonly called "Yasha's Group" after Yasha (Jacob) Serebriansky, was directly subordinate to the People's Commissar of Interior Affairs, and not to the INO. It had its own agents' school teaching subversive activity, sabotage and diversions, and some of the school's graduates would be active behind German lines during World War II.

In 1931 Artusov, counter-intelligence ace, became head of the INO. His achievements included the recruiting of an agent whose codename was Francesco and whose real name is still undisclosed. This agent supplied the Russians with so many secret documents from the British Foreign Office that they filled dozens of volumes.

■ *Above:* Artur Artusov, Yagoda's deputy and a ruthless operative. He and his chief organized numerous bouts of blood-letting during their reign. He too was shot during Stalin's purges, in 1937.

CHAPTER 3

THE NKVD AND THE GREAT PURGE

There were in fact three purges carried out by Stalin in the 1930s, and the leaders of the NKVD played a crucial role in each.

The 1930s witnessed the extermination of tens of thousands of people in the Soviet Union; many more were imprisoned and exiled. All this was attributed to a power struggle in the country between Stalin's supporters and Trotskyites, although Trotsky himself had been expelled from the party in 1927 and deported in 1929. A mass extermination of victims of the regime has become, more or less, the accepted picture of the Great Purge, not only in the West but in modern Russia too.

However, it is not that simple. Information about this period is contradictory and inconsistent, derived from books put out by Nazi or post-Stalinist Russian propaganda machines, or published in the West at the height of the Cold War. The truth is different. During the period from 1934 to 1938 there were in fact three purges in succession: two that dealt with two different types of opposition and another involving those who had carried out the second of the two previous purges. Most people have the impression that the opposition to Stalin was more-or-less monolithic, that there was a struggle for democracy which united the top politicians, the military commanders and the popular masses. In reality there were several opposition groups, each with its own ideals and aspirations. The OGPU, for example, was feared

■ *Left:* Alexei Rykov speaking at a conference. In 1936–37 he was implicated in fabricated treasonous conspiracies, found guilty and shot.

and hated, but some of the opposition did not think of destroying it: they wanted it to be "their" OGPU, and not Stalin's.

Another myth of this period is that millions of people were killed as a result of the Great Purge. Some Russian and Western authors, for example, talk in terms of anything between 20 and 80 million people murdered. The absurdity of such claims is evident when one compares the rates of population growth in Russia and Western Europe. In 1913 the population of the Russian Empire (less Finland and Poland) was about 160 million, and by 1960 the Soviet population was about 208 million; that is, the growth rate was roughly 0.6 percent per annum despite the revolution, emigration, the civil war, famine and World War II. For the same period, the population growth rate in Germany, France and Great Britain was between 0.41 and 0.46 percent per annum, which is substantially lower. These caveats do not mean that a fierce power struggle in the Soviet Union was not taking place, though. From 1935 to 1940, the number of political and military prisoners in the USSR practically doubled, from 965,000 to 1,846,000, and about 500,000 were executed (the number sentenced to death was actually greater, but in many cases terms in prison or labour camps were substitutes). About seven percent of those imprisoned died in the camps before the first shots of World War II.

In 1934 the OGPU was reorganized and then renamed: it became the NKVD (acronym for the Russian People's Commissariat for Internal Affairs), headed by Genrikh Yagoda. The difference between the opposition of the 1920s and that which the NKVD had to deal in the 1930s was substantial. There was now widespread contempt and dissatisfaction among the high-echelon bureaucrats in place of the opposition from fragmented and scattered groups of dissident intellectuals during the 1920s, and the NKVD was quick to detect this.

Opponents of the regime

It is often suggested that most of the purged party and state bureaucrats and military commanders were "innocent victims". Many were, because the Bolshevik terror machine created by Lenin and Trotsky ruthlessly struck the guilty and innocent alike. But to say that the majority shot or imprisoned by the NKVD in those years were "innocent" is offensive to the memory of the dead, because it downgrades the importance of the whole underground movement that had taken shape and was growing day by day in Soviet Russia. There were many thousands of conscientious opponents to the Soviet regime, resentful of the total absence of democracy in the country and the overwhelming dominance of the bureaucratic party machine. They knew that because the Frankenstein created by Lenin and Trotsky and perfected by Stalin could not be removed by democratic means, there had to be a violent solution.

As in the 1920s, when engineers and other professionals created shadowy but deadly effective sabotage organizations, anti-Communists over a wide spectrum united to form the Right Opposition and later the Bloc of Rights. Political figures leaning to the right or preferring Trotsky to Stalin, generals dreaming of power, technocrats who rejected the discredited economic theory of

■ *Right:* Karl Radek, the editor of *Pravda*, who was convicted during the second set of show trials held in January 1937. He got off relatively lightly – receiving a 10-year jail sentence.

Leninism, and thousands of other state and cultural figures were seeking a way to overthrow the Bolshevik regime by force.

(Collectivization and the First Five-Year Plan (1928–32) had been disastrous. The plan was a grandiose programme of creating new industrial centres and modernizing existing plants and factories. The state economy was to become a single mechanism. Stalin needed millions of workers, which was attainable only by radically reducing the agrarian workforce. So industrialization was to be followed by collectivization: merger of small peasant holdings into collective farms using modern cultivation methods and machinery supplied by the state. Stalin and his supporters were sure they could find ways and means to drive the reluctant peasants into collective farms.)

Many historians claim there is no way to prove that there was a right-wing conspiracy. They are sure that most of the interrogation files between 1935 and 1938 were doctored, and that confessions were produced under torture. There is not a shadow of a doubt that many of the files were rewritten or withdrawn, and that thousands of people were beaten and deprived of sleep in order to obtain "confessions". However, throughout the main trials of that period there was only one case, that of the former diplomat Nikolai Krestinsky, when the accused stood up in front of the judges, foreign journalists and diplomats and retracted the confession he had made earlier. But his revelations had been used to incriminate his colleagues, and they did not deny their guilt, so this retraction was useless. Indeed, these colleagues defended the cause they considered just and true. The majority of the bureaucrats and even intelligence officers arrested in the Great Purge came from a Social Democratic background and had served the Bolshevik regime for almost two decades, yet some of them openly stated to their investigators and also during the trials that, to them, the restoration of capitalism in Russia was inevitable, and that they had intended to accelerate this process. Such admissions almost invited a death sentence.

But there were other reasons – racial, religious, personal and tactical – for the

■ *Below:* Stalin (centre) and his bodyguard take a stroll through Moscow. After Kirov's assassination he never walked in Moscow again.

■ *Above:* G.L. Piatakov, Deputy *Narkom* (People's Commissar) of Heavy Industry, was shot in January 1937. He had had a nervous breakdown in August 1936 when the NKVD presented its evidence against him.

trials, which have remained obscure. By 1936 there were many Jews in the top political and military echelons, and some of them, talking to each other, at times expressed the view that they would be better off if they had an enlightened Jew as their country's leader: Zinoviev, for instance. Or there were Russian nationalists, many of them anti-Semitic, who dreamt of returning to an Orthodox Mother Russia and of the total rehabilitation of the church. Nationalists in Georgia, Ukraine, Chechenia and Armenia dreamt of independence and religious freedom. Marshal Tukhachevsky nurtured the idea of becoming Russia's new Napoleon Bonaparte, and he enjoyed the support of a number of military leaders. The prosecutors and members of the court also preferred not to mention that many intellectuals hoped an anti-Stalinist coup could finally bring back democracy, or that millions of ordinary people, tired of misery, poverty and persecution, were anti-Communist.

Five trials shook the USSR in the period from 1936 to 1938. The first was of the Trotskyite-Zinoviev Bloc in August 1936, which ended with relatively moderate prison sentences for the six accused, including Zinoviev (who was expelled from the party

three times) and Lev Kamenev himself, Lenin's one-time associates and party colleagues. The second, in January 1937, was much more dramatic. Thirteen people were sentenced to death, including party veterans G.L. Piatakov, G. Sokolnikov and Trotsky's old friend General Muralov, while Karl Radek, ex-editor of *Pravda*, and three others were sentenced to 10 years. Then there was the Special Military Tribunal of the Supreme Court in June 1937, at which eight prominent army commanders, including Marshal Tukhachevsky, were sentenced to death for treason (one of the accused committed suicide before he could be shot). Soon after, in August, Zinoviev and Kamenev were re-tried with 14 other people, and all were sentenced to death and shot. Finally, the fifth trial took place in March 1938 of 22 famous political figures in the state. These included Nikolai Bukharin, former editor of *Izvestia*, former premier Alexei Rykov, and diplomats Krestinsky and C.G. Rakovsky. But there were also some figures among the defendants who had been on the other side of the dock during the very first trial: Genrikh Yagoda, head of the secret service, and his henchmen. Following these show trials, there were many other, less high-profile trials in Georgia, Siberia, Ukraine and even Vladivostok. Sentences were passed on dozens, then hundreds, then thousands…

The Trotskyite bloc?

The people tried were not – could not be – all Trotskyites, although the main figures were undoubtedly cooperating with Trotsky and his emissaries abroad. They *were* inclined to support the Trotskyite camp simply because it was the most powerful agglomeration of political forces, an alternative centre of power capable of overturning the ruling regime. But it was very convenient for Stalin to later label them all and execute many as Trotskyites, since he did not want to recognize that 20 years after the October coup there were millions of citizens in the country, and many thousands among the top-echelon politicians, economists and cultural figures, who rejected Communism and wanted the country back on the path of capitalist development.

The paradox of the situation was that the people who had laid the foundation of the police state long before Stalin came to power, and who had created a unique repression machine used to humiliate, intimidate, persecute and shoot the people that were the cream of the crop of their country, ultimately became the victims of this very machine. The regime the Bolsheviks created did not tolerate any dissent. Stalin and those surrounding him truly believed that repression was the only method of survival for their Communist society, and it was this belief which made it possible for party bureaucrats at all levels to morally – and then physically – destroy every person who posed a threat to their authority.

Some historians state that Stalin and the NKVD were the killers, but in essence it was the regime that killed people. Neither Stalin nor the NKVD bosses could give the judges the order to sentence people to death for their beliefs. But the judges had to justify their comfortable existence, and they played according to the rules set earlier by the Bolsheviks. As for the bureaucrats, the purge cleared the way to more power and higher positions for those who were left.

In the 1930s the judicial body most often used was the so-called *troika* (trio). It was not an innovation – the *troikas* had been in action during the first years of the Bolshevik rule. Their reappearance now was a clear indicator of the return to mass terror. *Troikas* were quickly formed in every *oblast* (province) of Russia following a secret party directive issued in November 1936. They consisted of the local NKVD chief, a party bureaucrat (a secretary of an *oblast*) and a prosecutor. Another harking back to revolutionary times was the employment of the so-called Special Council (*Osoboe Soveshchanie*), which was also a non-judicial body. Similar to the *Cheka* Collegium that sentenced people to death without any trial, the Special Council created in 1934 tried about 450,000 people, and issued about 10,000 death sentences.

Troikas had the power to issue death sentences, and the initiative to use it usually came from party mandarins. In addition to NKVD officers, Nikita Khrushchev, Leonid Brezhnev (who worked under Khrushchev in the Ukraine) and hundreds of other party apparatchiks signed long lists of "enemies" to be shot immediately. Every area had its own quota of death sentences, and it is known that some party leaders – Khrushchev for one – repeatedly asked the NKVD to increase the quotas in the areas they were responsible for. After all, that showed what pure Communists they were. In 1936, when the flywheel of repression

■ *Below:* **Lev Kamenev (left), the former chairman of the Moscow Soviet, was accused of assisting in the death of Kirov. He was shot in August 1936. Nikolai Bukharin (centre), editor of *Izvestia*, was arrested in 1937 for being a "Trotskyite". He was shot in March 1938. Sergei Kirov (right), loyal party boss in Leningrad. His assassination in December 1934 was seen by Stalin as confirming the existence of a widespread Trotskyite conspiracy against him and his supporters. Stalin thus launched the Great Purge to destroy the conspiracy.**

was still gaining momentum, Khrushchev, who at that time headed the Moscow party organization, complained at a conference: "Only 308 people have been arrested. It needs to be said … 308 people for our Moscow organization is not many." In the period of the major trials of the Trotskyites, Khrushchev was more eloquent and theatrical: "We need to destroy these scoundrels … we need our hand not to shake, we need to step over the corpses of the enemies for the benefit of the people." He had to step over many corpses. By 1938, almost all the secretaries of the Moscow *Oblast* and city committees had been arrested, and only three were not subsequently executed or imprisoned, while 136 out of 146 regional and town committee secretaries and thousands of political, scientific and cultural figures were also arrested on his orders.

But was Moscow a special case? Alas, Khrushchev behaved like that in the Ukraine as well. When he was appointed the first secretary of the Ukrainian Communist Party, he was helped there by the NKVD chief, Uspensky, who had also been with him in Moscow. In 1938, when the terrible two years of mass repressions were almost over, he complained to Stalin: "The Ukraine sends

out 17,000 to 18,000 of the repressed every month, while Moscow approves not more than 2000 to 3000. Please take urgent measures." Only three people out of the Central Committee of the Ukraine – and it numbered 100 members – were not arrested. Incidentally, Khrushchev was probably the only member of the Political Bureau who interrogated the accused in Uspensky's office.

When the main organizers of the Great Purge were themselves brought to heel, Uspensky panicked, stole a number of blank passports, staged his own death by drowning and ran away. But he was spotted by an NKVD patrol in Siberia, and surrendered. Accused of many crimes, he insisted he had just obeyed Khrushchev's orders, but he was shot anyway. His wife, who was as friendly with the Khrushchevs as Uspensky himself, was sentenced to death for helping her husband run away. She pleaded for clemency, only for Khrushchev to recommend that the Supreme Soviet reject the plea. She probably knew too much, and Khrushchev wanted to get rid of a harmful witness.

The purge starts: the first wave

The first purge was of the political opposition inside the party. In January 1934 the 17th Congress of the Communist Party (Bolshevik) was to take place, and the anti-Stalinist opposition, especially the functionaries and bureaucrats who supported the exiled Trotsky, and the associates of Lenin's former colleagues Zinoviev, Nikolai Bukharin, Piatakov and their groups, were prepared to put up a fight.

They had time to prepare for it. For over two years their local supporters re-shuffled local party functionaries and appointed their people to key positions in order to ensure favourable representation. On the eve of the congress they started to spread rumours that the majority of the delegates wished to replace Stalin with Sergei Kirov, an old revolutionary, a member of the Political Bureau and the secretary of the Leningrad Committee, and many delegates were secretly asked to strike the

■ *Right:* Nikolai Yezhov, People's Commissar of Internal Affairs, who organized the Great Purge. A particularly unpleasant character, his nicknames included "Dwarf" and "Crawler". He was shot in 1939.

But Stalin outwitted the plotters. Instead of arresting the opposition leaders before the party congress, which would have resulted in public outrage, the NKVD arrested their most active supporters and organizers of unauthorized rallies. The base of the opposition vanished. Stalin threatened to resign, and the party bureaucrats, afraid of losing their jobs, were deeply concerned. Besides, Stalin enjoyed the full support of some popular men in the party, and also medium-level party apparatchiks and industrial managers whose aid was now important. So Stalin was triumphant at the congress, and the plotters were removed from their posts and exiled. Their hopes for a peaceful transition of power into their hands were doomed. Now they listened to more radical elements in the opposition, who talked about the seizure of power. They were ready to cooperate with Trotsky and most of his devoted followers, as well as any adventurers who might side with him in this dangerous political gamble. They accepted that a *coup d'état* was the only solution, and it came very close to being carried out.

The assassination of Kirov

The first mistake, however, was when the opposition allowed – and in fact encouraged – the assassination in Leningrad of one of the major figures in the Soviet Government, Sergei Mironovich Kirov. The latter was immensely popular in both the party and the state, and enjoyed Stalin's full support and confidence. He was assassinated by one Leonid Nikolaev.

There are many myths associated with Kirov's murder. One of them is that the assassination was organized by Stalin's agents because the Soviet leader abhorred any political competition. But Kirov, despite the rumours, never tried to replace Stalin. He was a loyal Stalinist, his unswerving lieutenant, and had played a principal part in routing the party opposition in Leningrad. He became the loyal "vassal lord" in Leningrad, where Zinoviev had formerly been a more-or-less

■ *Above:* **Genrikh Yagoda (left) with Khrushchev in 1935. Yagoda, head of the NKVD, organized the first show trials in August 1936. A year later he was accused of being a member of a "Trotskyite" conspiracy intent on mounting a coup against the regime. He was shot in March 1938.**

name of Stalin from the list of candidates for the Central Committee. Some of them did just that.

This was instigated by Zinoviev, former leader of the Comintern, Kamenev, former member of the Political Bureau of the Central Committee, and their associates. They were only superficially Trotskyites, and in the 1920s had in fact joined forces with Stalin to oust Trotsky. But they knew Trotsky's growing popularity among the intellectuals. His dreadful acts during the Red Terror and mass executions after the Kronstadt rebellion were long forgotten; he was an exiled underdog, and people always support such figures. Besides, he hated Stalin and promised his support to get rid of him and his "bureaucratic party regime".

independent feudal ruler. Another myth is that Nikolaev's wife Milda Draule, a waitress in the party committee headquarters, was Kirov's lover, and her jealous husband took revenge for his broken marriage. It is true that Kirov had enjoyed a wide range of female companions in Leningrad and Moscow, but Nikolaev's act was first and foremost political. He was an active opposition member, though previously employed in the party and even having had connections with the local OGPU. Milda Draule and some of her friends were also involved in the opposition movement and, reportedly, in a Latvian intelligence operation in Russia. When on trial before the Military Collegium of the Supreme Court, Nikolaev openly stated: "When I shot Kirov, I reasoned as follows: our shot must be a signal for an explosion, a revolt within the country, against the Communist Party of the Soviet Union and against the Soviet Government." Yet, jealousy might also have been a driving force, and Kirov's enemies undoubtedly used this angle afterwards in order to present the murder as being purely personally motivated.

Assassination attempts

After the assassination of Kirov a group of Trotskyites was arrested, to a certain degree randomly, resulting in the stunning revelation that Leonid Nikolaev had already been picked up on an earlier occasion by OGPU agents in Leningrad. They found on him a gun and a chart showing the route that Kirov travelled daily, but Zaporozhets, assistant chief of the Leningrad OGPU, let him go.

It was not the first time that attempts were made on the lives of Communist leaders in the 1930s. An assassin called Bogdan, from a Trotskyite group, tried to shoot Stalin at an important party conference in Moscow in May 1934, but was unable to get close enough to him. Bogdan was liquidated the next day by a Trotskyite hitman called Bakayev. Another attempt was made when Stalin was passing in a motorboat along the Black Sea shore. This time several shots were

fired by high-powered rifles, but missed. An attempt was also made on the lives of Stalin's close associates Vyacheslav Molotov and Kliment Voroshilov.

The killing of Kirov, who had helped Stalin retain his position as the party's general secretary after the 17th Congress, was the culmination of the violence instigated by radical opposition, and expressly encouraged by Trotsky. This time Stalin reacted by letting all his dogs off the leash. The OGPU started a wide-scale campaign of arrest and interrogation. Nikolaev, his family, Milda

**■ Above:
Reichswehr
commander Hans
von Seeckt (right,
with General
Werner Blomberg)
helped
Tukhachevsky form
a pro-German
clique within the
Soviet General
Staff.**

Draule and even her mother were executed, and that was just the beginning. Some 240 intellectuals were arrested by the OGPU in seven major cities of the Soviet Union and secretly tried by the military section of the Supreme Court. The defendants were not allowed legal assistance or to collect witnesses for their defence. About half were sentenced to death, their appeals for clemency having been abrogated in advance.

Most historians claim that Stalin used the pretext of Kirov's death to drive the last nail into the coffin of the political opposition inside the party. A group of old Bolsheviks, including Zinoviev, Kamenev, Evdokimov and Safarov, was arrested, accused at first of moral responsibility for Nikolaev's act, but later executed due to "incriminating evidence". The men who organized their trial were Genrikh Yagoda and his assistant Nikolai Yezhov (the latter kept the bullets that killed Zinoviev and Kamenev as personal souvenirs). But the documents and witness reports of this trial, as well as those of subsequent trials, give an entirely different picture. They show that secret service chief Yagoda had a hand in Kirov's murder and was closely associated with the radical opposition.

Genrikh Yagoda

Yagoda's real name was Enoch Yehuda. He was born in 1891 in the city of Rybinsk to the family of a craftsman. Second cousin of Jacob Sverdlov, Lenin's closest associate, Yagoda joined the Russian Social Democratic Workers' Party in 1907. He was a friend of the great Russian writer Gorky. After taking part in Lenin's October 1917 coup, he held important positions in the Bolshevik government, and became a member of the *Cheka* Collegium. He had been "one of the most reliable *Cheka* operatives", according to Felix Dzerzhinsky. After the death of Menzhinsky he became the chief of the secret service and started to improve the punitive machine. He created investigation units working on Western lines. When the OGPU disappeared and the People's Commissariat of Internal Affairs (NKVD) filled its place,

Genrikh Yagoda became *narkom* (acronym of *narodny comissar* – people's commissar) in the summer of 1934.

He was head of the secret service for only two years, but in that time he achieved much. He created the industrial empire of the NKVD, using the slave labour of prisoners. The empire was controlled and managed by his close friends, who built factories, bridges and even the White Sea–Baltic Canal, constructed at the price of about 90,000 lives. He established an NKVD laboratory to perfect methods for secretly murdering people by using chemicals, poisons and special devices. A *bon vivant* who enjoyed life immensely, he had a mansion in the centre of Moscow with a private swimming pool, enjoyed diverse female company, gambling and expensive restaurants. All this required a lot of money, which he got from the accounts of people held in detention.

In 1936 Yagoda was arrested, together with several army generals and secret service officials, for conspiring against the government and organizing the assassination of Sergei Kirov. He was also accused of high treason, spying for an imperialist state, killing Alexei Peshkov, the son of Gorky, and attempting to kill Yezhov, the man who was to succeed him. Yezhov had learned about Yagoda's role in Kirov's assassination, and Yagoda's secretary, Bulanov, then allegedly

■ *Left:* General Gamarnik, close associate of Tukhachevsky, committed suicide in May 1937, knowing that he was likely to be arrested and charged with conspiring with the Germans.

sprayed Yezhov's study with a powerful poison. During his trial Yagoda confessed to all these crimes except to being the main organizer of Kirov's murder and being a spy; these things he absolutely denied. Both he and his secretary were shot in 1938.

For historians, Yagoda has always been a mystery. They do not understand why he eradicated anything that could be associated with the White movement if he was not a Communist, and why he destroyed the opposition's main figures in the party if he was a Trotskyite himself. But these phenomena are not difficult to explain. Putting an end to the White movement, something that all of Russia's new élite had cause to fear, made the reinstallation of monarchic rule impossible. As for the main opposition figures in Russia, he staged the first trial in such a way that they were only sentenced to 3- to 10-year terms of imprisonment. That indicated to the rest of the opposition figures that he was not against them, but rather was saving their leaders from being shot. He supported the eradication of the main Stalinist vassals. When Nikolaev was first arrested by the Leningrad OGPU, it was Yagoda who instructed his appointee Zaporozhets to set him free. Holding all the threads of the web in his hands, he was not afraid of being implicated.

Yagoda's aim

The arrest and trial of the political opposition played into his hands, as it further aroused anti-Communist circles. The reason was that neither Yagoda nor his friends in the state bureaucracy and in the army wanted the Communist regime to continue. They were not essentially Trotsky-ites because the last thing they wished to was to replace one Communist fanatic with another. They were prepared to use the name and political influence of the Trotskyites against Stalin and the Stalinists, but if their coup had been successful they would have steered the state firmly towards capitalism.

Yagoda ultimately wanted be the USSR's leader himself, or at least the People's Commissar of Defence and the NKVD, with the reformist Alexei Rykov as the leader of a drastically reorganized Socialist Party. It is doubtful whether Trotsky would ever have been permitted to come back to Russia. Yagoda did not want this troublemaker to start a new power struggle, but *was* prepared to use him in negotiations with Japan and Germany, countries which favoured the exiled leader. Then, gradually, the Communist economy would be dismantled. As for the political structure, Yagoda wanted it to be modelled on that of Nazi Germany.

Uniformed conspirators

Those who study the history of Russia are often sceptical when they read about Soviet generals of the 1930s who were accused of being pro-German and pro-Fascist, especially since many of the accused generals and officers were Jewish. They forget, though, that the collaboration of Russian commanders with Hitler and the German Army started well before *Kristallnacht* (Crystal Night, 9 November 1938, a Nazi-organized pogrom against Jewish properties throughout Germany) and the confiscation of Jewish assets in 1938. In fact, its roots were in the 1920s when Soviet commanders were courting their German colleagues on instructions from Trotsky and his close friends.

"The Tukhachevsky affair shook me," wrote Colonel Gorlin. "I did not know how to take it. I could not believe what I heard, and yet there were hundreds of documents that supported the version that Tukha-chevsky, Deputy *Narkom* of Defence, and another deputy, Gamarnik, who was in charge of the Political Directorate, clandestinely cooperated with the Nazis. I also could not believe that General Kork, whom I knew personally and met many times, had secret relations with the German military. At the end of 1938 in Lubianka (headquarters) I ran across Amayak Kobulov, a young NKVD high-flyer whom I knew from the beginning of his career in the Georgian secret service, and, when I learned that he was being prepared for posting to Germany, asked his opinion about the coup of the generals. He seemed to be confident they had been deeply involved in Yagoda's and Trotsky's plot. 'There were two main reasons why,' he told me. 'Firstly, they wanted to run the country without commissars. Secondly, they had been involved with the Germans before the days of the Nazis, and when Hitler came to power Gamarnik and Feldman thought they could help Jewry in Germany and Europe if they managed to gain power in Russia, because they could then talk to Hitler as equals.' This made me view the whole affair in a different light."

It is hard to imagine today how popular Germans became in the Soviet Union from the mid-1920s onwards. By the middle of 1925, when Stalin was still a long way from being absolute master of the country or even its army and security service, 120 German pilots and an unknown number of ground technicians were trained at a military aviation school in Lipetsk. At least 30 German officers had been trained at a tank school near Kazan. Some German tank designs were tested there too, because the Treaty of Versailles did not allow Germans to have their own tank troops. Germans were trained near Samara to wage chemical warfare by dispersing poison gas from aircraft, and new chemical mines and grenades were also tested there. Meanwhile, 19 senior officers of the Red Army, including General Yakir, were instructed at special courses run by the German General Staff, and Uborevich, one of the generals tried and executed in 1937, studied there for a whole year. Kork used to be a military attaché in Berlin. Around half of the Revolutionary War Council in the 1920s had permanent contacts with the *Reichswehr* (German

■ *Below:* The writer Maksim Gorky, who died in 1936. Yagoda ordered the killing of his son, Alexei Peshkov, and stated at his trial in 1938 that he had also ordered Gorky's death.

Army), initiated by Trotsky himself, and Tukhachevsky, at that time the Chief of Staff, was a frequent visitor to Berlin. The training given to German officers was extremely useful: according to German sources, at least 20 German pilots who trained at Lipetsk and 10 tank officers who trained at Kazan became *Luftwaffe* (German Air Force) or *Heer* (Nazi German Army) generals.

The Soviet commanders who cooperated with the German General Staff and visited Germany on a number of occasions were fascinated by its growing military machine and the reception they received. This admiration of German militarism and the Third Reich led to multiple acts of treason during World War II. General Vlasov, a Soviet commander who went to Germany

■ *Below:* Yagoda's folly – the White Sea–Baltic Canal, which was constructed at a cost of around 90,000 lives. It was useless, being too narrow for ocean-going vessels.

twice in the 1930s, defected to the Germans after his field army was routed in 1942. He then created the Russian Liberation Army (ROA) at the end of the war (see Chapter 5).

Tukhachevsky's closest associate, General Putna, who had served as a military attaché in Berlin, London and Tokyo, was reportedly pro-German, and General Gamarnik was a personal friend of the *Reichswehr* commanders von Seeckt and Hammerstein. These people helped Tukhachevsky to form an active and highly influential pro-German clique within the Soviet General Staff, military intelligence and, later, with the help of Yagoda, even in the NKVD. Hitler's coming to power made little difference, since Tukhachevsky and his main supporters had already been deeply involved with the *Reichswehr*. Also, once Trotsky, the symbol of anti-Soviet opposition, was in league with the *Reichswehr*, they had to play by his rules.

For more evidence implicating Marshal Tukhachevsky we must go back to 1936. That year the marshal went to Great Britain as Soviet military representative at the state funeral of King George V. *En route* he made a stopover in Warsaw, and another in Berlin. While attending a formal dinner at the Soviet Embassy in Paris, he astounded diplomats from many countries by attacking the Soviet proposals for collective security measures in Europe. Talking to Nicholas Titulescu, the Foreign Minister of Romania, he said: "*Monsieur le Ministre*, you are wrong in linking your career and the fate of your country to countries that are old and worn out, such as Great Britain and France. It is to the new Germany that we should turn. For a certain time, at least, Germany will be the country that will take the lead in the European continent. I am sure that Hitler will help to save us all." At another banquet, discussing the air pact between the great powers and Nazi Germany with French political journalist Genevieve Tabouis, Tukhachevsky said of Hitler's army: "They are already invincible, Madame Tabouis!" Finally, there is what

■ *Left:* Nikolai Vasilyevich Krylenko, Public Prosecutor and Commissar of Justice. He himself was tried in 1938, found guilty and shot.

■ *Above:* "Uncle Joe" Stalin in jovial mood. The Great Purge removed all opposition to his autocratic rule.

French journalist Alexander Werth wrote in his book *Moscow 41*: "People of the French Deuxième Bureau told me long ago that Tukhachevsky was pro-German. And the Czechs told me the extraordinary story of Tukhachevsky's visit to Prague when, towards the end of a banquet – he had got rather drunk – he blurted out that an agreement with Hitler was the only hope for both Czechoslovakia and Russia."

Tukhachevsky must have been extremely confident in his friends in the NKVD and the army to make such statements in those turbulent times, especially after the assassination of Kirov and the first Trotskyite trial. But, as some historians observe, the marshal was also probably convinced that the hour was at hand when Stalin's regime would crumble, either as a result of internal strife or foreign aggression. At any rate, what Tukhachevsky was counting on was a future alliance between Germany, Russia and Japan, and a new militaristic order in Eurasia.

These ideas were in total conformity with the hopes and aspirations of Trotsky, who openly declared that the Nazis' coming to power had radically changed the situation and meant an imminent war that would bring about the defeat of the Soviet Union and, consequently, the triumph of the Trotskyite bloc in the entire Soviet empire. It

came out during the trials that Trotsky instructed his associates in Russia to build a power base in both the cities and villages, and to create a vast organization in the Red Army so that at the decisive moment strategic points could be seized. That was not an impossible aspiration. In 1930, for example, more than 4500 officers in the Red Army were still from the former tsarist officer corps, and although many of them were purged by Tukhachevsky himself, the personnel department retained and protected those who were personally loyal to top Red Army commanders. As for the soldiers themselves, since most of them were from rural areas, and hence naturally conservative, there was no doubt a great proportion would support opponents of the regime.

However, as much as Trotsky needed Tukhachevsky, he called him an adventurer and an excessively ambitious person, and ordered his supporters to organize the coup in such a way that, although Tukhachevsky would receive all the required help, he would not be able to subjugate the new government to his control. Bukharin, another opposition leader, concurred: "Tukhachevsky is a potential little Napoleon – and you know how Napoleon dealt with the so-called ideologists!"

The trials disclosed that there were substantial sums received by the Trotskyites from foreign donors: former diplomat Krestinsky confessed that some financial support even came from the German military. The *Reichswehr* was paying for the training of German officers in Russian instruction centres, and these funds were then redirected to opposition organizations in the state and army. Piatakov, Deputy *Narkom* of Heavy Industry, on Trotsky's instructions placed some orders with certain German companies that agreed to transfer a part of the received payment to Trotsky's organizations. Yagoda and his secretary, Bulanov, confessed that some money from the "secret packages" of the NKVD, i.e. special funds for financing illegal agents abroad, were also transferred to the opposition groups.

Myths of the Great Purge

It is usually claimed that Stalin destroyed the generals because they were too popular among his compatriots and he did not tolerate any competition, that the execution of these military commanders drastically undermined Soviet military capabilities, and that the executions were inspired by Lavrenty Beria, Stalin's henchman. The facts do not support this. At the time the First Purge started Beria was still the First Party Secretary in Georgia, and the military commanders were well outside his jurisdiction.

Were the generals popular? Yes and no. They were as popular as the media wanted them to be, but as far as the common people were concerned the Soviet generals of the 1930s were the same October Revolution upstarts, guilty of killing thousands of innocent people in the Red Army's punitive actions in rural areas, first and foremost servants of the Bolsheviks. We already know what role Tukhachevsky played in the suppression of the Kronstadt rebellion. He was even more bloodthirsty in Tambov Province, where he ordered the massacre of rebellious peasants. He told his troops to take hostages and shoot them publicly if the initiators of the mutiny were not turned in. He used artillery, poison gas

and machine guns against civilians, and sent his cavalry to charge down and sabre those who fled. These things must be remembered when anyone expresses grief over his court-martial sentence.

As to whether their arrest and execution undermined the defence of the USSR, these people were either military commanders with limited combat experience acquired in the civil war, or commissars who stood behind commanders with cocked Nagant revolvers, who later found their way to the very top. Many of them were NKVD generals with dubious records, like Frinovsky who was Yezhov's assistant. As for Marshal Blukher, Commander of the Far Eastern Military District: when the Russians were engaged in a relatively minor military confrontation with the Japanese in 1938 at Lake Khasan, his troops suffered heavy casualties due to utter disorganization and terrible combat support. Save for his political affiliations, he would have been tried by a military tribunal for his appalling incompetence.

Military incompetents

If Tukhachevsky, their leader, was the best of them, then the rest were totally worthless. In the Russo-Polish War (1919–20) Tukhachevsky had been mauled by Marshal Pilsudski. He also advocated the production of two categories of weapons which suffered the heaviest losses when World War II started: light tanks instead of medium and heavy tanks, and slow-flying heavy bombers instead of fighters and ground-attack aircraft. He was also against producing submachine guns. It was he who instigated the first purge of the military in 1930 when the ranks were "cleansed" of the officers who actually created the Red Army: the former tsarist officers and military technicians.

The number of officers arrested was significant but much less than is claimed. In 1937–38 more than 25,000 officers were expelled from the army for association with the conspirators and later arrested or exiled, but at least 11,000 of those sent into retirement were rehabilitated. Some of those arrested, who had been fortunate enough not to be sentenced to death at the height of the Purge, were set free and even restored to the army. The number sentenced to death and shot in 1938–40 was about 700. The Purge hardly touched young officers, who were well educated and highly trained. The most vulnerable group included those who served under the conspirators' direct command and were promoted by them to command positions. These were mainly senior officers who were, due to the lower standards of military education in earlier times, less suited to mechanized warfare.

Regarding the intelligence services, they had mostly well-educated and experienced personnel at all levels. Each day Stalin and some other members of the Political Bureau received intelligence and counter-intelligence information from the OGPU/NKVD and the military intelligence service, and on a number of occasions commended them. There was a special department created in the secret service for the protection of the party and state leaders, especially members of the Political Bureau, military commanders and scientists. They were assigned personal guards, servants from the secret service personnel and armoured cars. But all these measures could work only when the secret service was loyal to the regime. The way it developed from the early 1930s meant that this was not the case.

Genrikh Yagoda created an NKVD which was almost entirely loyal to him personally. Nearly all the most important NKVD officials, including the chiefs of departments in the main headquarters, provincial and regional administrations and labour camp directorates, were Jewish, and were either related to him or his friends, or to his long-time acquaintances. His first deputy was Yakov Agranov (Sorenzen), whom Yagoda knew had a criminal past. He used this knowledge to control him, as he did the head of the Special Department,

■ *Below:* Yagoda's NKVD controlled a vast empire of prison labour, which was ruthlessly mobilized to support Stalin's industrialization policy.

Miron Gai, and head of the Foreign Department (INO), Arkady Slutsky. Yagoda had an opportunity to use this huge operational and punitive machine for his own purposes, and for the sake of the Trotskyite opposition. He employed it, as he later confessed, to kill his – and Trotsky's – political enemies as well. He protected officers of the army and secret service who were plotting against the regime and formed several clandestine organizations.

Within military intelligence Yagoda's network was controlled by the counter-intelligence ace Artur Artusov, who migrated there from the OGPU on Yagoda's recommendation, and his close associate Shteinbruk. After Yagoda's downfall, Artusov was tried and sentenced to death after being accused of working for several military intelligence services at the same time, but mainly for the Germans. During the investigation he even confessed to working for the British intelligence service, but that could have been a tactical manoeuvre to distract attention. Many recent publications insist that Artusov was an innocent victim. Investigations,

interrogations and trials in those years were certainly illegal, and the truth is buried together with Artusov, who was shot in 1937. But it would be wrong to discard the possibility that he was an active opponent of the regime. During his interrogations he admitted that he had become Yagoda's main courier, and had delivered secret packages from Yagoda to the French premier Pierre Laval and British prime minister Ramsay MacDonald, and also letters from them to Yagoda. Artusov was well aware of the plot and its goals. He knew, and obviously approved of, plans to restore foreign concessions and convertible Russian currency, abolish entry and exit visas for foreigners, introduce real freedom of speech and political activity, and allow free choice of land use, enabling collective farms to revert to private ownership.

But he also knew the methods by which these goals were to be achieved. He said during interrogation: "In one of the conversations with Yagoda, replying to my question of who was his contact providing his communication with the Germans, Yagoda said it was Radek. According to

■ **Below:** During the 1930s the NKVD used spies to establish links with senior Nazi figures, such as Alfred Rosenberg (centre), Nazi ideologist.

Yagoda – and later, when I established contact with Radek, also according to Radek himself – the latter maintained contact in Moscow with an old German spy, Hilger, and through him, with the famous leader of the overseas department of the Nazi Party [Alfred] Rosenberg. Radek said he had made this contact soon after Hitler came to power [January 1933]. The goal of the conspirators was to establish the kind of relations between Germany and the USSR that would make the Germans give up the idea of attacking the Soviet Union after power had been seized by the conspirators. Hitler agreed to that, though on condition that the Germans living in the USSR would enjoy the right of ex-territoriality, German industrialists would have the opportunity to get concessions, and we would not oppose the *Wehrmacht* occupying Lithuania, Latvia and Estonia. If all these conditions were met, Hitler even promised to help the anti-Soviet plot."

When Artusov, head of the NKVD's INO, migrated to the Military Intelligence (*Razvedupr*), he took with him about 30 people. Almost all of them were arrested following his detention, and only a few stayed out of the labour camps. He was succeeded in the INO by Arkady Slutsky, a venerated intelligence officer famous for two important operations of industrial espionage in Sweden: the secrets of how to produce modern windings and lamination for electric motors, and how to produce ball-bearings. A former vice-chairman of the revolutionary tribunal in Turkestan who "distinguished" himself by organizing the repression of local nationalists, he was reportedly killed in 1938 in the study of Yagoda's successor, Yezhov, by deadly injection. The new chief of the INO, Zelman Passov, did not stay in this chair long either. A political schemer and favourite of Yagoda, he decided to outlive his promoter and started to report on and slander his own friends and even agents working abroad. Some of those with whom he maintained family links were shot as a

result of his reports. But soon this role in the repression of innocent people was revealed, and he in turn was tried and executed. His deputy, an outstandingly talented agent called Sergei Shpihelglas, who had a lobster shop in Paris in the early 1930s as a cover for an exceptionally effective spy network, was tried alongside Passov. Another top-class intelligence commander, already mentioned, Jakob Serebriansky, was also arrested and brutally interrogated. Serebriansky, unlike many others, survived the 1930s Great Purge, only to be arrested again in the 1953 purge.

This is what Colonel Chernov wrote in his notes: "I know for sure that some of the intelligence and counter-intelligence officers of Jewish background, who were arrested and sentenced to long terms, were

■ *Above:* Marshal Blukher (third from left) photographed during the Civil War. He was purged along with Tukhachevsky in 1938. An incompetent, he had been saved from an earlier court-martial by political contacts.

not as innocent as some people think: they were part of the coup, or at least knew about the plans of their superiors or friends to overthrow the regime and establish a state friendly with Nazi Germany. But in 1939 Beria declared to Stalin that he wanted to set some of them free. Stalin was astounded. 'Why you should do that?' he asked angrily. 'They can't have any illusions about Hitler, now that he has started his open offensive on Jewry,' Beria answered. 'And they are professionals. I need professionals more than ever. If I set them free we shall get the people who will be the most loyal to us and have nothing to lose.' Cynical though it was, it saved the lives of many top-class intelligence officers."

The sweep through the army and OGPU involved many secret agents and *seksots* as well. One was Natalia Sats, an actress and charming woman, second wife of the late People's Commissar of Culture Lunacharsky. Living in luxury (Lunacharsky robbed palaces and stately homes to make a nest for his much younger partner), she socialized with foreigners and dignitaries and frequently went abroad – all on OGPU assignments. When her husband died Yagoda made her his personal courier and messenger. With the beginning of the Great Purge, when Yagoda's fate was sealed, she tried to save herself by marrying a famous polar explorer, Otto Shmidt. But he reported her to the OGPU as a Trotskyite and a foreign agent right on the eve of the wedding ceremony. She did not die, though: she spent a long time in exile. After being miraculously rehabilitated in Khrushchev's time and elevated in Gorbachev's era, she returned to the stage and became director of the Children's Theatre in Moscow.

Finale of the Great Purge

There is no doubt that an anti-Soviet movement existed, was many branched and enjoyed enormous support from abroad. But how many were in it we shall never know because the finale of the Great Purge was both tragic and farcical at the same

time: people were arrested because there were scheduled regional quotas passed down from the new secret service boss, Yezhov, and approved of in most cases by the Political Bureau and sometimes by the Central Committee of the party. To be related to an imprisoned or suspected "enemy of the state", to have involvement in any project alongside confirmed Trotskyites, and even making anti-government jokes and "politically incorrect statements" was sufficient for a long prison term. Colonel Gorlin wrote: "The Georgian *Narkom* of Internal Affairs, Sergei Goglidze, an honest officer who came to this post from the frontier and special guards forces, was astounded when he received from Yezhov a quota of about 5000 people to be repressed,

■ *Above:* The Soviet agent and actress Natalia Sats. Accused of being a Trotskyite and foreign agent, she actually survived the Great Purge and was rehabilitated by Khrushchev.

with over 1000 to be shot. He convened all the heads of the departments and told them to be extremely meticulous in investigating every case. Unfortunately those were times when just one word meant a long prison sentence. I remember when he discussed with me a case of a famous Georgian academic who, surrounded by his best friends at a party in early 1937, pronounced a toast to 'the liberator of the Transcaucasian peoples, our Adolf Hitler'. Two people reported him, not just one, and there was nothing Goglidze could do. The man was sent to a Siberian labour camp for many years.

"After Beria replaced Yezhov as the People's Commissar of Internal Affairs, he assigned Goglidze to be head of the Leningrad Directorate of the NKVD. Goglidze started with the cases of several middle-echelon functionaries, and discovered that many were either obviously faked or inflated. He fired about half of the investigators, all inspectors and all heads of departments appointed by Yezhov. He knew what sort of man Yezhov was."

Nikolai Yezhov

The Yezhov mechanism of repression was one by which the arrested accused themselves, spurred on by torture and blackmail. The interrogators warned the accused that their relatives, even small children, would be exiled to areas where survival was virtually impossible. "You won't save yourself and you will kill them" – that was the universally used formula. Combined with acute physical suffering, that left only one way out: to confess to crimes never committed and be either shot or sent to a labour camp as soon as possible.

The man in charge of this regime, Nikolai Yezhov, was born in 1895. According to one version he was the son of a metal moulder, and according to another he was an orphan adopted by the Yezhovs. It was said he was originally from a Polish family (he spoke Polish and Lithuanian from childhood). He finished only one form of the junior school, and then worked as a tailor and at odd jobs. He entered the Bolshevik Party in 1917, became a military commissar, and progressed to be secretary of the Central Committee.

When Yagoda was arrested in 1936, Yezhov was pushed forward by Moskvin, an important man in the Soviet Inspectorate Committee and one of the most dreaded figures in the history of post-revolutionary Russia, since after the October coup he was in charge of the persecution of "ideological enemies". Yezhov sold out his patron, though, by sending him to the shooting stake in 1937.

The terror of the "Dwarf"

Yezhov, popularly nicknamed Dwarf and Crawler (he was lame and only 1.51m [4.95ft] tall), with his eternal sarcastic grin, envious and cruel, was even more hated than Yagoda. He allowed NKVD officers to use torture officially. He gained fame as an anti-Semite although he was married to a Jewish woman. He took part in interrogations and executions, and seemingly enjoyed it all. He created an entirely new type of "apparat": an assemblage of bone-breakers who were expected to use any means to get confessions, and who claimed a rate for solving crimes of about 100 percent.

In 1937 Yezhov arrested almost the whole counter-intelligence service, then military intelligence, and was about to finish off the intelligence department of the NKVD. But in 1938 he was demoted, and in 1939 he himself was arrested and sentenced to death for crimes committed against innocent people by his henchmen. Unfortunately, few of those unjustly sentenced to execution survived to see Yezhov's downfall. The purge of those who made the purge commenced, and his assistants, including security general Frinovsky, were also arrested. Many cases which they had investigated were reopened, and then they were summarily shot.

Did Stalin and the rest of the Political Bureau members appreciate what happened during Yezhov's reign of the NKVD?

Undoubtedly so. After Yezhov's arrest Stalin mentioned on many occasions to state and cultural figures that Yezhov killed thousands of innocent people, but he shifted the responsibility by saying that he trusted his people's commissars and they let him down. A staunch Communist believer, Stalin was unable to conceive of an opposition with legitimate grievances and the only response he was capable of was repression. General of State Security Sudoplatov wrote in his memoirs that to understand the nature of the Yezhov period, "It is necessary to take account of tendencies deep within Russian history. All political campaigns under a dictatorship invariably acquire a momentum of their own, and Stalin is guilty not only of crimes that were done under his directions but also because he allowed his subordinates to destroy, on his behalf, those who were unacceptable to local party functionaries at the regional and *oblast* levels. The party and NKVD bureaucrats were given an opportunity to solve even those regular disputes that arise almost every day by liquidating their opponents."

Stalin had thousands of complaints about Yezhov's interrogators and eventually he appointed Beria, a trustworthy man and top-class intelligence operator, as Yezhov's deputy to report on his superior. After just a month Beria reported that the scale of forgery and false confessions was so great that there could be only two explanations: either the organizer of the repression conveyor was an unprecedented fool, or he was a devious enemy whose mission was to undermine society by mass arrests of people not involved in any Trotskyite crimes. Moreover, some of those accused were amazingly loyal, honest and devoted to the cause, and their execution was a loss to the country and the party.

The reaction started. About a third of the arrested military officers were released, among them General Rokossovsky, future marshal of the Soviet Union and one of the

■ *Below:* The aircraft designer Andrei Tupolev was arrested in 1937 on charges of activities against the state. He was saved from death by Lavrenty Beria.

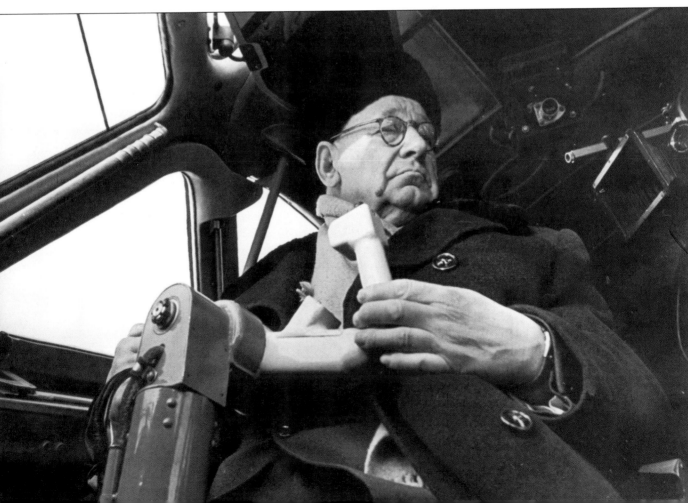

greatest military commanders in Soviet history. Victor Karpov was also released, who in World War II took 20 German officers prisoner and became a Hero of the Soviet Union, and later became a popular writer. Aircraft designer Andrei Tupolev had been sentenced to death, but Beria saved him, so he could resume his career building his airliners and bombers. By the spring of 1940 Beria had returned about 480,000 people to normal life out of 1,668,000 being held in prison and in camps on political grounds. During the war about a million people were released by Beria and sent to the army – not only the victims of repression, of course, but also those imprisoned for criminal offences – so substantially reducing the number of Gulag prisoners.

Of those who were not released, perhaps there is some justification for their continued incarceration when it is remembered that during the war about a million former Soviet citizens served in various Nazi military detachments and occupation forces, both in captured Soviet territory and in Western and Central Europe. How great would this force have been if all those still imprisoned on political grounds had been able to join it?

Stalin had two serious problems in the 1930s. One was Trotsky in exile, who was propagating worldwide the destruction of Stalin and his party bureaucracy, with the moral and/or financial support of every anti-Soviet organization. The other problem was an imminent war in Europe, and Russia's inevitable involvement in that war. Stalin knew as early as 1935 that Fascist Germany would be the Communists' main adversary, and the fact that the Germans aided Trotsky aggravated the situation. Trotsky's potential was not underestimated: he had a power base in almost every major city in the Soviet republics.

The Great Purge was a unique people's tragedy, a second Russian Civil War fought by the secret services. In addition to those who were executed, it broke the lives of nearly two million who were arrested, exiled and crippled or driven into the ground by hard labour and scarce rations. Not only were their lives tragic, but also those of their loved ones. Their families were exiled, their wives could not get a normal job, their children – the children of the enemies of the people – were ostracized, beaten and humiliated. Their fate was poverty, and very few got a second chance. It was an altogether inconceivable ordeal, especially – by a terrible irony – for those arrested after false accusations who were in fact Communists both in their hearts and in their minds.

But there is also another perspective. Imagine that the Trotskyites, Tukhachevsky and Yagoda had won this deadly game in 1937. Imagine them the masters of Russia which then became Germany's ally, ceding territories in the West and creating ideal conditions for Hitler's future campaigns. Imagine all Russia's mineral resources and weaponry in the service of the Nazis. Imagine America, left alone to face the Axis powers after the defeat of Great Britain and France, defending the free world at the price of millions of her sons. The losses could have been much greater than the 20 million Russian dead between 1941 and 1945.

Bearing all this in mind one may question whether it is right to regret that the anti-Stalinist coup in the 1930s failed.

■ *Left:* General Konstantin Rokossovsky was arrested in 1938 and imprisoned, but was released upon the German invasion of the Soviet Union in 1941 because his military talents were needed. He became a marshal of the Soviet Union and was later Polish Minister of Defence.

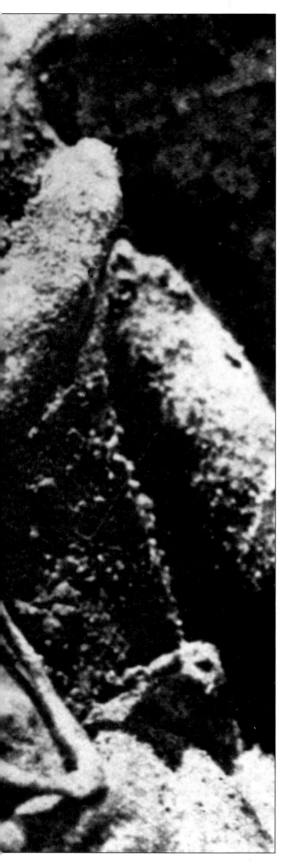

CHAPTER 4

PRELUDE TO WORLD WAR II

Having destroyed internal opposition, the NKVD set about dealing with external threats, including liquidating Leon Trotsky.

I n the late 1920s and early 1930s the Kremlin was still unsure where the greatest danger to the Bolshevik regime came from. Although it showed its capacity for expansion by force in the Far East, Japan was mainly preoccupied with China and Korea. Germany was not considered strong enough to seek expansion eastwards and, besides, Russo-German relations were steadily improving, to no small degree because of the sympathy of a significant part of the German working class and intellectuals for Communist ideas. Great Britain and the United States seemed more dangerous. The first was a colonial power with outposts and strongholds around the borders of the Soviet Union, while its élite harboured an unconcealed hatred for Communists, evidenced by its intervention on the side of the Whites in Russia during the Civil War. The second was a citadel of young and aggressive capitalism whose future as one of the major forces in the world was guaranteed. The USA had also intervened on the side of the Whites. For these reasons these two countries became important areas of operation for Soviet intelligence in the early 1930s.

The Soviet secret service operated in Great Britain both legally, via diplomatic and other representatives, and through illegal agents. An illegal *residentura*, or local intelligence station, was formed in

■ *Left:* **One of the victims of the Katyn Massacre, an atrocity which was blamed on the Soviets by the Germans during World War II.**

■ *Right:* The outstanding Soviet spy Nahum Eitingon. His greatest achievement in the 1930s was to create an illegal espionage network in America among Jews who had emigrated from Russia on the eve of the revolution or immediately after.

■ *Below:* The NKVD controlled a number of foreign spy networks, including the German Shulze-Harnack group, which acquired the top-secret plans for the Messerschmitt 210 aircraft.

Great Britain as early as 1933, and some top-class agents like Arnold Deutsch (acting under the name of Stephan Lang), Theodor Maly and Alexander Orlov were sent to London to look for contacts who could supply valuable information. One of the greatest successes of Soviet intelligence was the recruitment of the so-called "Cambridge Five": Kim Philby, Donald Maclean, Guy Burgess, Anthony Blunt and John Cairncross. The members of this group, in some Soviet publications called "The Big Five", initially met while studying at Cambridge. They and their contacts, some still undisclosed, would play an exceptionally important role in providing top-secret information to the USSR before, during and after World War II, especially on atomic energy applications. Philby, Burgess and Maclean later defected to the Soviet Union.

Their first controller, Arnold Deutsch, was an able and devoted intelligence operative. Born in 1904 in Vienna, the son of a small businessman, he graduated from the University of Vienna in 1928 and spoke six languages fluently. Deutsch was an agent of the Comintern's underground organization from 1928 (the Comintern was an international Communist organization founded in Moscow in 1919 and dissolved in 1943), and joined the Foreign Department (INO) of the OGPU in 1932. He went to "study" in London in 1933, followed by three illegal agents from his group, two of them young Austrian women. One of the latter, a spy called Edith Tudor Hart, was the wife of an English doctor, and provided Deutsch with access to upper-middle-class London society. Deutsch focused his attention first and foremost on Cambridge and Oxford, and soon had a team associated with scientific and academic institutions, including the "Cambridge Five", and at least three other important agents. Deutsch died at the end of 1942 when the transport ship *Donbass*, taking him to his new intelligence post in the USA, was attacked and sunk by German bombers.

The biographies of the other two top Soviet agents in Great Britain are even more convoluted. Theodor Maly, Hungarian by origin and a former chaplain in the Austro-Hungarian Army, was captured by the Russians in World War I, and after the revolution became a Red Army officer and

later a commissar in the *Cheka*. He reportedly took part in the extermination of the Russian Royal Family, and was then sent as an illegal agent to Austria, Germany and France, as well as Great Britain, where he recruited German and Austrian immigrants. In 1937 he was recalled to Moscow and executed. He was, according to most sources, an absolutely innocent victim of the Purge, although he had a lot of blood on his hands from the Civil War.

The other top operative, Alexander Orlov (real name Feldbin), spoke perfect English, French and German, and was the author of an agents' textbook on recruiting foreigners. He cooperated with Philby with great ingenuity while in London in 1934–45. In 1936, after a tragic romance with a young colleague, Galina Voitova, who committed suicide right in front of NKVD headquarters, he was sent to Spain as resident, i.e. the head

of the intelligence outstation. This "exile" was arranged by Orlov's close friend Slutsky, head of the INO.

This posting to Spain, despite the trials and tribulations of the civil war and several tough assignments, ultimately saved Orlov's life. He was successful in all his missions, including two particularly delicate matters: secret transportation of the Spanish Republic's gold reserves to Russia, and the assassination of the Spanish Troskyite leader Andreu Nin. In July 1938 he was to meet his INO chief, Sergei Shpihelglas, in Belgium. However, when the latter arrived on board a Soviet ship he was afraid to disembark because some of his agents had been recently arrested in Brussels. Orlov, who had just received information that his brother-in-law Katsnelson, Deputy *Narkom* of the Ukrainian NKVD, had been arrested, was afraid to board the ship in his turn, suspecting a trap

■ *Above:* Eitingon (third from right) in his *Cheka* days. He first encountered Trotsky in 1920 while in Gomel. He would later play a leading role in the assassination of Trotsky.

■ *Right:* Jakob Serebriansky, who in the early 1930s worked with Eitingon in the United States to recruit Chinese and Japanese workers for the OGPU.

■ *Far right:* Willie Leman (codename Breitenbach), a German counter-intelligence operative who offered his services to the Russians as early as 1929.

for himself. Instead of meeting his superior he hastily fled, not forgetting to grab US $60,000 from the *residentura* safe, and later surfaced in America. He sent a message to Moscow promising not to disclose any spy networks unless his relatives in the Soviet Union were subject to reprisals, or a hunt was launched for him. He managed to survive, although almost all defectors in that period were not as lucky.

After Hitler came to power in January 1933, operations in Germany were also given priority. Illegal *residentura* staff enjoyed the help of anti-Fascists and German Socialists, and had agents reporting from the Ministry of Foreign Affairs and from other Nazi ministries, though there was always the question of whether it was real information or German disinformation they were being fed.

There were three main sources of information. The first was one Willie Leman (codename Breitenbach), a German counter-intelligence operative who offered his services to the Russians as early as 1929 both for ideological and financial reasons. Working from 1933 in the Gestapo (Nazi secret police), he supplied his controllers, Vladimir Zarubin and Alexander Korotkov, with valuable information about rockets and missiles being designed in Germany, as well as armoured personnel carriers, aircraft

and aircraft armour, flame-thrower tanks, military shipbuilding, and the organization of German national defence. He was also instrumental in warning Russian diplomats and agents about surveillance, Gestapo informers, and persons in Russian missions who had been "worked on" by the German intelligence services. In March 1941, Leman informed his Soviet contacts that German military intelligence was hastily building up its Russian department, and on 19 June he told a Soviet agent in Berlin that the attack on Russia would start on 22 June after 03:00 hours. That was the most accurate information on the subject anybody could get.

The second outstanding source was a flamboyant Polish intelligence officer, von Sosnovski. A handsome aristocrat, he was successful in getting, through German society ladies, important intelligence information for his country, until caught by the Gestapo. He was then exchanged for a German agent detained in Poland. When back in Poland, he was arrested for his overspending on an excessive lifestyle and imprisoned. In 1939, when part of Poland was overrun by Red Army troops, he was found by the NKVD and transported to Moscow, where he was dealt with first by a famous female intelligence operative, Zoya Rybkina, and then by her boss Pavel

Sudoplatov. As a result, von Sosnovski agreed to cooperate and provided the names of two of his most important agents still active in Germany. They were contacted by the Soviet secret service and supplied valuable information until the end of the war.

The Schulze-Harnack group

The third source was the Schulze-Harnack group. It consisted of First Lieutenant (Res.) Harro Schulze-Boysen, who enjoyed the patronage of *Luftwaffe* chief Hermann Goering and had an office at the Ministry of Aviation; Senior Privy Councillor Arvid Harnack of the Imperial Ministry of Economics; writer and producer Adam Kuckhoff; and many others. The group used wireless equipment supplied by the Soviet Embassy to transmit valuable information to Moscow almost every night, about 500 messages in all. Some of the messages, such as the ones containing descriptions of the new fighter aircraft, the Messerschmitt 210, radar equipment and rockets, were of outstanding importance. This group of anti-Fascists was, however, doomed in 1942 after German counter-intelligence, due to the recklessness of a Russian agent, disclosed which French novel was used as the code-book when transmitting messages. The Gestapo arrested 117 people and executed about half of them (the men were hanged and the women guillotined).

This tragedy was in part the result of administrative problems in the Soviet intelligence services dating back to the mid-1930s. Some of the networks in Germany and Switzerland were originally planned by the NKVD, and even such famous agents as Leopold Trepper, conductor of the Soviet networks in Belgium and France (the Germans gave them the codename Red Orchestra), had originally been recruited by the NKVD. But after 1934, when Artur Artusov, head of the INO, was transferred by Stalin to military intelligence, he took about 30 officers with him, and also some of their network files. The network and communication system planning was now done by military intelligence. As a result, by the late 1930s the military intelligence *residentura* in Germany and the NKVD were at times getting information from the same source or, worse still, had the same key figures in their networks and the same transmitter codes. In 1941, German direction-finding units located the Soviet transmitters and arrested some members of the network. The Germans also found coded messages which had not been destroyed, and that meant the game was soon over, not only for the Schulze-Harnack group but also for other Soviet military intelligence teams, including the Red Orchestra in Brussels and Paris and the Red Trio in Switzerland under Alexander Rado.

The NKVD in the USA

In the United States, the NKVD employed much cunning in its long-term planning. In the early 1930s two ace Soviet spies, Jakob Serebriansky and Nahum Eitingon, were there to recruit Chinese and Japanese workers for the OGPU. By that time Japan had already seized a significant part of China and Manchuria, and these were potential agents who, in the case of war between the USSR and Japan, would conduct acts of sabotage and diversions against Japanese ships in American ports. But both Russians were too experienced not to see the possibility for other initiatives. Since the Chinese workers comprised the most oppressed, heavily exploited and poorest community in the USA and thus not deeply attached to their new country of residence, there would be little problem in finding potential agents among them to carry out subversion in America. Eitingon also set up another network of so-called "sleeping" agents. He facilitated the emigration to the USA of a few Polish Jews who were starving in France, set up businesses for them and arranged useful connections. They would be helpful in the years to come.

Nahum Eitingon (sometimes referred to as Leonid Eitingon), an outstanding Soviet career spy who would play an important role in the assassination of Trotsky, was born in the Belorussian town of Shklov in 1899 to a family of paper-mill employees. In 1917 he, like his famous colleague Serebriansky, joined the Socialist Revolutionaries, but in 1919 became a Bolshevik and the *Cheka* officer in Gomel. He saw Trotsky for the first time in May 1920 when the latter came to Gomel to supervise fortifications and stop desertions. Trotsky did this in his usual fashion: executing hundreds of peasants who were reluctant to abandon their plots and build fortifications, plus hundreds of soldiers who were fed up with six years of continuous fighting. After distinguishing himself in *Cheka* operations in Bashkiria, Eitingon was transferred to the Oriental Department of the OGPU and studied at the Intelligence Department of the Frunze Military Academy in Moscow. He operated in China, the USA, France, Iran, Germany, Poland, Mexico and Belgium. Between 1933 and 1935 he was the head of the Illegal Intelligence Section, "the holy of the holies" of the OGPU.

Eitingon's greatest achievement in the 1930s was his creation of an illegal espionage network in America among Jews who had emigrated from Russia on the eve of the revolution or immediately after: families from Odessa, Vinnitsa, Petrograd and even Gomel, where he had started his career. He approached some of them through his friends and acquaintances, and was introduced to others by distant relatives who had settled in the USA much earlier. Very few of the new immigrants prospered in the Great Depression in the USA, and Eitingon's help was very timely. His connections and his payments were appreciated, and dozens of people agreed to render him various services. This laid the foundation for a system that, existing in parallel with the Soviet intelligence units based on trade and diplomatic representations, ensured Russian penetration of US government and scientific institutions for many years to come.

From 1936, and especially after the Great Purge, there was no doubt concerning where

the next war would come from. The pro-German officers in the Red Army and secret service were gone, and so were the Trotskyites who collaborated with them. The prelude to the future confrontation was being played out in Spain. Francisco Franco, the leader of the right-wing Nationalists, used not only military equipment but also "volunteers" from Italy and Germany. Soviet Russia replied by sending her own advisors and "volunteers" to fight alongside international brigades of Socialists from the USA, Great Britain, France and Latin America on the Republican side.

■ *Above:* First Lieutenant (Res.) Harro Schulze-Boysen of the Schulze-Harnack group. He enjoyed the patronage of *Luftwaffe* chief Hermann Goering and had an office at the Ministry of Aviation.

The only question that remains unanswered is whether the defeat of the Republicans in Spain was a result of the internal strife among the leftists and the massive support enjoyed by Franco from foreign Fascists, or whether it was pre-determined by treason. Some Soviet historians claimed that Trotskyites and anarchists had started a mutiny in Barcelona in 1937 to weaken the Communists, and largely succeeded. They believed the mutiny had been inspired and instigated by Trotsky and his lieutenants to undermine Stalin's political and ideological expansion in Europe. The Russian consul in Barcelona, V.A. Antonov-Ovseenko, once Lenin's trigger-happy revolutionary, was a secret Trotskyite who undoubtedly received instructions from his Germanophile Moscow centre. Orlov, head of the NKVD intelligence network in Spain, was linked to a confirmed Trotskyite named Katsnelson. Whether they acted on instructions from the Trotskyite centre in Moscow, which in turn was implementing a German plan, or were honestly doing their assigned jobs, is a secret they took to their graves. The former was executed and the latter died decades later in the United States.

Fitin's Department V

The Spanish Civil War offered a clear manifestation of the expansionist character of both Fascist and Communist ideologies. In early 1937, Soviet agents reported that the Nazi leadership had been conferring on possible campaigns in the East. One of the most important subjects of discussion was the fate of Poland – to launch an offensive against Russia the Germans had to deal with Poland first. That prompted Stalin's next move: the signing of the non-aggression treaty with Germany, the so-called Molotov-Ribbentrop Pact (23 August 1939), to gain time in order to be better prepared for the invasion. It also shifted Soviet borders many miles westwards.

Upon becoming the head of NKVD, Beria replaced any residents and foreign agents appointed only because of their revolutionary past rather than their ability to speak foreign languages. By the end of 1939, a new chief was appointed to direct exterior intelligence: Department V of the NKVD Main State Security Directorate. Pavel Fitin was only 31, and he made a spectacular breakthrough by recruiting young and educated people. By the time of the German invasion (June 1941) Fitin's department was about 700 strong and had 40 *residenturas*. The biggest of these were in the USA (18 officers), Finland (17) and Germany (13). More than 240 of his best officers were stationed all over the globe, receiving information from 600 agents and collaborators. The intelligence service was thus prepared for war, but was the state?

Stalin's "special operations"

The Great Purge shook the intelligence community in Russia to an even greater extent than the army and its intelligence service, *Razvedupr*. The fear of arrest pushed some NKVD officers to desperate measures; as in the case of Orlov, some defected or tried to go underground. The NKVD Main State Security Directorate always considered the elimination of such defectors a matter of honour, and hunted them down worldwide. Very few were lucky enough to make a deal with Beria or able to hide for long.

In 1937, for example, Vladimir Poretski (codename Ignace Reiss), a spy sent to operate in Europe, spent and gambled away a substantial sum of money. He knew how strict financial discipline was in the NKVD, and decided to defect. He was basically a professional without any special political affiliations, but to give himself credibility he wrote a letter to the Soviet Embassy in Paris in which he condemned Stalin. After this letter finally found its way onto the pages of the Trotskyite press, Poretski was sentenced to death as a traitor *in absentia*. When he defected he stole a large sum of money from operative funds which he enjoyed squandering in Paris, so was soon spotted by the NKVD. They traced him to Lausanne in

■ *Above:* Ace spy Eitingon (second from left) with NKVD operatives in Spain during the civil war.

Switzerland, where two liquidators impersonating Bulgarian businessmen befriended him at a restaurant, and then promptly staged a brawl. The agents threw Poretski out of the restaurant and pushed him into their car, drove a couple of miles, and then pulled him out and shot him.

Georgi Agabekov, the OGPU resident in Istanbul, also sealed his own doom by defecting after his friend Blyumkin, killer of the German Ambassador Mirbach in 1918 who was pardoned by Dzerzhinsky, was arrested for communication with Trotsky. Blyumkin was informed on by his own wife. Agabekov also had a romance with the daughter of a British diplomat who seemed to be an intelligence officer. His defection did not bring him substantial dividends, and he had to write books and make translations to earn a living. Several years later he was approached by Armenian emigrants who had hidden treasures in Soviet Russia and wanted them to be clandestinely transported to France. Agabekov started probing among his old NKVD contacts, and that soon exposed him. Grig Takhchianov, an ethnic Armenian and NKVD illegal agent in France, was sent to Antwerp to meet Agabekov, posing as a Greek middleman. Agabekov was trapped in a safe flat and stabbed to death, and his corpse was put in a suitcase which was thrown into a canal and never recovered. One of the agents who trapped Agabekov was Alexander Korotkov, the man who directed Soviet illegal intelligence in the 1940s.

The same Korotkov also took part in the assassination of Rudolf Clement, leader of the European Trotskyites and secretary of the Fourth International formed by Trotsky. Elijah Taubman, a young Soviet agent of Lithuanian descent, became Clement's assistant and served under him for more than a year. He trapped Clement by inviting him to dinner at a safe flat, where he was stabbed to death, and the corpse was again put in a suitcase before being thrown into the River Seine. This time the body was found and identified, but the assassins had escaped. All of them were highly rewarded in the Soviet Union. Taubman's identity was changed and he became Semenov, a student at the Institute of Chemical Machine Building. He was later employed by the secret service for at least two important intelligence operations.

The NKVD also targeted Ukrainian nationalists in Europe whose subversive activity had intensified after Hitler's coming to power. Stalin and Beria considered Konovalets, the leader of the Organization of Ukrainian Nationalists (OUN), the most dangerous figure, and in May 1938 he was assassinated by Pavel Sudoplatov, INO officer and future head of the special intelligence service. The lengthy preparations started with the planting of Sudoplatov in the nationalist underground in the USSR through agents the NKVD already had in the OUN. Travelling through Finland and Sweden to Germany, Sudoplatov met Konovalets and soon won his confidence. He later escorted him to Paris. Sudoplatov met almost all the leaders of the OUN and learned their plans. When he returned to Russia he was informed by Stalin in person that he had been selected to assassinate Konovalets. The acting INO chief, Shpihelglas, warned Sudoplatov that he must not allow himself to be captured during or after the assassination. So he had to be prepared for suicide. The assassination weapon was a bomb in a chocolate box, since the NKVD knew that Konovalets had a weakness for good chocolate. Meeting

Konovalets in the Atlanta restaurant in Rotterdam, Sudoplatov gave him the box with the timing mechanism already cocked, talked for a short while, and then said goodbye. Konovalets was blown to pieces, and Sudoplatov was promoted to assistant chief of the INO.

But the most important "special operation" carried out on Stalin's orders was, of course, the assassination of his arch-enemy, Leon Trotsky. It was a very sophisticated operation, implemented by Nahum Eitingon, though the actual assassin was a Spanish Communist called Ramon Mercader. An earlier attempt on Trotsky's life, made by the famous Mexican mural painter David Siqueiros and his Communist gang on instructions from Moscow, had failed. The assassins broke into Trotsky's villa in Mexico and fired 300 shots, but Trotsky and his wife survived by hiding under the

bed. This time Stalin was sending top professionals to do the job. His determination to eliminate Trotsky not only derived from his personal hatred of the man who criticized his regime, but was also caused by the subversive activity of Trotsky and Trotskyites inside Russia and abroad.

■ *Above:* Triumphal Nationalist troops march through Malaga in 1939 at the end of the Spanish Civil War.

■ *Left:* Pavel Sudoplatov, INO officer and future head of the special intelligence service, who in May 1938 assassinated Konovalets, the leader of the Organization of Ukrainian Nationalists (OUN).

Trotsky is often lauded as Lenin's "heir apparent", architect of the October Revolution and creator of the Red Army. Stalin, it is said, exiled Trotsky because he rebelled against Soviet bureaucracy and dogmatists that paralyzed the productive and spiritual forces of the country. But that makes him no different from the other victims of Stalinism. Certainly there is no point in commending Trotsky for the October uprising, since that brought so much suffering to the people of Russia. Still less should he be praised for creating the Red Army, used in his time not to defend the country but to triumph in one of the bloodiest civil wars in history. Trotsky was expelled from the party and exiled when a group of political figures, who later became opponents of Stalin, combined forces in order to put an end to Trotsky's activities in the state and party. A man of unprecedented ambitions, a noisy, choleric rabble-rouser, he could not accept the fact that Stalin was elected the general secretary of the party, and so made the struggle against "Stalin the shoemaker's son" his crusade. There is no doubt that Stalin controlled a cruel totalitarian regime, probably one of the cruellest in world history. But Trotsky was no better. It was People's Commissar Trotsky who ordered the execution of peasants in Tambov, sailors in Kronstadt,

■ *Below:* Leon Trotsky, who was banished from the Soviet Union in 1929. Stalin then realized this was a mistake, and organized his assassination on the eve of World War II.

and families of tsarist officers in Kiev, gave instructions to blow up churches and formed "labour detachments" (refusal to join meant the execution of the whole family). Now the Soviet Union was getting ready for what promised to be the defining struggle with the Third Reich, and Trotsky had become the black apostle of defeatism. He claimed that in the face of Fascist aggression Stalin and his clique would betray their people, that the USSR would be defeated in the clash with Nazi Germany. "One thing I am sure of," he wrote, "the political regime will not survive the war." Trotsky's words that "the Kremlin clique has demoralized the land's army and its population" were accepted in Berlin with joy and enthusiasm. In effect, Trotsky encouraged the Nazis to attack Russia by convincing them that the Soviet regime was weak and its military machine fragile.

The plan to kill Trotsky

These words were also a deadly poison for the Soviet people. There were many thousands who started to believe that the victory of Fascism over the USSR was ensured, that its leadership was incompetent and cowardly, that its society was rotten, and that the ruling clique would betray them anyway. Hundreds of thousands of Soviet prisoners ended up in Nazi prison camps in the initial phases of the war, in part as a result of Trotsky's propaganda. If he was not silenced there could be devastating results for Russia, so in March 1939 Stalin gave his intelligence units the order to terminate Trotsky.

In fact, the NKVD operation started long before that. When Trotsky still lived in Norway, an NKVD female agent (code-name Patria) was planted in his secretariat. But she was recalled in 1939 after Orlov's defection. So other people had to be found who could get access to Trotsky in Mexico, where he lived in Coyocoan at the villa of the painter Diego Rivera, which had been converted into a fortress. Eitingon counted on two of his personal friends, agents recruited during the Spanish Civil War:

Caridad Mercader and her son Ramon. And Eitingon played the whole thing his way.

Ramon was not known to the Trotskyites, and he was first sent to Paris to impersonate a young and wealthy businessman using the name Jacques Mornard. The image Ramon had to build was of a playboy and adventurer who, due to his eccentricity and the hostility he felt towards any authorities, financially supported political radicals. Soon Eitingon received information that a young and dedicated female Trotskyite, Sylvia Ageloff, would come to Paris from New York in the summer. She and her family were friendly with Trotsky. Ramon was now introduced to her as a Belgian photojournalist and son of a diplomat. As he was romantic and very good-looking she fell for him almost immediately. When Sylvia was going back to the USA, Jacques declared he could not imagine living without her, and so would soon join her as a correspondent for a Belgian news agency. When he joined her in

New York he had changed his name to Frank Jacson (it seems that the NKVD section in charge of foreign passports made a spelling mistake), and explained that, reluctant to take part in the "crazy European war", he had bought a Canadian passport for US $3000, giving him permanent residence.

A month later he told her he had found a good job in Mexico, establishing a British export company there. Jacson gave Sylvia a substantial sum of money so she could stop working in New York and go with him. Sylvia, who had friends in Mexico, agreed. In October 1939 he moved to Mexico City, and Sylvia followed him three months later. He hired a room for his "office" to justify his frequent long absences. Soon Eitingon and Ramon's mother arrived, and they started to draw up a battle plan.

Sylvia visited Trotsky at Coyocoan, and soon became one of his part-time secretaries. She also discovered that her apolitical lover had developed a taste for Trotskyism. She and Jacson befriended

■ *Above:* Ramon Mercader (left), the assassin of Trotsky, with members of his family in Spain.

83

some guests of Trotsky, a couple from France, and took them on picnics in Jacson's car. Soon he became well known at the villa, and the guards did not search him at the gates.

The failure of Siqueiros and his gang to kill Trotsky helped Eitingon. Trotsky and his associates and guards thought that, since his enemies were compelled to use such rough methods, they had no ambition to infiltrate the villa. Although Jacson, as an NKVD agent inside the Trotskyite headquarters, was a potentially valuable source of information to the NKVD, Stalin agreed with Eitingon that he should be used as an assassin as soon as possible.

Eitingon initially planned that he and Ramon's mother, Caridad, would stage a diversion in the street outside the villa by firing at Trotsky's guards, allowing Jacson to kill Trotsky and then escape. But Jacson dissuaded him; there were too many guards and police patrols in the street. He had to act alone. Jacson decided to use an ice-axe to kill Trotsky, but he also had a revolver and a stiletto knife. He was sure that the guards would let him in with his small arsenal hidden under a folded overcoat, and, while alone with Trotsky, he would dispatch him and flee. But when Jacson was about to strike, Trotsky turned, and thus was not killed instantly. The noise he made alerted the guards, who fell on Jacson, wounded him and then handed him over to the police. Trotsky died the next day, while

■ Below left: A mortally wounded Trotsky lies in a hospital bed following Mercader's attack.

■ Below right: Mexican detectives with the ice-axe used to kill Trotsky.

Eitingon and Caridad hastily left for Cuba. Ramon Mercader was tried and imprisoned for 20 years in the ill-famed Lecumberri prison. After being released he received the gold star of the Hero of the Soviet Union, and lived in the USSR for most of his remaining years.

Eitingon was involved in another assassination attempt, this time in Turkey. In February 1942 he led a team of six people, including Muza Malinovskaya, a young and very attractive woman who became his wife, on a mission to kill Franz von Papen, former German chancellor and now ambassador in Ankara. Moscow was deeply concerned by the possibility, however remote, of a separate peace between the USA and Great Britain and Germany. The Kremlin knew that as long as Hitler was the leader of Germany, the Western powers would not consider any separate peace proposal. But if someone more moderate came to power – for instance, von Papen – the situation would be different. Von Papen, a Catholic, could have used his Vatican connections to help negotiate such a peace. That would leave Russia facing the Germans alone, so Stalin decided to remove von Papen from the political stage. But the attempt on his life was unsuccessful. The bomb exploded prematurely, killing the agent who was carrying it. Two Russian agents and two collaborators were imprisoned, although there was little clear evidence of their guilt. The Russians were later released by the Turkish president after the Soviet victories

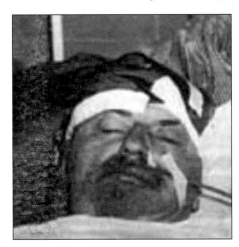

of 1943 at the city of Stalingrad and the Battle of Kursk.

In September 1939, when the Red Army crossed the Polish border and occupied western Ukraine and western Belorussia, it was followed by battalions of OSNAZ troops (acronym of the Russian *Osoboye Naznachenie* – Special Purpose). These troops were not subordinate to the area military commanders but were part of the GUPV (Main Directorate of the Frontier Troops) of the NKVD. They also moved into the "liberated" territories of Lithuania, Latvia, Estonia and Bessarabia. Newly appointed Communist Party officials from these countries normally accompanied them. The main mission of the OSNAZ battalions was similar to that of the *Chon* and OGPU Special Forces of previous times: the smooth

transition to Soviet power and suppression of any local civilian resistance. Jointly with the NKVD operatives assigned to each area, they screened the local population and arrested anyone considered potentially dangerous.

There were other NKVD troops which were used to perform less pleasant work, the so-called Convoy Battalions and Regiments. Originally established to transport and guard prisoners, these troops were also trained to suppress civilian unrest. In 1940 NKVD forces supervised road construction and other hard labour by about 12,000 Polish officers in the Smolensk and Kozi Gory area. These troops, as well as some regular Red Army units, were later accused by the Germans of murdering captured Polish officers on Stalin's instructions before the Nazi invasion. This crime is known as the

■ *Above:* A battered Mercader photographed immediately after his assault upon Trotsky. He received a 20-year sentence for the murder. Upon his release in 1960 he became a Hero of the Soviet Union. He died in 1978 and was buried in Kuntsevo Cemetery in Moscow.

Katyn Massacre after the name of the nearby forest. Many respectable Western historians accept as fact that the Russians were responsible for the Katyn killings. However, this is still in dispute.

In 1944, there was a special report published in Moscow that contained statements on Nazi atrocities, the Katyn Massacre included, which showed that the mass killing of the Polish officers had been done by the Germans, who in 1943, on the eve of the Battle of Kursk, had arranged some theatrics in the Katyn Forest to enable them to accuse the Russians of the killing. Later, during the Nuremberg trials after World War II, the Soviet reluctance to admit that these Polish prisoners of war had been reclassified as convicts, placed under the jurisdiction of the NKVD and used, in violation of the Geneva Convention's rules on officer prisoners, for hard labour, resulted in the whole affair being muzzled. In particular, the fact that the NKVD had handed the Polish officers over to the Germans for inevitable murder never emerged. Although there was a lot of hatred in the Red Army for Poles since the Russo-Polish War (1919–20), Stalin and his Political Bureau preferred them to be killed by the Germans. The decision backfired when the German propaganda machine decided to incriminate the Russians. The story of the Russian involvement in the massacre is based only on German accusations and a number of "documents" retrieved in Russia and Poland, and some of these have been lately rejected as primitive fakes by scholars and investigative journalists. It was, not surprisingly, hugely inflated by the West at the time when the Soviet Empire and the Socialist bloc were crumbling, in order to speed up Polish liberation from Soviet dominance.

That does not mean that there were no executions by the NKVD in the newly acquired territories. It rounded up Polish nationalists in western Belorussia and western Ukraine, as well as intelligence and police officers, and prominent figures in

■ *Above:* Exhumed corpses during the Nazi investigation of the Katyn Massacre.

■ *Left:* Over 4,000 Polish officers were murdered at Katyn Wood. The Soviets handed over the Poles to the Germans knowing they would be killed.

regions, wanted to handle relations with local political and cultural figures with extreme delicacy and asked Communist Party functionaries to be tolerant towards them, the latter would not listen. Khrushchev, who led the Ukrainian Communist Party Central Committee, ordered his NKVD units to arrest and imprison some local dignitaries, known not only in Poland but in many European capitals. One of the arrested, Kost-Levitsky, had been for a short time the premier of the independent Ukrainian Republic. A retired professor in his eighties, Kost-Levitsky's arrest had an extremely negative effect on the local population. Although he was later released by Molotov on the recommendation of NKVD main headquarters and courteously escorted back to his city of Lvov, the harm had already been done. The behaviour of Khrushchev and his Kiev NKVD units helped to make it relatively easy for the Germans to later recruit a number of military units in the Ukraine to fight against the Soviets, including the ill-famed SS Division *Galicia*.

NKVD deportations

There were also the so-called "preventive measures" of other kinds: deportations of potentially harmful persons. In March 1940, for example, the Council of People's Commissars adopted a secret resolution that prescribed deportation and exile from the western areas of the Ukraine and Belorussia for the families of former landlords, shop owners, members of bourgeois political parties, and former officers of the Polish Army. More than 40,000 were exiled from the Ukraine and more than 50,000 from Belorussia. They were transported to distant areas of Siberia and southeastern Russia. Most of them were concentrated in the regions of Vorkuta, Karaganda, Kemerovo and Irkutsk, where the climatic conditions were extremely harsh and where the government needed a lot of working hands. More than 5000 were deported from Moldavia (former

anti-Soviet organizations in Poland, especially Russian émigrés and former tsarist army officers. Some of them were imprisoned and 600 people were shot, according to a former NKVD officer called Chernov. These were mainly counter-intelligence officers and shock troops accused of the torture and execution of Red Army personnel during the Russo-Polish War. That the harsh treatment of Russian prisoners in this war had, in fact, been in reaction to the awful cruelty of Russian cavalry commanders towards captured Polish officers, was omitted.

While NKVD generals, wholly aware of the vulnerable situation in the captured

Bessarabia). In 1941, after Soviet troops entered the Baltic republics, about 12,500 people were deported from Lithuania, primarily shop owners and police officers and their families; 16,500 from Latvia; and 6700 from Estonia.

The ethnic make-up of deportees

Ethnic Germans were also deported from Georgia (23,500) and Azerbaijan (22,700). The government provided either accommodation or five-year mortgages (housing construction was very cheap in Russia at that time). Needless to say, all the deportation programmes were drawn up and implemented by the NKVD, but the decisions on every aspect of deportation and the everyday life of the deported were taken by the Council of People's Commissars. The more serious deportations would follow in 1944–45; the first had involved the most vulnerable ethnic groups before World War II: descendants and families of Koreans who had fled to Russia from Japanese expansion, Kurds who had emigrated from Turkey and Iran, Armenians who came to Russian territories after the Turkish genocide, and Persian refugees. In 1937–38 they were moved to Uzbekistan and Kazakhstan, especially to the areas where the government planned to start building the Baikal-Amur Main Railway. More than 21,000 families later had to migrate again from this area – this time, however, with substantial help from the government, which built houses, schools, hospitals and even clubs for them.

The NKVD empire was enormous. Beria, as soon as he became the *Narkom* of Internal Affairs, issued a decree that forbade mass arrests and exiles, liquidated *troikas* and instructed that arrests be carried out only on the directive of a court or sanction of an attorney. This resulted in the liberation of many thousands of innocent people. But despite this, there were still 2,300,000 inmates in the prison and labour camps of the Gulag, most of them working on government projects. The NKVD economic plan for 1941 consisted of capital construction by its building enterprises valued at 6.8 billion roubles, and industrial output valued at 1.8 billion roubles. The NKVD was using at least 1,976,000 inmates and 288,000 hired personnel in 1940, when about 13 percent of all basic capital construction in the country's economy was done by the People's Commissariat of Internal Affairs. Its Main Directorate of Highways and Roads, its Survey and Map Service, and its Resettlement and Administration Directorates were extremely busy, and Beria added to his empire the Main Directorate of Archives in 1939 and the Main Directorates for Hydro-Technical Construction and for Railways in 1940. The labour camps had been geared to satisfy the demands of Stalin's five-year plans, but now some were reoriented towards production of army equipment and supplies.

The Urals project

There was one more mission assigned to Beria by Stalin: the most secret, the most important, and therefore one he could give only to his most trusted man. It was the creation of industrial potential many hundreds of miles from the western border, in the Urals and Siberia. In 1940 Beria and his people, the generals who would be executed by Khrushchev after he came to power, began assembling stockpiles of weapons, preparing construction sites for future relocation of plants and factories, and storing raw materials, machines and even hand tools. They were planning a powerful parallel armaments industry to produce all sorts of military equipment capable of coming on stream in weeks, not months. Administrative embryos of new industrial combines, reserve control and design departments were set up, and special agents were counting the number of houses, rooms and beds in each vicinity for receiving the workers belonging to relocated enterprises, should the need arise. Stalin and Beria knew the strength of the army that was poised for a massive onslaught against Russia, and they were taking no chances. They wanted to retain the strength of the USSR during the invasion at any cost, and so they did. There could be chaos in the frontline after the invasion, but not in the NKVD.

Last-minute moves

From November 1940, the NKVD intelligence department and some counter-intelligence sources warned the Soviet leadership that war with Germany was imminent. Beria reacted by restructuring some intelligence units and giving them new assignments. The first unit to be substantially strengthened was the so-called "personal intelligence of the Soviet leader". This is not a unit much talked about, and, unlike other intelligence units, its files are still secret. Judging by scant information leaks, it was headed on the eve of the war by Colonel-General Lavrov.

"In December 1940 I was sent to Moscow with some papers which analyzed reports from our agents along the Turkish border," wrote Colonel Gorlin. "When our plane landed, I was, to my surprise, taken to the Hotel Moscow instead of the Lubianka. There was a man waiting for me there who said he wanted to use the opportunity of my visit in order to talk to me. He introduced himself as Pavel Sergeevich, and did not mention his surname. 'We know that you speak Greek and some Turkish,' he said without preamble. 'Would you help us if necessary and travel to Greece or Turkey or Cyprus and meet our people?' I replied that I was ready to perform any mission within my powers. 'This will be done on the direct order of Stalin,' he added. I realized that his was probably the most secretive intelligence unit in the country, which reported directly to Beria and Stalin. I was called on to help it only once, in 1947, when I spent a week in northern Greece. I learnt later that this unit existed until at least 1952."

The NKVD knew that the invasion was about to begin when it learned that the Nazis had started to select bureaucrats for

■ *Left:* Soviet agent controller Raikhman, who obtained important documents from two German diplomats in a Moscow hotel.

potential appointments in the occupied territories of the Soviet Union, including the engineers who would restore or operate Soviet enterprises, and geologists who would exploit the mineral resources in White Russia and the Ukraine.

On 12 June 1941, the head of Stalin's personal intelligence service reported the visible concentration of Axis troops on the western borders of the USSR, and proposed the immediate mobilization and reinforcement of the army. Stalin refused. He explained that such a move could be interpreted by Germany and other Western powers as a tacit declaration of war. He referred to World War I, when the Russian mobilization in support of Serbia was interpreted by Austro-Hungary and Germany as Russia's declaration of war. Stalin was still trying to gain time, but he knew there were only a few days of peace left.

The other intelligence and counter-intelligence bodies were also concentrating on the task of defining the timing and groupings of the German onslaught. From about the middle of 1940 NKVD intelligence had a special file that contained all the most important reports concerning German war plans against the Soviet Union. Any new information which was considered important was given to Stalin and Molotov. Vital though the information coming from legal and illegal *residenturas* was, it lacked many components important for the Soviet military. The NKVD thought that gathering information on the balance of forces was the job of military intelligence, while the latter was in fact mostly doing the same job as the NKVD: providing political intelligence. The lack of a thorough analysis of German offensive power, strategy and tactics meant that the Soviet General Staff could not properly evaluate the abilities of the German armed forces.

The impending war necessitated drastic expansion and strengthening of the Main Directorate of State Security within the NKVD, especially the intelligence and counter-intelligence services. In 1937–38 there were only a few German spies caught while crossing the border or dropping by parachute, while there were about 400 infiltrations in 1939 and 2000 in the first half of 1940 alone. Special mobile detachments for hunting infiltrating spies were therefore formed.

Despite the growth of counter-intelligence, in Stalin's eyes Beria was more important as the organizer of the major defence measures in the Urals and beyond than as intelligence supremo. Accordingly, in February 1941 Stalin made the state security directorate a separate ministry: the People's Commissariat of State Security, headed by Beria's deputy and trusted associate, Vsevolod Merkulov. Beria kept the post of the head of NKVD, and a dominating position over the new *narkom* as well, while Stalin still consulted him on all matters of security.

As far as its main mission was concerned – gathering political intelligence – the new state security service was doing its best. Many of the intelligence officers who were active in these last, tense days before the German invasion would be the backbone of Soviet intelligence throughout the war and for years afterwards. About a week before the German invasion, Soviet intelligence officer

Zoya Rybkina attended a cocktail party at the German Embassy in Moscow. She knew the inside of the embassy very well, and was quick to notice that some important paintings had been removed from the walls. She also spotted some employees packing boxes and suitcases. That confirmed that the Germans, meticulous as usual, were making ready to depart.

Another important NKVD operation during this period was the interception of two German diplomatic couriers in Moscow's Metropolis Hotel by counter-intelligence units controlled by Raikhman and Yakovlev. One of the couriers was trapped inside the hotel's elevator for about five minutes. This was arranged by the NKVD operatives while the second courier was in the bathroom of the hotel suite; the officers quietly entered the suite and locked him in there. The counter-intelligence operatives had long enough before the elevator moved again to photograph all the documents the couriers were taking to Germany. Among them was a message from

■ *Below:* German foreign minister Joachim von Ribbentrop, whose top-secret messages to the German Embassy in Moscow were intercepted by Raikhman.

the German ambassador to the German foreign minister, von Ribbentrop. The most important line in the message was that the reduction of the diplomatic personnel in Moscow would be carried out as planned.

At this time the NKVD was also trying to plant as many agents as possible in Switzerland and Germany, which was very difficult to do in 1941. The normal transfer routes, via Belgium for example, were blocked, while sending intelligence officers directly from Moscow to Berlin meant they would be under surveillance from the moment they arrived. Some agents went to Germany from Italy, but, as it was impossible to supply radio equipment or batteries, their effectiveness would be very limited.

The NKVD was also making some efforts to cool the German enthusiasm for war by showing Russia's power and hinting about heavy German losses. In early 1941 Stalin was informed by the intelligence *residentura* in Berlin that the German General Staff had organized training exercises to work out the solutions for strategic and tactical supply in case of a protracted campaign. He reacted immediately, instructing the NKVD to organize a trip for the German military attaché in Moscow to the industrial centres in the Urals and Siberia. He gladly accepted, and in April 1941 NKVD officers took him to plants that were producing the newest medium and heavy tanks and fighter aircraft. The general was obviously impressed. Using this as a pretext, both legal and illegal *residenturas* in Berlin started to spread rumours in German ministries that the war against the Soviet Union would be a catastrophe for the German people, especially if a second front was opened up in Western Europe as well. Intelligent people in the German establishment realized that the Russians were not bluffing, but the Nazi leadership would not listen.

Less than a week before the war Beria called Sudoplatov, the deputy head of intelligence, and ordered him to start creating a detachment of officers to perform

■ *Left:* Vsevolod Merkulov, head of the People's Commissariat of State Security and Beria's trusted deputy.

special assignments for the chief of the NKVD: intelligence gathering and sabotage in the enemy rear after the war started. Its immediate assignment would be to prevent any German provocation similar to the one staged to justify the invasion of Poland in 1939 (a German special-purpose unit pretending to be Polish radicals had captured a radio station in German territory, transmitted anti-German statements, and then executed a group of Germans already condemned to death after dressing them in Polish military uniform).

To find people capable of creating diversions or conducting sabotage and reconnaissance missions was not an easy job in departments that were basically engaged in peacetime espionage, so Sudoplatov and Eitingon contacted the commanders of army reconnaissance units and parachute detachments, first and foremost trying to recruit officers with combat experience from the Russo-Finnish War (1939–40).

On the night of 20/21 June 1941, almost all secret service personnel, both the NKVD and NKGB (People's Commissariat of State Security), plus those belonging to all local agencies and bodies of the two ministries, stayed in their offices after the working day was over. At 03:00 hours they were informed that the Germans had bombed Russian cities, and their panzer units were driving wedges through Red Army formations.

CHAPTER 5

THE INVISIBLE FRONT

When the Germans invaded the Soviet Union in June 1941, the NKVD committed all its efforts towards defeating the Nazi foe.

There are many unanswered questions raised in the thousands of books on The Great Patriotic War (1941–45). Two in particular stand out at the beginning of the conflict. Was the German invasion a surprise for the Soviet leadership, and were Russian forces unprepared for the Germans on 22 June because Stalin refused to believe his intelligence sources?

The first question was essentially answered in the previous chapter, though a whole book would be needed to catalogue all the measures taken on the eve of the German offensive. As to the second question, it can be answered only if we are able to answer yet another, much more important one: was Soviet intelligence able to decipher the strategic plan of the Nazi leadership?

A persistent myth is that Stalin had all the relevant information about German intentions and targets supplied to him from various intelligence sources, but did not believe his spies and preferred "to trust Hitler". But if one takes a look at the information supplied by the most able spies located in the best positions, the reality is different from the myth. The information received by Stalin and his Political Bureau did not allow them to make right decisions, not because the intelligence officers were stupid or badly trained, but because the Germans made great efforts to obscure the "big

■ *Left:* Troops of the Independent Special Purpose Motorized Rifle Brigade of the NKVD (OMSBON) on patrol during World War II.

picture" and fed the Soviet intelligence services all sorts of disinformation. Many Russian spies had no idea they effectively operated under the control of German intelligence and counter-intelligence services, supplying Moscow with information the Germans wanted them to supply. In the first stage of the battle of wits the Nazis were victorious.

Consider first the timing of the invasion. Intelligence information about the date of the German attack was abundant from autumn 1940, but the reports were all different. Some agents reported that the war would start in the second half of 1941, whereas others, no less trustworthy, pointed to the spring of the same year. Between February and March 1941 some messages were more precise: the war, they said, would start in the period from mid-May to mid-June. But other

information undermined the validity of these reports. The Schulze-Harnack group, for instance, insisted that the invasion would start after Germany had concluded peace with Great Britain. In May there were other reports, all completely false. The spies warned that the invasion would start either in the middle or at the end of May at the latest. Soviet spy Richard Sorge reported from Japan on 21 May, basing his report on information from within the German Embassy there, that the invasion would commence at the end of May. Later came reports ranging from 15 June to 25 June, while some were extremely precise, stating that 22 June was the date. It is certain that the Germans originally intended to invade in May, but were delayed seven weeks by the Greek and Yugoslav campaigns (both of which began on 6 April). But in the USSR, after so many dates passed, few believed the

■ *Above:* This photograph of Soviet frontier troops was taken on 21 June 1941, the day before the Germans invaded. It is unlikely either men or dog were alive the next day.

■ *Right:* A German motorized column advances into the Soviet Union during the opening phase of Operation Barbarossa. Hitler deployed over three million troops to crush Russia.

accurate information when it came, and the Germans, most probably, counted on that. The wrong dates lessened the readiness of the army and especially the border troops, and the commanders understood that they could not keep their officers and men under the highest level of readiness indefinitely. It was only after the border troops and advance reconnaissance detachments had discovered German troops poised for the attack, that the Political Bureau realized, 10 days beforehand, the real invasion date.

Unfortunately, the deployment of German forces and their groupings were not clearly defined either. Once again, disinformation supplied by the Germans obscured the picture, making it almost impossible to take the right decisions. Some reports speculated that the German Army would have about 14 million soldiers by the spring of 1941, while others implied that the invasion forces would not be more than 1.5 million. Sorge reported that the Germans had between 170 and 190 panzer and mechanized divisions at the Soviet border, though they had only 19 armoured and 14 mechanized divisions in 1941. It is

interesting to note that the reports containing the wrong estimation of forces had the right date of attack, and vice versa. This was obviously one of the main aims of German disinformation: half-truths and half-lies. Sorge reported that the Germans would have only about a million men in the first echelon of the invasion, while the rest would be in the reserves. In reality, the Germans had less

■ *Above:* Despite Stalin's efforts to placate him, German dictator Adolf Hitler (pointing at map) always intended to conquer the western USSR.

than five percent of their forces in the reserves out of 4.6 million troops.

The directions of the main thrusts were also wrongly reported. None of the Soviet spies was able to get information about the real Operation Barbarossa, the codename for the German assault. No wonder: only nine copies of the plan were made, and three of them were handed over to the commanders of the armed services while the rest stayed in Hitler's safe until the end of the war. The Soviet agents reported on all earlier versions of the plan but not the last one adopted by the German General Staff. The invasion's objective was the destruction of the bulk of the Red Army in the western areas of the Soviet Union, specifically in the border region up to the Dnieper and Dvina rivers. That would lead to – and did result in – the cutting off of the Soviet armies and their encirclement around Smolensk, Uman, Bialystock and Kiev. Soviet intelligence reported, however, that the priority of the German Army would be capturing Moscow or the Baltic republics, or – as was stressed in many reports – an advance through the Ukraine towards the Donets coalmining basin and then to the Caucasus and the Baku oilfields.

German disinformation

Almost all the information received from agents in Germany and its allied states was aimed at deflecting the main attention of the Soviet High Command away from the real goals of the first phase of the invasion. These were not to seize territory but to envelop the main Soviet forces in the European part of the USSR in a 10-week campaign. A number of Soviet agents died in German cells without knowing they had earlier been used by their captors to supply misinformation. The German strategic plan was based on the experience of routing France in just 39 days. The chief of Russian exterior intelligence, Pavel Fitin, could not believe his ears when he heard in late 1939 from the former White émigré Count Neledov, who had helped the Germans to

draw up their invasion plans, that Hitler's generals planned to enter the Belorussian capital of Minsk five days after the beginning of the invasion, but that is exactly what happened. Neledov was found by the NKVD in Lvov prison when the Red Army entered the western Ukraine, as he had been arrested in Poland as a German spy.

In view of the vagueness of its intelligence, Moscow faced a difficult task when it came to minimizing the immediate impact of the invasion, but something was done. On 12 June, 10 days before the invasion, a top-secret order was issued by the General Staff to send out some troops to frontier defence positions in order to start mining roads, bridges and other strategic points. For the last seven days all the army was on full alert. The secret mobilization of about 800,000 men was under way, but Stalin refused to increase this number in order not to provoke Hitler's offensive

■ *Above:* Some of the thousands of Russian prisoners that fell into German hands in 1941. The NKVD established Blocking Detachments to deter desertions and attempts at surrender.

■ *Right:* During the invasion livestock and machinery were evacuated east. Anything left behind was destroyed as part of Stalin's scorched-earth policy.

before 22 June, i.e. before at least some of the preparations were complete on the Soviet side. But the assault by 153 well-trained German divisions, supported by 3712 tanks and self-propelled guns and 4950 aircraft, ensured their superiority.

The first troops that encountered the Germans were the lightly armed frontier detachments of the NKVD. But they were supported by their better-equipped colleagues of the frontier guards regiments. Some of the units were armed with artillery and even light tanks, but they were not able to wage sustained warfare. Their stubborn, almost sacrificial resistance irritated the German field commanders, who sometimes had to use artillery and aircraft to crush small units. Once inside the Soviet Union, the Germans had to fight not only Red Army forces but NKVD troops as well. Some of the latter were not ordinary combat units.

In May 1941, Lavrenty Beria submitted to Stalin a plan to create units to wage urban warfare and carry out numerous subversive activities if the Germans were successful in reaching the major economic centres of the Soviet Union. This plan included the creation of the highly mobile Destroyers' Battalions (*Istrebitelnye Bataliony*), which ensured security in the rear and could quickly destroy German paratroopers or rapidly advancing reconnaissance elements. Such battalions were formed in every major Soviet city.

Some NKVD troops soon found themselves desperately fighting to avoid encirclement by the well-trained and superbly equipped German forces. An NKVD cavalry regiment suffered appalling losses trying to block the German advance in the western Ukraine. In the Baltic region, two NKVD divisions managed to delay a very substantial German force, holding their positions against great odds. Even convoy battalions, used to guard and escort prisoners and military trains, were thrown into battle in Belorussia and the Baltic region, and distinguished themselves in that uneven confrontation. The most organized and determined resistance to the Germans in Kiev was offered by three NKVD divisions, while four NKVD divisions took

part in defending Leningrad and seven in the Battle of Moscow. It is universally accepted that most of them displayed toughness, iron discipline and exceptional loyalty to the regime, and their endurance helped raise the morale of other forces.

The steadfastness of the NKVD troops was noted by German commanders. In the Ukrainian port of Odessa, the local convoy regiment fought literally to the last cartridge, and less than a tenth of it survived. NKVD troops also fought in the Battle of Stalingrad (1942) and Battle of the Caucasus (1942). The Seventieth Field Army, formed entirely of NKVD troops, later took part in the Battle of Kursk (1943) and the Battle of Berlin (1945). Yet their deeds are much less well-known in the fighting army than the actions of the so-called Blocking Detachments (*Zagraditelnye Otriady*), also formed from NKVD troops. They were feared and hated, with reason.

The Blocking Detachments

It became clear from the first days of the war that many troops, poorly trained and led, were unable to fight, while some simply did not want to. The number of Soviet prisoners of war was growing rapidly, and so was the number of deserters. Retreat from positions without orders, panicking and fleeing from the battlefield became common in some parts of the front, and the NKVD was ordered to put an end to this by stationing Blocking Detachments behind the frontline. These troops were ready to fire on their own compatriots whether they were deserting or making attempts to surrender. Blocking Detachments had machine guns and sometimes even mortars, and did not hesitate to use them. Cruel though this was, it helped maintain a certain discipline in the fighting army, which, in this first phase of the war, was disorganized and unable to keep in communication with superiors and neighbouring units, and sometimes was infected with defeatism.

In February 1941, Stalin ordered that military counter-intelligence units of the

NKGB (State Security) became elements of the administrative staff in every army and naval unit. They still maintained a dual chain of command, reporting also to their NKVD headquarters on all operational and political matters, but they were assigned to the army and navy.

As well as being responsible for the equipping and provisioning of the troops, on 30 July 1941 Lavrenty Beria also became security supremo again, heading a merged and oversized NKVD/NKGB, and this time his powers were much greater than before. Military counter-intelligence became particularly important when Soviet troops were retreating. Young counter-intelligence officers in regiments and divisions even had the power to arrest the unit commander if he failed to comply with the orders of his superiors, but their primary mission was to

■ *Above:* German troops advance on Moscow during Operation Typhoon in late 1941. Four NKVD divisions took part in the defence of the city, fighting with courage and discipline.

deal with traitors, spies, deserters and soldiers who inflicted wounds on themselves and then pretended they had been hit by the enemy, in order to be transported to hospitals in the rear. During the first, chaotic phase of the war, maintaining discipline among soldiers became the priority not only for unit commanders but for NKVD personnel as well.

As for the intelligence service, its primary mission at this stage was to start large-scale guerrilla movements and diversionary activities in the enemy's rear. Beria had a list of intelligence officers who could be assigned to wage underground warfare during a German occupation as early as the beginning of April 1941, although it was inconceivable for any party functionary or army commander at that time to talk about the Germans seizing any Soviet territory. Later, ammunition depots and canned food stores were created in catacombs in Odessa, in the deep basements of derelict houses in many Russian cities, and in forests.

Two weeks after the beginning of the invasion the so-called Special Group directly subordinate to Beria was formed under Pavel Sudoplatov, deputy head of external intelligence, and his assistant, Nahum Eitingon. Its missions were intelligence and diversionary operations against Germany and her satellites, organization of guerrilla warfare, setting up espionage networks in the occupied territories, and using radio to feed disinformation to German intelligence.

The Shadow Army

The Special Group's backbone was formed from officers of the 1st (Intelligence) Directorate of the NKVD, and most of the jobs in the field would be done by guerrillas or special diversionary units. As soon as the Special Group was created, the formation of yet another very unusual unit commenced under its auspices: the Independent Special Purpose Motorized Rifle Brigade of the NKVD (OMSBON – Russian acronym of *otdel'naya motostrel'kovaya brigada osobogo naznacheniya*). The party's Central Committee and Comintern offered all the political émigrés and Communist refugees in the Soviet Union the chance to join OMSBON. About 2000 foreigners joined immediately, including Spaniards, Germans, Poles, Chinese, Bulgarians, Czechs and others. OMSBON also recruited about 10,000 of the best Soviet sportsmen. The crack shots, martial arts experts, boxers, archers and athletes formed diversionary groups which, complemented by German, Italian and Romanian speakers, were ready for clandestine and subversive operations in the enemy's rear areas. Intelligence aces like Georgi Mordvinov and Zoya Rybkina were also setting up diversionary and sabotage units. Five days after the German invasion started, for example, four such detachments were already formed, each numbering between 100 and 200 men and women.

Soviet sportsmen, especially parachutists and marksmen, proved to be very useful from the first days of war. In the Kiev Military District, for instance, the sportsmen from the local garrison were helping military intelligence and NKVD

■ *Below:* Partisans in action against the Germans during the early phase of Operation Barbarossa.

teams to capture German officers in the advancing units. One squad formed almost entirely of NKVD sportsmen operated in the rear of German and Romanian troops for about a week in the southern Ukraine, terrorizing the German administration and inspiring a massive hunt by field police and SS (élite Nazi troops) units. In July 1941 the Central Committee instructed underground party committees to be set up in the occupied lands, and for these bodies to use all methods to disrupt enemy operations, including ammunition and fuel supply. There is a rich tradition of partisan warfare in Russia, and Stalin and his Political Bureau were aware of how difficult it would be for the Germans to smother guerrilla movements in their rear, especially in autumn and winter, when the Red Army would be receiving reinforcements on the frontline.

Some of the groups were parachuted into the forests, as their missions were the destruction of enemy personnel and material on the railways; other groups had to set up in German-occupied cities. The latter were almost invariably a "family", consisting of a "grandfather", a "grandmother" and a "grandchild". The grandfather, the group leader, and the grandmother, his deputy, were old and battle-hardened Bolsheviks, some from intelligence or civil-war partisan backgrounds, and normally over 60 years old, while the grandchild was a very young man or woman who acted as a radio operator. Both the elder members of the group and the younger one would have been freed from military service due to their age or their health, and in most cases were local people, so their presence did not arouse any suspicions. They maintained communications with underground teams in the enemy rear and sent back valuable information about enemy intentions and movements. One of the most dangerous jobs was to be planted in German subversive and sabotage schools as trainees, so as to learn the possible targets of German diversionary forces.

At first, the OMSBON squads were engaged mostly in passive espionage

■ *Above:* An OMSBON squad behind German lines in 1941. OMSBON units targeted German rail lines in the first phase of what became known as the Rail War.

■ *Right:* OMSBON stage an assault for the camera during the Battle for Moscow in late 1941. OMSBON troops played a critical part in slowing the German advance.

■ *Below:* Intelligence ace Pavel Sudoplatov (front row, extreme left), photographed with members of the NKVD's Special Group in late 1941. It later became the NKVD's 4th Special Directorate.

operations, but as the German offensive progressed they took part in diversionary activity. Dmitri Medvedev, a former exterior intelligence officer and future Hero of the Soviet Union, was the first to take his special squad behind enemy lines. He operated in the area where he was born: near Briansk. His unit was instructed to destroy a section of the railway used by the Germans to transport tanks, artillery and ammunition closer to Moscow. The Medvedev unit

■ *Below:* Intelligence ace Pavel Sudoplatov (front row, extreme left), photographed with members of the NKVD's Special Group in late 1941. It later became the NKVD's 4th Special Directorate.

derailed a military train, blew up two bridges and destroyed a long section of the railway. This operation gave the name to a new type of warfare: the Rail War.

As the Germans approached Moscow in November 1941 and concentrated about 50 divisions, including 13 panzer divisions, the Red Army called on the support of NKVD professionals. A detachment of 290 OMSBON demolition experts mined the highways to the north, west and south of the Russian capital, installing 11,000 anti-tank and 7000 anti-personnel mines, and 160 high-explosive charges; they also mined 19 bridges and 2 pipelines. This detachment was thus able to destroy 50 German tanks and armoured personnel carriers (APCs), and about 70 trucks, for the loss of about 30 people.

The Germans sent a group of *Abwehr* (counter-intelligence) officers who spoke Russian and were dressed in Red Army uniforms to seize the bridge over the Yakhroma River. These men killed 12 Russian demolition experts who were preparing to blow up the bridge, allowing German tanks to advance towards Moscow.

At this critical moment an NKVD armoured train appeared and started a duel with 20 German tanks, blocking their advance until two OMSBON groups were able to force the Germans to withdraw. The bridge was then destroyed.

Meanwhile, 12 underground district party committees were formed in the Moscow *Oblast* (province), of which five were already operating in the enemy rear. As soon as Moscow became a frontline city, the urgent evacuation of enterprises, workers and government offices got under way. Part of OMSBON was left in Moscow in case the Germans did break through. Beria and his long-time friend and associate Bakhsho Kobulov, head of counter-intelligence, were assigned to prepare Moscow for possible enemy occupation. The scale of the measures they planned was tremendous. Explosives, traps, strongpoints, disruption of the water supply and heating systems, and continuous night guerrilla attacks were all designed to inflict enormous losses on the occupying troops. Radio sets were installed and stockpiled to ensure communications with the government and General Staff, and all railway lines, installations and bridges were mined. Some 244 people, including 47 of the best state security and intelligence officers, were specially selected to work in the underground had the Germans taken Moscow. Sudoplatov, head of the Special Group, and his deputy Eitingon were earmarked to stay and control this Moscow underground network.

The situation near Moscow was so grave that on the night of 22 October 1941 an order was issued to Colonel Ivanov, commander of an OMSBON regiment (and father of Igor Ivanov, appointed Minister of Foreign Affairs in September 1998), to use

■ *Below:* Soviet partisans. By the spring of 1942 there were hundreds of partisan units operating behind German lines. Each one had an NKVD representative.

■ *Far left:* General Sidor Artemevich Kovpak, who organized Soviet partisans and ended the war with his own division.

■ *Left:* General Petro Vershigora, a partisan leader who in January 1944 was given command of the "Kovpak First Ukrainian Partisan Division".

his troops to block Gorky Street, the main thoroughfare in Moscow leading to the Kremlin. The OMSBON fighters were prepared to stop the Germans there or all die. But the Germans did not get through, never getting closer than the outermost tramstop. After the German defeat near Moscow in December 1941, the trained agents of the Special Group and OMSBON groups were used elsewhere in the enemy rear.

When moving behind the German lines in winter, the OMSBON fighters, if not air-dropped, frequently skied. They were well trained in hand-to-hand combat, and well equipped. Each fighter had a submachine gun and pistol, 300 rounds of ammunition, 5 grenades, explosives, a knife, 10-day compo ration pack, compass, maps, a flask and a pot. All told, this load was about 30kg (66lb), and one had to move very fast with it. Every unit had a radio set, and almost all of them had fluent German speakers.

During the war the Special Group (later called the 4th Directorate of the NKVD) sent over 2000 units – about 15,000 agents – into the enemy rear. Twenty-three of the officers in the field received the highest Soviet award, becoming the Heroes of the Soviet Union, and more than 8000 were awarded other orders and medals. At a later stage of the war, when the Soviet troops advanced through Belorussia and the Ukraine, the commanders often applied to the NKVD for special detachments to disrupt the enemy rear and communications and to destroy local German headquarters. OMSBON and the units of the 4th Directorate were extremely lethal: they killed about 157,000 German troops, liquidated 87 high-ranking German officers and administrators, and captured or killed more than 2000 enemy spy groups.

By the spring of 1942, the Germans started to realize the scale of Soviet partisan operations. The guerrillas had already established large camps in remote forests, with well-organized and long-distance warning and messenger services, wireless communications with the Partisan Movement Headquarters, and even agents close to local German garrisons. Some of the guerrilla units had as many as 2000 men, although most of them, operating in the vicinity of small towns, were only 20–30 strong. The Soviet Air Force regularly dropped food, ammunition, explosives, weapons, newspapers and medicines to the guerrilla camps. Almost all had NKVD representatives acting as both instructors and counter-intelligence operatives. There was an intelligence section in the Partisan Movement Central Staff, although it was

■ Above: Gauleiter Erich von Koch (pointing with swastika armband) headed the Nazi civil administration in the Ukraine between 1941 and 1944. Targeted for assassination by the NKVD, he unwittingly unveiled intelligence about the Kursk Offensive in mid-1943 that saved his life. Koch eventually died in a Polish prison on 12 November 1986.

merely coordinating the acquisition of information and not collecting any independent intelligence except in conjunction with either the NKVD or military intelligence. The NKVD also supported and covered the party and *Komsomol* propagandists who were active in the occupied territories.

By the middle of the war the Russians had at least 1200 partisan detachments and special squads in the enemy rear, and, as the Soviet troops advanced west, these units maintained contact with advancing Red Army commanders and coordinated their operations with them. The partisan movement was especially effective in the Belorussian forests and swamps, and by the middle of 1942 it controlled big areas there, and later in the northern Ukraine as well. By mid-1943 the guerrillas in Belorussia had killed about 300,000 Germans, caused about 3000 train accidents, destroyed 1200 tanks and other armoured vehicles, burnt about 4000 trucks and blew up about 900 depots of various kinds. Hitler, who had

believed Trotsky's declarations that the people of Russia would support the invaders against Stalin's tyranny, grossly underestimated the possible impact of guerrilla warfare on his troops. The German field commanders also failed to grasp the scale of partisan operations. Had they known that there would be a Russian shadow army of almost 700,000 in their rear, they would have taken some precautions earlier. But by the middle of the war neither seven security divisions of the German Home Guard nor emergency squads totalling 4000 men and specially trained SS guerrilla warfare units sent by *SS-Reichsführer* Heinrich Himmler could make any difference to the situation.

There were hundreds of partisan instruction centres in the Soviet Union, with the largest in Georgia and the Gorky region. An NKVD camp in Georgia trained officers of the Special Sections, i.e. the counter-intelligence staff sent to guerrilla detachments as either instructors or spy catchers. A lot of work was done to simplify spy catching and the prevention of German infiltration of guerrilla units. For instance, a special questionnaire was composed that consisted of 200 questions combined in 20 groups. This had to be completed by every guerrilla and every candidate who wanted to become a partisan. The NKVD officers boasted that it was 99.99 percent accurate in exposing enemy agents: very few infiltrators could answer all the questions in the right way. The NKVD also managed to plant more than 100 agents in various parts of the German administration and local police.

Nikolai Kuznetsov

Some of the diversionary groups sent by the NKVD behind enemy lines coordinated their efforts with local partisan and underground forces, and received extensive information about German locations and movements of troops. One such was the unit of Dmitri Medvedev mentioned above, numbering about 100 fighters (85 of them OMSBON people), which had as its primary target Rovno, made the capital of the conquered Ukraine by the Germans. The office of the Ukrainian *Gauleiter* (district leader) Erich von Koch, the military headquarters and the All-Ukraine Gestapo were located there.

One man attached to Medvedev's unit was Nikolai Kuznetsov, a legend within Soviet intelligence, sometimes called the "Liquidator". His unusual linguistic abilities had flourished in part because his teacher of German had trained in Switzerland. He became a *seksot* of the OGPU in 1932. Working from 1935 in the design section of the Uralmach machine-building plant, Kuznetsov improved his spoken German talking to the many German specialists who worked at the plant. A year later he became an NKVD agent. Though arrested in the period of the Great Purge, he was soon released and transferred to Moscow to work in the central office of counter-intelligence. His speciality was working with foreign diplomats and correspondents, at which he was considered "brilliant". He also helped in the secret photographing of letters from the pouches of German diplomatic couriers, and received information about the movements of German diplomats in Moscow from their lovers and acquaintances.

In the summer of 1942, Kuznetsov was parachuted behind enemy lines and was based at Medvedev's OMSBON detachment camps. Before the mission, he spent some time in German prisoner-of-war (POW) camps, talking to inmates and developing his new identity as Lieutenant Paul Wilhelm Zibert, the winner of two Iron Crosses. A man of rare personal courage, he approached German officers or administrators in the streets of Rovno and Lvov, proclaimed their death sentences and shot them at point-blank range. The effect on the populations of these cities was tremendous. He also collected very valuable information.

One of the missions he was assigned in 1943 was the assassination of *Gauleiter* Erich von Koch, who had ordered the execution of so many Soviet operatives that his killing was considered a matter of honour for the NKVD. Kuznetsov befriended Koch's dog

■ *Left:* Soviet intelligence legend Nikolai Kuznetsov, here wearing a German uniform. Nicknamed the "Liquidator", he was totally fearless. He was killed in action in March 1944.

trainer at a restaurant and asked him to organize an audience with Koch. He said he wanted to ask the *Gauleiter* for permission to leave his Ukrainian bride at Rovno, rather than send her to Germany, along with many other young Ukrainian women, to work at an industrial enterprise. The audience was granted, although Kuznetsov and his partner were brought to Koch's office separately. When he entered the room, Koch embraced him and said: "Paul, I remember you as a child, when you were running around in the castle." Luckily, Kuznetsov was able to come up with a suitable reply. Despite this warm reception he was closely watched throughout the interview by Koch's three guards and a dog, so there was no chance to kill him and escape. Kuznetsov was prepared to die, but he changed his mind after Koch advised him to hurry back to his unit because a massive offensive was about to begin. Kuznetsov realized that this information was more valuable than Koch's life, and so he left. The offensive Koch mentioned was to be Operation Citadel at Kursk, the greatest tank battle in history.

Tidying up loose ends

Kuznetsov's next operation was the abduction of the German Major Martin Gettel, who had been suspiciously interested in Lieutenant Paul Wilhelm Zibert. Registered as an officer of the *Reichskommissariat* (Reich Civil Administration – responsible for administering occupied lands in Russia), Gettel was in fact an officer of the *Abwehr*. He was invited to lunch with a Dutch businessman, actually a member of the Soviet spy network, and never showed up again. About three weeks later Kuznetsov and his group made an attempt to assassinate Koch's deputy, Kurt Knut. Although his car was badly damaged by an anti-tank grenade, and what was left of it was riddled by at least 100 bullets, Knut survived. Several days later Kuznetsov captured and shot Major-General von Ilgen, the German commander of the local

special detachment made up of Soviet defectors and collaborators.

In 1943 the OMSBON intelligence unit operating in Vinnitsa discovered that Otto Skorzeny, head of German special operations, was training his people in the Carpathian Mountains for some secret mission. Kuznetsov befriended von Ostel, a German officer attached to the Skorzeny unit, and lent him a substantial sum of money. The grateful von Ostel promised to pay him back with Persian rugs, which he would bring back from a business trip. These words alerted Kuznetsov, and he reported them to the Centre. In combination with other agents' information, Kuznetsov's report made it clear that the Germans were preparing an attack on the American and Soviet Embassies in Tehran, where the first conference of the "Big Three" (Churchill, Stalin and Roosevelt) was scheduled. The NKVD increased security to prevent any attack taking place.

The death of Funk

On the morning of 16 November 1943, while the president of the Supreme Court of the occupied Ukraine, *SS-Oberführer* Alfred Funk, was in a barber's shop, Kuznetsov visited his office and waited in the reception. When Funk appeared, Kuznetsov shot him three times at point-blank range and left. His escape car was pursued without success. Finally, in February 1944, Kuznetsov approached the deputy district governor of Galicia, Otto Bauer, and his justice advisor in the centre of Lvov and killed them both. He and his team also killed more than 20 army and SS officers. Kuznetsov reportedly died in March 1944 when his unit ran into a trap set by Ukrainian nationalists collaborating with the Germans.

In April 1943, when the Red Army was consolidating its positions before the Battle of Kursk, the Central Committee of the Party and the Council of People's Commissars took the decision to divide the NKVD into three ministries. The first was the NKVD proper headed by Lavrenty

■ Above: Otto Skorzeny, Hitler's top special operations ace. In 1943 Kuznetsov foiled his plans to disrupt the Tehran Conference between the Allied leaders.

advancing Soviet troops, who would be in alien territory. Therefore the quality of agents and investigators became much less important than their numbers.

Abakumov had to increase the number of SMERSH personnel, and used the best army special units' staff for this purpose. He knew, as did Stalin, that as soon as the Red Army rolled into the Ukraine and beyond, German diversionary and sabotage units and spies would be sent behind Russian lines in their thousands. He also knew of the intensive work done by the *Abwehr* in recruiting an enormous number of Russian POWs in camps where they were starving. Some admittedly agreed to enter the German spy and sabotage schools just to get back to the Red Army, but thousands were prepared to fight against the Soviets. The Germans could also select from a million former Soviet citizens who had collaborated with the Nazis, and who were in no doubt that a Russian victory meant their execution as traitors. An independent department assigned to sending agents and diversionary groups into the enemy rear was also set up within SMERSH in 1943, and cooperated closely with military intelligence.

Merkulov's agency, the NKGB, was an enhanced version of the intelligence service of the NKVD. Its missions were not limited to intelligence deep in the enemy rear but also included intelligence worldwide. His people were further ordered to acquire technical secrets overseas by any possible means. From 1941 to the autumn of 1944, 566 intelligence officers were sent abroad for illegal operations, 1240 agents and informers were recruited, and about 42,000 documents and other items were obtained. About 1200 technical documents were obtained and more than half were used by Soviet industrial enterprises and scientific laboratories.

Beria did not cease to be the intelligence supremo: he was still in charge of coordinating all the intelligence services of the state. Besides, he retained control of strategic intelligence and technical

Beria, the second was the NKGB headed by Vsevolod Merkulov, and the third was SMERSH (Military Counter-Intelligence) headed by Victor Abakumov.

The intention behind this is sometimes interpreted as Stalin's wish to curtail Beria's powers and place SMERSH and the state security agency under the control of the State Committee of Defence, over which Stalin presided. But the truth is different. By now Stalin and his associates had no doubts that the war was being lost by Germany. The Red Army would move into territories previously occupied by Germany and her satellites, and be confronted by desperate attempts to stop its advance. There would be German sabotage and espionage activity in the rear of the intelligence, and his NKVD troops and local units were in charge of filtering millions of people as they were liberated from occupied territory and POW camps and came back to the USSR. Another of his tasks was the re-establishment of Communist structures in the liberated areas and preparations for the restitution of everything the Soviet Union had lost as a result of the German invasion. That meant making plans for transporting German plants and national treasures to the USSR.

In 1944 there were several major operations of NKVD troops far from the frontline. There were, in addition to the screening and filtration, also deportation operations. By the middle of 1945 more than 2,230,000 people had been deported to sparsely inhabited areas in Kazakhstan, Uzbekistan, Siberia and the Urals region. The largest number was made up of ethnic Germans, more than 687,000. The majority lived in the so-called Special Populated Areas (*Spetsposelenia*). Basically these were open villages and towns, not concentration camps like those used for ethnic Japanese detained in the USA during the war. But the inhabitants' movements were restricted, and they were monitored by special contingents of NKVD sergeants. The second-biggest group were the Chechens and Ingushi (about 406,000). Other deported North Caucasian peoples were the Karachai (60,000) and Balkars (33,000). Deported Kalmyks numbered about 70,000.

The deportation of yet another people, the Crimean Tartars, was always considered one of the worst crimes of Stalin's regime, senseless and groundless. In fact, as well as Tartars, Bulgarians, Greeks and Armenians were also deported from the Crimea. This was partly due to the animosity felt towards them by their neighbours, by Stalin and by the Soviet Union as a whole. The Germans had not inflicted any substantial losses on the local population, nor had they destroyed the buildings, farms and infrastructure of the Crimea, since they

wanted to keep all that for themselves and to use both the Crimea and Caucasus as their tourist resorts.

The Crimean Tartars, like Muslims elsewhere, fell for the promises of religious freedom, autonomy and exceptional quality of life offered by the Nazis. They fully cooperated with the Germans, especially in organizing the local police force, searching for Communist families and hunting for Soviet spies. Bulgarians in the Crimea, encouraged by the example of their motherland, which fought on the Axis side, followed suit. They readily supplied German troops with food, and some of them also joined local police detachments and participated in mopping-up operations

■ *Above:* SMERSH officers at a liberated Nazi concentration camp in 1944. As the Red Army moved into Germany, SMERSH began the screening of liberated Russian prisoners taken by the Nazis.

against Soviet guerrillas. Greeks, living mainly in seaside cities, used the opportunities offered by the German regime to start trading and setting up small enterprises, and, as such activities were encouraged by the Germans, this also became a crime in the eyes of the Soviet authorities. As for the local Armenians, they fell victim to the cunning game played by the Germans and the Armenian nationalists they had brought along. An Armenian military nationalist organization called Dromedar was set up in Simferopol, capital of the Crimea, to propagate the idea of an independent Armenia, and well-to-do Armenians even donated money for German military needs. Some Crimean Armenians were also recruited for subversive activities in the Soviet rear.

Deportations from the Crimea

In April 1944 Beria received approval from the government for the Crimean deportation operation. Some 23,000 NKVD troops and about 9000 NKVD secret service officers took part, and it lasted more than three months. They arrested about 1000 trained German agents and almost 8000 active collaborators who had served in the security units and police under the Germans. About 16,000 firearms were found, including more than 700 machine guns and 5 million rounds of ammunition. But Beria was reluctant to stop at this point, since the government had sanctioned the deportation, and about 183,000 Tartars, 12,000 Bulgarians, 15,000 Greeks and 10,000 Armenians were also removed, along with about 4000 Germans and other subjects. Beria agreed, however, not to deport women from these ethnic groups who were married to Russians either living in the Crimea or serving in the Red Army. This second phase of the operation has always been considered totally unnecessary, but Stalin and Beria had their own mysterious reasons.

As far as the Chechens and Ingushi were concerned, their confrontation with the Soviet secret service had a long history. After the October Revolution most of the mountain folk in the Caucasus, influenced by Bolshevik propaganda, supported the Communists against the White Guards. Soon, however, they realized the true intentions of the Russian Bolsheviks. Their religious leaders continually called for liberation from the "infidels", and there were hundreds of large and small revolts between 1922 and 1930. Some of these were brutally crushed, and most of the leaders of the mountain peoples' *teips* (clans) warned the Bolsheviks that they would never forget.

Chechen revenge

And they had not. The NKVD had to deal with enormous terrorist activity in the north Caucasus between 1937 and 1940. More than 1000 bandits were arrested or killed, 109 gangs were routed and about 14,000 firearms captured. But as soon as Nazi troops invaded the USSR the *teips* and religious leaders urged the mountaineers to sabotage all government measures and render any possible help to the Germans in their conquest of the Caucasus. As a result the areas inhabited by Chechens and Ingushi soon became uncontrollable. When the army draft started some young men evaded it, and those who were drafted soon deserted, went underground and joined armed bands. Mobilization of the local population for the construction of fortified positions was foiled, and some local leaders even encouraged the conscripts to kill NKVD officers and the draft teams.

In October 1941 an armed revolt started in the village of Borzoi, and about 800 people took part in it. Fighting between them and NKVD troops was so fierce that a squadron of aircraft was sent to bomb the rebels. In another village, Nikaroi-Kiy, the rebels surrounded and disarmed a Red Army unit, then executed 16 servicemen. When the German offensive in the south in the summer of 1942 was clearly heading towards the Caucasus, the rebels started to form battalions and destroy local administration offices and collective farms. Participation in the resistance operations was almost total as far as the male population was concerned. None of them was prepared to collaborate with the Soviet authorities, knowing they could expect no mercy from their own people. To indicate how strong the Chechen and Ingushi rebel forces were, when some went into hiding in Georgia, five rifle regiments and a mountaineer regiment of the NKVD were involved in the operation against them, plus NKVD counter-intelligence staff from Georgia, the Grozny *Oblast*, and the North-Ossetian and Daghestani Autonomous Republics.

From 1942, when the Germans started to send their paratroopers and intelligence teams to the Caucasian mountains, they invariably coordinated their operations with the local rebels. In many cases their sabotage and subversive teams consisted of both Germans and locals, the latter predominating. The Germans made several air drops of weapons and medical supplies to the bands, which soon became even more numerous. With their support German units were preparing to strike in the Red Army's rear and in the mountain passes. It took NKVD and Red Army forces several months to surround and destroy these units. From the day of the German invasion up to January 1945, more than 3000 guerrillas were killed in Chechenia and Ingushetia. The NKVD revealed that many bandits were hiding in villages and farms, and many gangs had a method of rotating their personnel: some of them from time to time returned to normal life on collective farms to give an appearance of legality and were temporarily replaced by their compatriots.

It was very hard to crush such resistance, in part because some of the nationalists were under the protection of local Soviet and party officials. Some bandits were even appointed to high positions, and were viewed by the public as true nationalists

and Chechen patriots. Some local NKVD officers of Chechen origin even secretly met German intelligence and army officers to discuss their support of the armed rising. Killed and arrested terrorists were proclaimed martyrs, and the struggle against Russia became a sacred duty. Deportation was regarded by Chechens and Ingushi as an offence against both their nationality and their religion, and many

leaders of the *teips* swore on the holy Koran that they would have their revenge. Their chance came 50 years later when the war in Chechenia broke out, and the Chechens used it to the full.

The NKVD and SMERSH were jointly responsible for the screening of many thousands of Russian POWs and military personnel who had managed to escape while their units had been encircled by the Germans. The POW problem was one of the regime's biggest during the war because of the magnitude of the number of captured Soviet soldiers in the first months of the German offensive, and also because of the moral, political and emotional implications that they entailed. From the very first days of the war the Political Bureau took the decision that the soldiers and especially officers who surrendered had to be considered traitors, and that their families would be exiled. When Stalin learned that the family of his elder son, Yakov Dzhugashvili, had been exiled after he had been taken prisoner, he said to his bewildered relatives that there were many thousands of families of war prisoners so exiled, and he had no right to make an exception for the family of his own son.

On 27 December 1941, the State Committee of Defence and Council of the People's Commissars issued a decree which instructed that all POWs and the soldiers who escaped from encirclement by the Germans should be screened in the NKVD camps. This gave birth to the myth that these camps were just transit points for sending former POWs *en masse* to labour camps and prisons. The truth was different. Most of them were exonerated and returned to fighting units. For instance, from about 303,000 sent to the screening camps before 1 October 1944, 231,000 were sent back to the army, about 18,000 to the penal (assault) battalions, 30,000 to industrial enterprises, and about 6000 to be convoy troops. About 12,000 were arrested and some 5000 died as a result of their wounds or treatment in German POW camps. In total, more than 95 percent of soldiers successfully passed the checks and were exonerated. As for officers, a significant number of them were sent to penal battalions where they fought as rank-and-file personnel: that was the punishment for surrender. However, officers who acquitted themselves well had their rank restored.

A reappraisal of numbers

In November 1944 the State Committee of Defence took a decision that former POWs were to be sent to the army directly, bypassing the NKVD camps. Only four percent were arrested for collaboration with the enemy, and a roughly similar proportion was sent to the penal battalions. As for those liberated after the war from POW camps and from industrial slavery in Germany, these were received by about 100 camps and 46 army reception centres. Beria required that every applicant be checked within 10 days and, if exonerated, sent either to his (or her) pre-war address or to reserve military units (later the term was increased to about two months). By the

■ *Left:* Lieutenant-General Andrei Vlasov (right), the leader of the Russian Liberation Army, which was raised by the Nazis in 1944.

■ *Below:* Red justice – Vlasov (far right) and his commanders hang in the Lubianka prison following their capture at the end of the war.

spring of 1946, 4,199,488 Soviet citizens had been repatriated, including 1.5 million POWs, and only about 15 percent were punished. The latter were mostly people who had agreed to serve in the German police, as guards, in the so-called Russian Liberation Army (ROA), in national legions or various punitive forces. And even these were not executed, as might have been expected, and their treason was actually forgiven, as they were simply exiled for six years. On 6 November 1944, British ships delivered 9907 former Soviet POWs to Murmansk who had fought in the German Army on the Western Front. The Russian Criminal Code stipulated that defection of the military to an enemy army in wartime was punishable by death, and most of the prisoners had expected the NKVD to execute them right there, even on the Murmansk pier. But what these people got was also just six years' exile.

Games and hunts

Myths about the secret services of the USSR are popular not only in the West but in Russia as well. Novels, films and short stories about Russian intelligence during World War II made the public believe that their intelligence penetrated not only the German General Staff but was even getting information from Hitler's party deputy, Martin Bormann. OGPU and later NKVD coordinators in Berlin had established contacts with Martin Bormann and his secretaries in the mid-1930s, but Stalin had not attached great importance to this as he realized that at the beginning of the war any contacts at this level would be totally broken.

After the Gestapo had arrested most agents of the Russian networks, almost no information was coming out of Germany from these sources. But amazing as it may seem, there were Soviet agents who really had access to the very top figures in the German establishment. One of them was Olga Chekhova, former wife of the famous Russian writer's (Anton Chekhov) nephew and an international film star who lived in

Germany. She was immensely popular in the 1930s, playing in Hollywood and European productions, and received the title of German State Actress in 1936. She frequented official receptions, was a friend of Eva Braun, Hitler's lover, and was admired by Hermann Goering and many other leading figures of Hitler's Germany. Arrested by SMERSH after the war and brought to Moscow, she did not disclose her relations with Soviet intelligence, but was soon allowed to go back to Germany. Very few people knew that she was received by Stalin in the Kremlin and awarded the Order of Lenin for her intelligence services during the war. Beria always believed that a valuable

■ *Above:* Magda Goebbels, who unwittingly supplied intelligence to the Soviets through her friend Marica Rokk, who was a Russian spy.

agent should never be exposed, even within the intelligence service, and he had his own special network to control them.

Another source of top-level information from the Third Reich was the Hungarian-born actress Marica Rokk. She was loved and frequently entertained by Magda Goebbels. The news she received from Goebbels and his wife was transferred to Moscow immediately by the "strategic intelligence channels", i.e. via Beria's own network. When Soviet troops entered Germany she was allowed to go to Austria, where she was helped to establish her own film company.

Igor Miklashevsky

Information from such sources came through the channels established by illegal agents individually planted in Berlin on the eve of the war. They were directed and controlled by Igor Miklashevsky, something of a James Bond figure within the NKVD. A former boxing champion, Miklashevsky played the role of a Soviet defector, thus apparently following the steps of his uncle, who had defected from the Soviet Union at the beginning of the Great Patriotic War and had become a leading member of the German Committee for the Liberation of Russia from the Bolsheviks. After befriending the German boxing champion Max Schmeling, Miklashevsky gained access to German high society. He contacted Olga Chekhova and other agents at official receptions.

There was a plan, involving Olga's knowledge of Hitler's itinerary and her relations in Russia, to assassinate Hitler if Moscow ever fell to the Germans and he then visited the city. The mission was assigned to the composer Lev Knipper, brother of Olga Chekhova, and his wife. Later the Kremlin was not interested in killing Hitler, although Miklashevsky was sure he could arrange it in Berlin. Stalin thought that the elimination of Hitler and his replacement with a more moderate figure might lead to a separate peace

between Germany and the Western powers. In 1944, Miklashevsky dispatched his uncle and fled to France. He stayed there for about three years, his mission being to locate the top officers of the Russian Liberation Army, recruited by Germany, who were trying to hide in France. He returned to the Soviet Union in 1947, received the Order of the Red Banner and took up boxing again.

NKVD transmitters

Russian spies were well equipped for strategic intelligence missions. After the radio transmitters of the Red Orchestra and other European networks were located by German direction-finding units, the special laboratories of the NKVD were assigned to produce, in a matter of months, multi-frequency radio equipment that could transmit up to several thousand code signs in half a second. The information to be transmitted was first recorded on a metallic tape or disk, and then swiftly broadcast on several automatically switched frequencies. No direction-finder was able to get the bearing of such radio sets, which had no equivalents elsewhere in the world. They used batteries because the Germans switched off electric power district by district to help them quickly locate the area from which a transmission might be coming. Sometimes the Soviet agents transmitted from a car or motorcycle.

As for the intelligence and counter-intelligence officers in the war zone, the last three years of the war were exceptionally difficult. In 1943, SMERSH officers in southern Russia and the Ukraine were engaged in massive hunts for German field spies, saboteurs and diversionary groups. The losses among SMERSH officers in field patrols before the summer operations of the Red Army were appalling: the groups of German agents and pro-German Ukrainian nationalists in Soviet uniforms were numerous, well equipped and superbly trained. Fights with such groups normally led to the total destruction of one side or the other, as each of the fighters knew what would happen if his side lost. In some cases, when SMERSH lost, it had to call in army units to encircle and sweep the area, and again losses were very high.

By the middle of 1943 the combined efforts of the NKGB, military intelligence and SMERSH bore fruit and they managed to plant several agents in *Abwehr* intelligence schools. After receiving information about 200 agents sent to the Soviet rear, the secret services either arrested them or forced them to cooperate. The result was that, despite the enormous number of POWs in German camps from which to recruit and the collaboration of many Muslims with the *Abwehr*, the latter was unable to organize either large-scale intelligence operations or serious diversionary activity in Russia.

The NKGB was also engaged in hunts of a different sort: for major traitors such as the creator of the Russian Liberation Army (ROA), former Soviet Lieutenant-General Andrei Vlasov. He was captured in 1942 when in command of the Soviet Second Shock Army, and soon started to collaborate with the Germans. There were other high-ranking traitors like Generals Trukhin, Zhilenkov and Zakutny, but Vlasov was a special case. He was leading the whole anti-Soviet movement; and some SMERSH officers believed that it had been he who had recognized Stalin's son Yakov in a German concentration camp. Vlasov was kept by the Germans as a propaganda figure until 1943, when defeats prompted them to start using the so-called Eastern Battalions, formed mainly of Soviet POWs. On 24 February 1943, the Military Collegium of the Supreme Court of the USSR sentenced Vlasov to death *in absentia*.

The hunt for *Voron* (Russian for "raven"), as Vlasov was called in NKGB reports, was on an unprecedented scale. When the intelligence units disclosed that Vlasov regularly visited Pskov, Smolensk, Minsk and other cities where the Germans had formed branches of the Russian

Committee, an embryo of the projected puppet government, and where there were combat units of the Russian Liberation Army, at least 15 operational groups and about 20 secret agents in various areas received orders to terminate him. One of these groups was led by Francisco Guillon, a 22-year old Red Army captain and a holder of the Order of Lenin who, as a boy, had fought in the Republican Army in Spain. There were four more Spaniards in his group. The NKGB operational groups had detailed information about Vlasov's associates and their movements, and even planted agents on his staff. However, Vlasov survived, since the Germans were concerned with the rapid decomposition of the Eastern Battalions in the face of Soviet success, and so transferred them to the West European theatre. Vlasov was eventually caught in 1945, and he and almost all his ROA and

■ *Above:*
Lieutenant-Colonel Heinrich Scherhorn, a German officer who worked for the NKVD at the end of the war, luring German agents and paratroopers into captivity. So successful was his deception that Hitler awarded him the Knight's Cross while he was working for the Russians.

■ *Left* The Soviet agent Demianov, who convinced the German High Command that there was a large Nazi unit operating in the Berezina forests and which needed supplying with men and equipment.

■ *Above:* The deception operations against the German were organized by some of the best intelligence operatives the Soviets had, including Eitingon (centre) and Sudoplatov (right). This photograph was taken in 1945.

Russian Committee main figures were hanged in the summer of 1946 in the Lubianka prison in Moscow.

As the war reached its climax, Stalin and Beria encouraged the intelligence bodies to render greater assistance to the advancing Red Army. One way was to make the German Army High Command believe there were substantial German forces left in the Soviet rear, capable of effective operations and needing help in the form of equipment and experts. A Soviet agent called Demianov, of Russian noble descent and a graduate from an *Abwehr* school, was sent to Belorussia in 1944. He enjoyed the full trust of the *Abwehr* and used it to persuade the Germans to start helping a large unit purportedly stuck in the Berezina forests. This classic deception operation and radio game was conducted by some of the best secret service officers the USSR had in those

days: Generals Sudoplatov and Eitingon, Colonel Michael Makliarsky (a famous playwright after the war), Jacob Serebriansky and William Fisher, who in the Cold War era would be arrested in the USA as a Soviet master spy – Colonel Rudolf Abel.

German and Austrian Communists were also involved, playing the roles of the personnel of the phantom unit, and Lieutenant-Colonel Heinrich Scherhorn was the unit commander. His unit of about 1500 really had been fighting near the Berezina River, but he had surrendered and ordered his men to surrender too. Scherhorn and his radio operators then started to work for the NKGB. They got in touch with the German zone command and asked for weapons, medicine and food, which were air-dropped into the forest. Officers and men of *Abwehrkommando* 103 were also sent to Scherhorn's unit, and immediately captured. Two of them were then recruited to play the radio game. The plan of the operation was to seize as many German agents and paratroopers as possible, especially experts in diversionary and demolition operations. On one occasion several magnificently fit sergeants in SS uniform appeared: these were Skorzeny boys, and particularly difficult to deal with. Later, two more phantom regiments were created by the NKGB, each "commanded" by a captured German colonel ready to collaborate. Though the war moved onto German territory, the *Wehrmacht* High Command still thought Scherhorn's unit was fighting in total isolation. In the early spring of 1945 Hitler even awarded him the Knight's Cross for his courage and endurance, and on 25 March he was promoted to colonel by Field Marshal Guderian. But the game was now over for both Scherhorn and his former superiors.

As for Sudoplatov and his men, there was another game coming up: fishing for German missile, aircraft, atomic and electronic specialists among the POWs and displaced persons, and delivering them to Moscow. And some of the intelligence officers were getting ready for a trip across the Atlantic Ocean.

CHAPTER 6

THE GREATEST SECRET EVER STOLEN

In 1945 the Americans had the lead in the race for the atomic bomb, but the NKVD deployed its assets to redress the nuclear balance.

I n the summer of 1945, a group of Soviet scientists of the highest calibre was brought by special aircraft to Germany. They were to visit a number of the scientific research-and-design establishments and weapon production lines which had survived Allied bombing. Special attention was paid to Peenemünde, where the V-2 rocket had been produced under the guidance of Wernher von Braun, future American missile programmes director. The trip was organized by Lavrenty Beria on Stalin's instructions, and each team of specialists was allocated a particular aspect of Germany's weapons design to study. The man who led the team assessing von Braun's former domain at Peenemünde was Sergei Korolev, who later created the Soviet missile industry and designed Yuri Gagarin's first spacecraft.

As early as September 1944, more than 40 special-purpose groups had been created by the NKVD and NKGB, composed of intelligence officers and technical experts, with the aim of capturing German scientists and engineers engaged in all types of secret design programmes. The NKGB's so-called Lightning Unit (*Gruppa Molnia*) boasted that they had captured von Braun's brother, Heinrich, who had also worked on the missile programme. The groups were also to acquire actual weapons, drawings,

■ *Left:* The rewards of espionage – Russia's first atomic bomb is detonated in 1949, courtesy of stolen Western nuclear secrets.

■ *Right:* Sergei Korolev, who led the Soviet team investigating the work carried out at the Peenemünde rocket research establishment after World War II.

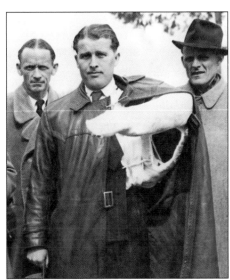

■ *Above:* The German scientist Wernher von Braun (with arm in plaster), who worked with the Americans after the war. The NKGB captured his brother Heinrich, also a rocket scientist.

■ *Right:* A German V-2 rocket. The Soviets were interested in all aspects of German rocket and missile technology.

calculations, laboratory equipment and even tools. In addition to long-range ground-to-ground missiles, the Soviets studied the German ground-to-air missile programme, still in the experimental stage, and Messerschmitt jet fighter technical documentation. But there was something the Soviet scientists and engineers were particularly interested in: atomic energy laboratories, not because they did not know anything about it, but rather because they already knew a lot and wanted the smallest details about German attainments in this field.

The Soviet secret service paid attention to the so-called "atomic problem" from 1939 onwards. Originally it was merely a counter-intelligence question, since there were at least three groups of Soviet scientists engaged in theoretical research about the uranium fission chain reaction using a reactor as a control medium. Some of them, including Zeldovich and Khariton, later became the creators of Soviet Russia's thermonuclear weaponry. The NKVD was responsible for keeping secret almost all scientific research and experimentation. But then the technical and strategic intelligence sections almost simultaneously reported to Beria that European scientists had achieved the nuclear fission of uranium-235 (uranium-235 was the essential fissionable material for the atomic bomb; it cannot be separated from its natural companion – uranium-238 – by chemical means; the atoms of these respective isotopes must be separated from each other by physical means), irradiated by neutrons, and the subsequent chain reaction. After this event the names of nuclear physicists and their articles disappeared from the pages of Western magazines and journals.

So the atomic problem was singled out by the Soviet secret service as one of supreme importance as early as 1940. Since the late 1930s the People's Commissariat of Internal Affairs had ceased to be a purely punitive organization, and had departments and sections where engineers and even some invited scientists studied intelligence information about various weapon systems, radio equipment, aircraft and automobiles. Beria became especially interested in nuclear fission. He called on the Political Bureau to form a special commission, which was convened under Politburo member Molotov and the scientists Yoffe and Kapitsa. The commission studied the intelligence acquired from Germany, France and Great Britain but, on the advice of the scientists, decided not to take any action. They thought the atomic energy problem, though it existed in theory, would take decades to solve, and it was not worth spending money on something that would

weapons. His belief was not based on intuition only, since he maintained contact with leading scientists in Russia and abroad. According to Beria's son Sergo, Robert Oppenheimer, the nuclear physicist, stayed at Beria's house in Moscow for about two weeks in 1939. If Oppenheimer did visit Russia then he did so secretly, because he would not later have been appointed director of the top-secret atomic laboratory in the United States if the American authorities had known of this visit.

Stalin blocks the atomic bomb project

In 1940, a special message was sent to Soviet intelligence stations in the USA and Great Britain instructing them to detect and penetrate scientific and research centres engaged in atomic energy projects with military applications. Armed with the new information which resulted, Beria once again applied to Stalin and the party's Central Committee and urged them to launch an atomic weapons programme. This time there was no opposition from Soviet scientists: both they and their Western colleagues had already admitted that an atomic bomb project was realistic. Besides, the NKVD intelligence service reported that uranium was no longer being exported from Czechoslovakia as it was all being consumed by German research centres (the Germans also tried to acquire most of the heavy water production). African uranium, according to other agents, was secretly being transported to the United States. But the Soviet programme was blocked again, this time by Stalin himself, who felt he did not have enough resources and people to assign to such a project with war imminent. His priority was new tanks and fighter aircraft, and he believed, mainly due to assurances by the military, that Germany would soon be routed.

In September 1941 Gorsky, the head of the London *residentura*, reported that he had received reliable information about the British atomic weapons programme. The information he supplied to Moscow

not bear fruit in the foreseeable future, especially in view of the imminent war. Beria tried to convince them, but in vain. He then instructed NKVD agents in the West to pay particular attention to any data associated with atomic explorations. His point was that Germany must not overtake the Soviet Union in the creation of atomic contained a memorandum of the British Joint Chiefs of Staff and papers of the Uranium Committee. He even had details of the participation in this work by some universities and such companies as Imperial Chemical Industries, Metropolitan Vickers and the Woolwich Arsenal.

In December 1941, more valuable information became available when a British scientist working for the government atomic programme volunteered, on ideological grounds, to supply the Soviet Union with hundreds of secret papers. It seems this was Allan Nunn May. Between 1942 and 1946 Gorsky received from him more than 2000 pages of documents, material so important that it became the basis for a new report from Beria to Stalin in 1942, showing the scale of research and experiments in Great Britain and America, where the cream of scientific Europe had gathered to work on the atomic bomb project. Stalin made up his mind. A Chief Directorate for the Uranium Project was created under Boris Vannikov, an outstanding weapons production admini-strator, and made subordinate to Lavrenty Beria himself.

Why the chief of the secret service was responsible for a mainly technical project is a question still being asked today. The main reason was that Stalin trusted him. He knew Beria's ability to grasp any problem and to use every possible route to achieve success. And there were two more factors. The first was the omnipotence of the NKVD, its enormous leverage on society, especially in wartime. The second was that intelligence reports about the bomb came first to Beria's office to be translated, evaluated, processed and distributed. He already had the staff capable of doing most of this new job, and he knew whom to send abroad to get more information, and fast.

The people who became the core of Beria's strategic and technical intelligence in the USA and Great Britain were mostly young graduates of the so-called Special Purpose School of the NKVD. Yatskov, a highly qualified officer, was sent to America before the war, to be followed in 1943 by Kvasninkov, who became head of a separate technical intelligence station in New York. Semen Semenov, a young engineer, was in contact with some famous American scientists, while Ishak Akhmerov, a master spy, worked in the USA from 1941 to 1946 as head of the illegal *residentura*, receiving information from his sources in govern-ment agencies and atomic research centres. As an illustration of the volume of

■ *Right:* The US atomic research laboratory at Oak Ridge, a facility that was easily infiltrated by Soviet spies in the 1940s.

■ *Above:* Claus Fuchs (second from right) provided Moscow with information about the Americans' uranium and plutonium bombs.

atomic bomb had been formulated in Great Britain, the NKGB and NKVD received orders to help Soviet scientists catch up with their Western colleagues. Beria asked Stalin to appoint Igor Kurchatov, a talented young scientist, director of the programme. Stalin agreed, commenting that Beria's protégé would encounter opposition from older and more famous scientists. But the choice proved to be right. Kurchatov was the man who built the first European nuclear reactor in 1946, the first Soviet nuclear bomb in 1949, the world's first thermo-nuclear bomb in 1953, and then an atomic power station (he was three times Hero of Socialist Labour for his achievements).

All this catching-up would have been impossible without intelligence. Kurchatov conceded that the very first reports he received had changed the views of Soviet scientists on many problems and greatly facilitated implementation of the atomic bomb programme. The most important information was that about plutonium, because there had been no research on it in the Soviet Union. The Russians acquired not only the methods of calculating the atomic charge critical mass, but also a diagram and technical description of the American bomb, information about a nuclear reactor that could produce 100 grams (3.5oz) of plutonium a day, and even the rates of admissible irradiation. In April 1945, a detailed description of the Fermi experimental reactor was received in Moscow, which most probably became the prototype of the reactor later built in the Soviet Union.

On 24 July 1945, US President Harry S. Truman decided, after consultations with Winston Churchill, to inform Stalin at the Potsdam Conference of the "Big Three" that the USA had acquired a weapon of enormous power that had been already tested. Churchill, who observed Stalin calmly receiving the news from Truman and then not asking any questions about it, came to the conclusion that the Soviet dictator had had no idea about the real

information acquired and supplied to Moscow from the American *residenturas*, from 1943 to 1945 Akhmerov alone sent to his centre 2500 rolls of film, i.e. about 75,000 pages. These intelligence operations were supported by hundreds of agents and informers, and also by some members of the Communist Party of the USA. Most of the local supporters cooperated with Soviet intelligence because they thought that it would be in the interests of a common victory over Nazi Germany, and that their governments should not keep atomic weapons secret from their Soviet ally.

As soon as Moscow received information that experimental equipment had been installed at the American atomic centre at Los Alamos and the principal design of the potential of the new super-weapon because he was invariably amiable and affable. But Stalin did not need to ask any questions. Two hours before the meeting of the "Big Three" Stalin had spoken to Beria, who had just received the news of the nuclear test explosion in the USA.

It took the Russians two years from that date to build their own bomb, which they tested two years later, in 1949. Decades of research were compressed into just four years because the greatest secret in the world had been already stolen.

The scientists' plot

The scientists who let the nuclear genie out of the bottle were, of course, proud of their achievements, but they were also concerned that they were giving the politicians a doomsday weapon. Some of them were idealists, respectful of the "Russian experiment"; many thought that, after all her losses in the war against Fascism, Russia had a right to the military secrets of her allies. As for those who were Communist sympathizers, they were concerned that as soon as the war was over the Soviet Union would again become the West's "potential enemy". So their idea was that sharing the atomic secret with Russia meant preserving world peace.

Oppenheimer, it seems, was one of them. A man of extraordinary intellectual abilities (he spoke eight languages including ancient Sanskrit and learnt Dutch in six weeks), he was a Harvard and Cambridge graduate capable of predicting the discovery of neutrons, positrons and nuclear stars. Since his youth he had moved among Communists and liberals, the more so as the Depression years increased the number of pro-Socialist intellectuals. He was married to Ella Friedman, a left-leaning painter whose brother was a Communist. Robert Oppenheimer was a staunch anti-Fascist, as were other famous physicists who worked on nuclear energy problems, including Enrico Fermi, Bruno Pontecorvo and Leo Szilard. This had attracted the

■ *Left* One of the young graduates of the so-called Special Purpose School of the NKVD: Semen Semenov. An engineer, he was in contact with some famous American scientists. He spent most of his life back in the USSR working as a boilerman.

attention of Russian intelligence in the 1930s. After his father's death in 1937, Robert Oppenheimer inherited substantial wealth, and used it extensively to support the anti-Fascist cause in Spain. In 1942, at the age of only 38, he became the head of the theoreticians who were creating the model of the future nuclear bomb. All the research in that period was conducted according to a unified plan called the Manhattan Project (a US Government research project that produced the first atomic bomb, in which some British scientists took part in compliance with an agreement signed between the two countries). Incidentally, this centralized operation was advocated by Oppenheimer himself as the best method of beating the Nazis in the race for the super-weapon.

As soon as the unified command of the project was created, both the American and British security services showed concern that there were some scientists with leftist backgrounds on the project staff, including Oppenheimer himself. He assured them that he had broken all ties with the Communists, and so counter-intelligence left him alone. Technically neither Oppenheimer nor Fermi were Russian agents, as they never handed over any confidential papers to the Soviet secret service. But General Sudoplatov agreed that they made

■ *Left:* The brilliant American scientist Robert Oppenheimer (wearing hat) was a staunch anti-Fascist who believed that sharing atomic secrets with the Russians would preserve world peace.

it possible for Soviet technical intelligence to have reliable sources of information in the most important atomic laboratories in Oak Ridge, Los Alamos and Chicago.

Oppenheimer and Szilard almost certainly knew about the leakage of information to the USSR, but they reckoned that only parity of forces in the world, ensured by the presence of nuclear weaponry on both sides, could prevent nuclear war. The Dane Niels Bohr, the titan of physics, and Fermi, the man who made the first chain reaction and was later named "the father of the atomic bomb", were of the same opinion. After talking to his tutor Fermi, Bruno Pontecorvo informed his Russian friends that Fermi was most agreeable to the idea of sharing information about nuclear energy with the Soviet Union. Szilard's sympathy for the USSR may also have been increased by disputes which he had with the military administration of the Manhattan Project.

The hard information was physically supplied by less well-known scientists. Most Western historians believe that the most important of the Kremlin's atomic spies was Klaus Fuchs, who provided Moscow with information about both the Americans' uranium and plutonium bombs. He handed over not only the theoretical calculations but also the diagrams showing the dimensions of the bomb's components.

Born in Germany into a Quaker family in 1912, Fuchs became a Communist at the age of 20. In 1933 he emigrated to England, and there finished his higher education. Recruited into a nuclear project called "Tube Alloys" in 1941, Fuchs began passing information to Soviet intelligence agents in the same year. He was sent to the USA in 1943 as a member of the British team joining the Manhattan Project. In 1944, in New York, he met a man called Harry Gold, who identified himself as a link to the Soviet secret service (codename Raymond), and who later contacted Fuchs in Boston and Santa Fe. Posted to Los Alamos, a secret city where 45,000 people were building the bomb, Fuchs was able to pass to Russia an enormous volume of top-secret technical information. He returned to Great Britain in 1946 as head of the Theoretical Physics Division at Harwell Atomic Energy Centre, where the British were resolved to build their own bomb. In 1947 Fuchs re-established contacts with the Soviet agents in Great Britain. This time his link was a young officer called Alexander Feklisov who, in order to talk to Fuchs on an equal footing, had undergone special training in nuclear physics. The plan of every meeting was discussed and approved in the Moscow Centre. Feklisov met Fuchs six times in the period between 1947 and 1949, and Fuchs appreciated the professionalism of the people who had compiled his questionnaires. He even commented that, judging by them, Soviet scientists were very close to making their own bomb. After the Federal Bureau of Investigation (FBI) got information that there had been a British scientist providing secret information to the Soviet Union from Los Alamos, Fuchs came under suspicion due to his Communist background. In 1950 he confessed and was sentenced to 14 years

■ *Above:* At the Potsdam Conference (July–August 1945) Stalin (at the far side of the table with moustache) was told of the US nuclear test explosion by Beria.

in prison, though the Soviet Government denied he had spied for them. Released in 1959, he emigrated to East Germany and became deputy director of the Nuclear Physics Research Institute.

Fuchs's communications agent, Harry Gold, was a chemist himself. He was recruited by the NKVD in 1935, and soon

■ *Above right:* Soviet scientist Igor Kurchatov, the man who built the first European atomic reactor in 1946, the first Soviet atomic bomb in 1949 and the world's first thermonuclear bomb in 1953.

■ *Left:* Another Western nuclear physicist who believed that sharing nuclear secrets with the Soviet would preserve peace – Bruno Pontecorvo.

started to provide it with important technical information about the main directions of research being carried out by American physicists and chemists, which he learned through his friends in industry and in research centres. One of those who supplied information to him from 1942 was David Greenglass, a US Army machinist who worked first at the atomic centre at Oak Ridge and then at Los Alamos. He was related to another physicist, Julius Rosenberg, who also shared professional secrets with Greenglass.

Some information on the Manhattan Project was received by Soviet spies in America from an idealistic young scientist called Theodore Hall (codename Mlad), who believed that a US monopoly of knowledge about atomic weapons could lead to his country becoming a Fascist state. A member of the team designing the implosion trigger for an experimental bomb, he was able to pass two batches of extremely important information to the Soviet "mailbox". Some historians believe that he was even more important to the Russians than Fuchs, with access to information at Los Alamos no other spy enjoyed. A star pupil of Professor John Van Vleck at Harvard, he undoubtedly received some information from his tutor, an authority on quantum theory who had also been recruited by Oppenheimer to take

part in designing the nuclear device. Although his spying became known to the FBI, Hall never confessed and was never put on trial, because he knew too much that the Americans wanted kept secret that could have come out in court. He left America for Great Britain, where he became a leading scientist at Cambridge.

Bruno Pontecorvo – Soviet spy

Other physicists who helped the Soviet secret service were Allan Nunn May and Bruno Pontecorvo. The latter, a brilliant apostle of Fermi, was born in Pisa in 1913 into a wealthy Jewish family and was a member of the Italian Communist Party from 1939. After emigrating to the USA, he worked at various research centres, becoming one of the world's leading scientists in the nuclear field. In 1949 he moved to the British centre at Harwell; but after Klaus Fuchs confessed Pontecorvo took his family on holiday – first to Italy, then to Sweden, and finally to Finland. From there they were reportedly transported to Russia by a specially assigned submarine. He subsequently worked in the Soviet atomic centre at Dubna. He became a member of the Communist Party of the Soviet Union in 1955, an Academician of the Soviet Academy of Sciences, and received Lenin and Stalin Prizes. His work on slow neutrons, neutrinos and astrophysics were considered to manifest marks of brilliance.

Allan Nunn May, a leftist in pre-war years, joined the nuclear project "Tube Alloys" in 1942, and a year later was sent to Canada to work as a member of the British mission. Here he was approached by an officer from Soviet military intelligence, and agreed to cooperate. He later informed the secret service about the types of the bombs used at Trinity, Nevada, and at Hiroshima, the output of uranium-235 at Oak Ridge, and of plutonium-249 at Hanford. There are reasons to believe that he passed a sample of uranium-233 to Soviet agents.

The names of two more scientists in the American nuclear centres who facilitated the information leaks have not been disclosed so far by Soviet intelligence, but their codenames are known: Quant and Persey. The FBI suspected that it was Van Vleck who had the codename Quant. As for Persey, the only thing known about this mysterious person by retired Soviet secret service officers was that he had started to work for the Manhattan Project about a month-and-a-half before Klaus Fuchs's arrival in the USA, and that this man was still alive in the early 1990s. However, this could be a smokescreen to cover a person with an entirely different biography.

Beria versus Hoover

The valuable theoretical and design information would have been impossible to channel to the Soviet Union without the closely woven web, created in America and Great Britain by Beria, Merkulov and Abakumov, of reliable agents, highly placed scientists and businessmen, and properly organized intelligence, counter-intelligence and communications networks. Although some agents already working in the USA and Great Britain were engaged in the operation, Beria ordered the NKVD and NKGB to build a special network to service it alone.

There was already a foundation that could be used. The Soviet agents knew that the US Army did not have military counter-intelligence from about 1920, and that the FBI dropped counter-intelligence from 1924, so in the 1930s they had an opportunity to establish a wide web of Communists and sympathizers whom they could use practically throughout World War II. Also, when Soviet master spy Nahum Eitingon operated in the USA and Mexico in 1939–41, and unprecedentedly was given the right to recruit agents without the sanction of his superiors and to employ his American relatives who were well connected in scientific and business circles, he used that very effectively. When the Zarubins, career Soviet spies, were sent to America to take part in atomic espionage, Liza Zarubin re-established contact with

two "sleeping" agents on the west coast. These were Polish Jews recruited by Eitingon at the beginning of the 1930s. They were given money and instructed to settle in California, get jobs and wait for instructions. No instructions came for a decade, which was all to the good. With no burden of espionage work and no fear of arrest, these agents became well established and well connected. One of them, codename Shakhmatist (Russian for chess player), was a dentist, trained as such in France with money provided by the NKVD. His wife managed to befriend the Oppenheimers, and thus they became a communications channel with the scientist, which could not arouse any suspicion on the part of the FBI or the new security service of the US Army.

The density of the Soviet network around the leading scientists of the Manhattan Project was stunning, consisting of about 200 agents, informers and sources. After Stalin created Directorate C in 1944, which had the main goal of obtaining secret

■ *Above:* The Dane Niels Bohr, the Nobel prizewinning physicist who was the first to apply the quantum theory to atomic structure. He was targeted by Soviet intelligence in the late 1940s.

information from such major scientists as Robert Oppenheimer, Niels Bohr, Enrico Fermi and Leo Szilard, there were about 40 illegal Soviet agents targeting laboratories at Los Alamos and Berkeley alone.

The spy network in the USA

Another strength of Soviet espionage in America was the multiplicity of its channels and operational facilities. AMTORG, the trade representation body of the USSR in America created before diplomatic relations between the countries were established in 1933, was used as a screen for setting up illegal groups that then formed small parallel networks of agents and informers. The representatives of various Russian agencies and missions, including TASS (Telegraphic Agency of the Soviet Union) and AMTORG, took an active part in various events organized in New York, Los Angeles and San Francisco by Communists, Socialists and Latin American human-rights activists. Russian agents were able to meet left-leaning statesmen, scientists and businessmen at these functions. The first contact made by Gregory Kheifets, Soviet Consul in San Francisco, with Robert Oppenheimer took place at a charity party organized to help the victims of the Spanish Civil War. Eitingon's network in Mexico was stood down after Trotsky's assassination in 1940, but only three years later it was re-activated by a new *resident* (station chief), Vasilevsky. Using this network, Vasilevsky established a channel of communication with Bruno Pontecorvo in Canada and some scientists at Fermi's laboratory in Chicago. That was particularly important for the Russians because it made it possible to bypass Soviet intelligence's New York office, where too many threads were crossing. Now the secret papers could be sent to a "mailbox" in a little pharmacy in Santa Fe, New Mexico, and from there a courier transported them to Mexico. The pharmacy had been opened in Santa Fe by Eitingon and another Soviet master spy, Grigulevich, when they were preparing for the

assassination of Trotsky. As Grigulevich's father had a chain of pharmacies in Latin America, all this looked quite inconspicuous.

When the density of agents in the atomic espionage networks seemed excessive, Beria agreed to change the structure. An order was sent to the United States to transfer all the informers and contacts around Oppenheimer and other important scientists in California from the legal *residentura* to the illegal one. This was timely, as there were reports coming from Soviet moles in the USA and Great Britain that the FBI and US Army counter-intelligence were seriously concerned by the operations of the Russian secret service in America, and especially around the nuclear centres. In February 1943, the electronic interception and radio intelligence service of the US Army – the Signals Security Agency (which became later the National Security Agency) – started to work on a programme codenamed Venona. Its mission was to decode messages sent via Russian diplomatic channels beginning in 1939.

Breaking the Soviet codes

The volume of information intercepted and recorded by the Americans was tremendous: there were tens of thousands of coded messages. Each of them was made up of groups of five digits. The Soviet secret service also used three- and four-digit codes, but irrespective of the digit numbers the Moscow Centre believed the codes to be safe and secure. The point is that the Soviet agents used a one-time pad system. In essence, these were sheets that had a random number of five-digit groups on them. After coding his message in digits, the agent added to each group of digits in his coded message the groups on a sheet from a one-time pad. Once a sheet had been used, it was torn off and destroyed. Since the one-time pads were continually replaced, code-breakers were unable to trace any systematic repetition of digit groups. Breaking into the text in such cases is an extremely difficult and lengthy process, and it took the Americans several years. But with the help of computers, the capabilities of which had not been adequately appreciated in Moscow, a major step forward was taken in 1943. Lieutenant Richard Helleck used a computer to analyze about 10,000 coded messages from the Soviet trade mission in the USA. The computation showed that in seven cases there was a systematic repetition. By the end of 1944 the Americans were able to discern some patterns in the messages. In 1944 an AMTORG employee called Kravchenko defected; he knew a lot about the role of his company as a front for intelligence activity around the nuclear research centres. In 1945 Igor Gouzenko, a cypher clerk at the Soviet Embassy in Ottawa, defected after stealing some military intelligence coded messages and confidential papers. Most of them dealt with atomic espionage. Director of the FBI J. Edgar Hoover was slowly getting the upper hand in the battle of wits with Beria.

Piecing together the jigsaw

Some valuable evidence also came from quite unexpected sources. When Allied troops captured Nazi archives in Germany, some of them contained police and Gestapo files on Socialists. Fuchs's pro-Soviet sympathies were known to the Gestapo, and his file reportedly contained instructions that if captured he should be immediately escorted to Berlin.

The real breakthrough for the FBI and the Signals Security Agency came thanks to two critical mistakes made by the Soviet secret service. The first was that, considering their code unbreakable, the Russians recklessly duplicated some one-time pads and sent them to a number of *residenturas* abroad. The second was that a Soviet agent in Finland did not burn one code-book properly, and parts of it landed on the table of the American code-breakers. Still, it took the outstanding American linguist Meredith Gardner years to decipher some coded messages. On 20 December

1946, he was able to read part of a message that contained a list of leading scientists working on the development of the atomic bomb. The message had, in fact, been sent two years earlier, but it became a basis for new discoveries. Gardner then succeeded in reading the codenames of some Soviet agents, and finally identified some scientists. Combining that information with the debriefing of Kravchenko and Gouzenko, the Americans finally got a clue about a physicist spy codenamed Alec who had been previously involved in nuclear research in Canada. US and Canadian counter-intelligence identified the man as Allan Nunn May.

In 1949 the FBI informed British counter-intelligence that it had received evidence that an unknown British scientist had been passing top-secret information to the Russians from Los Alamos. In combination with the Gestapo archives and the newly acquired documents, that was sufficient to give a lead to Klaus Fuchs and his sister, who lived in Cambridge. There was also a report that she had been visited in 1945 by Harry Gold, who had been under suspicion for a long time. The arrests of David Greenglass and the Rosenbergs were also imminent. The last piece in the jigsaw was the arrest and revelations of Elisabeth Bentley, an important Russian link agent, who confessed to working for Moscow and named dozens of people who operated on her instructions. The Russian atomic

■ *Below:* The photographs on these pages are the so-called "Cambridge Five": British intelligence operatives who in reality worked for the Soviets.

espionage network began to crumble. In her sensational disclosures to the FBI Bentley incriminated Harry Gold, and he and David Greenglass confessed and were imprisoned. The latter, the elder brother of Ethel Rosenberg, stated that Julius Rosenberg, Ethel's husband and a US Government weapons inspector, was an active Soviet agent. The Rosenbergs were sentenced to death in 1953, despite the fact that the information they supplied to Russian intelligence was peripheral and much less important than that supplied from other sources.

The FBI also trapped Morton Sobell, an engineer engaged in secret research at the General Electric Laboratories. And it now looked as if the FBI had wiped out the entire Soviet atomic espionage network. But part of it survived. The reason was that the hierarchy of Directorate C knew about the Venona Project from 1945, from agents deep within the Washington administration and from William Weissman, a US Army officer attached to the project as a specialist in Russian. Before joining the US Army, Weissman lived on the west coast where he was a link agent for a Soviet spy who operated in the aircraft industry. Both had been recruited years earlier by Nahum Eitingon and his people. Weissman knew that Venona was moving ahead, though slowly, but he did not know what exactly had been disclosed about the Soviet espionage network and about the scientists who supplied it with information.

There was, however, a man who knew accurately where Venona had got to, and that was Kim Philby, an enormously important Russian spy within the British intelligence community. At that critical moment for the Soviet network in America Philby was the British intelligence liaison officer there. In fact, he had been getting information about the Venona Project even before his arrival in Washington, but once there naturally the information to which he was privy was much more extensive. For instance, he received copies of decrypts of a number of coded messages which contained the names of individuals. Philby was getting such classified information until 1951, and thus learnt that other Soviet spies, such as the British diplomat Donald Maclean and colourful Guy Burgess, were under suspicion, and instructed them to flee to the USSR. Maclean, a Communist sympathizer, was instrumental in sending information to the USSR about nuclear research, which he had access to as First Secretary of the British Embassy in Washington and supervisor of the cooperation between British and American scientists in the nuclear project.

Directorate C was clever enough not to focus exclusively on the research centre at Los Alamos, but also targeted the nuclear centre at Berkeley as well. By the time the Americans realized the risk of serious leaks from the latter, it was too late. Informed by a mole in American intelligence, Moscow left its contacts at Berkeley alone, and none

■ *Below:* From left to right: Donald Maclean, Guy Burgess, Anthony Blunt, Kim Philby and John Cairncross. Their collective treachery did great damage to Western interests.

of them was caught in the counter-intelligence web. It has recently been claimed that half of the total Soviet network in the USA at this time remained unexposed.

In all 286 secret scientific documents and classified publications were acquired, and the secret service was duly rewarded. Most of the officers who took part in the operation were promoted and received orders and medals, and their boss, Lavrenty Beria, became Marshal of the Soviet Union.

The golden assets of the NKVD

The agents and moles of the Soviet secret service that facilitated atomic espionage were, for the most part, recruited either in the early 1930s or during the civil war in Spain. For instance, Kim Philby, a graduate of Trinity College, Cambridge, cooperated with the NKVD from 1934. He continued to do so during the Spanish Civil War, which he covered as a war reporter. After joining the British intelligence community in 1940 on the instructions of the Soviet secret service, he was linked to the NKVD *resident* in London – Gorsky. Philby was a highly respected member of Military Intelligence 6 (MI6 – intelligence and espionage agency), and made many friends in the intelligence community, including the novelists Ian Fleming and Graham Greene. In 1944 he became head of the 9th Section, in which 15 crypto-analysts worked on decoding the messages sent by Soviet diplomatic and trade missions. His opportunities to supply secret information grew with time, but, like many other Soviet agents, Philby never sought any financial reward. In 1945 he was close to catastrophe when he learned that one Volkov, Soviet vice-consul in Istanbul and an intelligence officer, informed the British consulate that he was going to defect and that he could provide the names of at least four NKVD agents within British intelligence and the Foreign Office. Philby hurried to Istanbul, but the Russians he had reported the news to managed to get to Volkov first. He was taken to NKVD headquarters and executed.

In 1949 Philby was sent to Washington, where his position as the British representative at the CIA and FBI was almost equal to that of deputy head of MI6. When clouds gathered over his head after the defection of Maclean and Burgess, Philby initially denied all allegations by both counter-intelligence officers and journalists, but finally had to run. He was secretly transported to the USSR from Beirut in 1963, and lived in Moscow until 1988, working as a consultant for the KGB. He was awarded the Orders of Lenin, the Red Banner, the Peoples' Friendship and the Patriotic War, and was something of a patriarch among Western intelligence defectors in the USSR.

Besides Kim Philby, Maclean and Burgess, there were two other Britons who cooperated with Soviet intelligence in those years: Anthony Blunt and John Cairncross. This group is sometimes called the "Cambridge Five", as all had studied at Trinity College in Cambridge. Anthony Blunt was recruited by the NKVD *resident* in London – Arnold Deutsch. Blunt spent the war working for Military Intelligence 5 (MI5 – counter-intelligence agency) while supplying the Russians with highly sensitive documents and, appointed Surveyor of the King's Pictures after the war in 1945, had contacts at the very top of the British establishment. He was able to memorize hundreds of secret documents by heart, a very important aid to his espionage activity. Russian intelligence valued him exceptionally highly, and his contacts in Moscow noted that about 90 percent of the materials he supplied were of importance. He passed on 1770 documents between 1941 and 1945. When Burgess and Maclean defected, British counter-intelligence traced Blunt down. The Russians offered him a pension and a chance to flee immediately to the USSR, but he refused. In 1964 he was exposed by an American called Michael Straight, also a Trinity College graduate and once a member of a leftist group. Blunt died in 1983, in sickness and disgrace.

■ *Above:* Mr and Mrs Kroger, alias the Cohens, were Soviet spies who worked in Great Britain in the 1950s and 1960s.

John Cairncross was recommended to Russian *resident* Deutsch by Anthony Blunt. From 1940 Cairncross was secretary to Lord Hankey, who headed the British Science Committee and was at one time on the board of "Tube Alloys" that was linked to the nuclear energy programme. His contribution to the Soviet military effort was also enormous: he reportedly supplied the USSR with more than 3000 documents from the British Foreign Office and other government organizations, including a report to Churchill about the nuclear weapons project. After migrating to MI6 in 1943, he succeeded in sending to Moscow a list of the British agents in the Balkans. Uncovered in the early 1950s, he was fired from the Treasury where he was employed at the time, but never imprisoned, and died in 1995 at the age of 82. He was awarded the Soviet Order of the Red Banner for disclosing the plans of the German Army at Kursk through

access to British documents, including German Enigma coder decrypts, which were not officially revealed to the Russians.

Soviet intelligence historians claim that the "Cambridge Five" provided the Soviet secret service with about 17,000 documents, 35 background briefs, 9 voluminous reports, and information about 40 Soviet citizens who were linked one way or another to the Western intelligence services. Although some of the "Cambridge Five" were active up to the beginning of the 1950s, their main contribution was from 1939 to 1947, i.e. in the period when the Russians were getting the keys to the American nuclear vaults.

In the USA, other agents became valuable assets of the Soviet secret service for future years. Morris and Lona Cohen, two Americans who were in 1996 awarded the title of the Hero of the Soviet Union (posthumously) for their work in atomic espionage, had been the link agents receiving valuable information and transporting it to their Russian contacts in New York and Los Angeles. One of the most memorable episodes in Lona's espionage career took place in 1945, when she boarded a train to New York after receiving from Ted Hall a tissue box containing papers on the Manhattan Project. Soon she was approached by a security officer who wanted to search her luggage. Lona asked him to hold the box, and then opened her suitcase. On finishing the inspection the officer returned her the box and left.

Morris Cohen, alias Peter Kroger, alias Israel Altman, was recruited by the NKVD in 1938 in Spain where he fought in the International Brigades. A devoted Communist, Morris (codename Louis) was the manager of the network, collecting and transporting information to the local Soviet intelligence resident. Lona (codename Lesley) was a courageous woman who shared all her husband's adventures. After the Rosenbergs were executed, the Cohens fled to the USSR. But they would return to spying, becoming part of the so-called Portland Spy Ring.

CHAPTER 7

THE LAST PURGE

The death of Stalin in 1953 sparked a power struggle in the Soviet Union, in which Nikita Khrushchev was triumphant.

In Moscow in October 1951, special counter-intelligence units arrested Major-General of State Security Eitingon, Major-General Raikhman, Colonel Maironovsky and Colonel Sverdlov – all of them Jews. They were accused of the illegal storage of poison and also of being participants in a Zionist plot whose aim was to seize power and eliminate the top echelon of the state leadership, including Stalin himself. The detention of these experienced and loyal officers of the secret service was only part of a larger sweep. In addition, counter-intelligence squads arrested Minister of State Security Abakumov, a number of party functionaries, and also numerous doctors who worked in various Kremlin and government hospitals and clinics – more than 100 people in all.

In order to understand the significance of these arrests, events both inside and outside the Kremlin must be analyzed. Stalin was now old and very ill: wartime events had badly affected his body and brain. By 1950 he was unable to take full charge of state affairs, especially those of the party and personnel, and he had transferred most of these tasks to his assistants and members of the Central Committee of the Communist Party. Soon three groupings took shape in the committee, formed around Nikita Khrushchev, Georgi

■ *Left:* **Stalin takes a walk inside the Kremlin walls in the late 1940s. By this time he was paranoid about Zionist plots.**

Malenkov and Lavrenty Beria. The party bureaucrats and army generals supported Khrushchev; Malenkov was considered a man without his own power base, although he managed to put some of his friends and relatives in key positions; Beria had friends, though no political supporters. Each of these leaders pledged themselves to Stalin, but the ageing "Big Master", as his subordinates called him, regarded them with growing suspicion.

Stalin's paranoia

Stalin was suspicious of many things during his last years, especially the new state of Israel. In 1946 he supported Jews struggling in Palestine and sent substantial aid to them. Their emissaries asked for more and even promised to build a "Socialist Israel". So Stalin let them fly captured German aircraft to Israel from Eastern Europe and sent hundreds of battle-hardened officers there; almost all of them were Jews, including the graduates of Soviet military academies. But he soon discovered that Israel was much more pro-American than he thought it would be, and considered himself deceived. He now took all contacts of Jewish figures from the USSR with Israeli leaders as personal insults. He was concerned about the spreading of the Zionist agenda in the Soviet Union, and warned the secret service that it had to be prepared to deal with this. The creation of Israel led to some growth of anti-Semitism in the USSR, especially in the top echelons of the army, and yet it was not Stalin who launched the persecution of the Jews; it was Khrushchev. But he did it by proxy, in his usual scheming manner.

Although the final clash over the Russian "throne" would take place two years later, its outline was already there in 1951. From 1946 Beria was in effect removed from his control of the secret service and put in charge of building the missile and nuclear potential of the USSR, as well as the development of high-tech and chemical industries. That made it possible for Khrushchev and his

clique to quickly take the first steps towards seizing power, by slandering some key figures of the government and replacing them with "reliable people". Khrushchev started by making an agreement in 1950 with Malenkov, a member of the Political Bureau, to appoint his friend – and Khrushchev supporter – Ignatiev to some of the most important positions in the country: the director of the Central Committee Department of the Party, Trade Unions and *Komsomol* (Young Communist League) bodies. This meant that control of all the appointments to any major position in the state now lay with Khrushchev and Ignatiev.

Then, in October 1951, Minister of State Security Abakumov was arrested. He was the former head of the military counter-intelligence unit SMERSH (Russian acronym of *Smiert Shpionam* – Death to Spies), and known for his first-degree interrogations: he was a big and very powerful man, and did his own beating of suspects. His arrest was a result of slander

■ *Above:* Georgi Malenkov (right, shaking hands with Great Britain's Lord Citrine) had no power base in the party, and thus failed to mount a serious challenge to Khrushchev. Following his expulsion from the party in 1961, he became the manager of a remote hydroelectric plant in Kazakhstan. He died in 1988.

by his own subordinate Riumin, chief investigator for especially important cases. This man was even more famous for his use of torture in interrogations. When Riumin was conducting an interrogation at a prison, all the inmates instantly knew about it as a result of the awful cries of the victims. The slanderous report was written as the result of a sordid deal done in the study of Ignatiev. Riumin was immediately appointed Deputy Minister of State Security of the USSR, and in return Ignatiev received a paper in which Abakumov was accused of protracting investigations on important crimes and preparing a coup to overthrow the regime. The Political Bureau accepted these absurd accusations; after all, Riumin was Khrushchev's man. It is now known that the elimination of Abakumov was done at the request of the army generals.

After Riumin helped Khrushchev and Ignatiev to destroy Abakumov, they encouraged him to launch the idea of the "Zionist plot", allegedly initiated by Jews in the state security bodies and Kremlin and government hospitals and clinics. Immediately after Abakumov's arrest, Khrushchev and Ignatiev persuaded the Political Bureau to appoint Ignatiev "a representative of the Central Committee in the Ministry of State Security". It was a political trick, and as early as October 1951 he was elevated to minister. In the Khrushchev era he was talked about as "the first *Chekist* of a new type", suggesting he

was a reformist leader of the secret service. In fact, at one of his first conferences he called on the security officers to "pull off the white gloves" and beat the prisoners while taking "necessary precautions" (ensuring secrecy of the beatings). This protégé of Malenkov and friend of Khrushchev was an organizer of repressions in Turkestan, Buriatia and Bashkiria in the 1930s, and after he became chief of the secret service he raised the number of prisoners in the camps under his jurisdiction to two-and-a-half million.

A new purge

It was clear to many top officers of state security that the arrest of Minister Abakumov was the beginning of a new purge. But even they could not conceive what would be the scale of the repressions against people loyal to their country and to their jobs. As Ignatiev, Khrushchev and Riumin talked about the "Zionist plot", Jewish officers were targeted first. Ignatiev and Riumin, lovingly copying Yezhov's bone-breakers of the 1930s, demanded that interrogators not limit themselves to orthodox methods in getting confessions. The individual given the case of the Jewish officers succeeded – and we can imagine how – in getting fantastic confessions from Maironovsky, the head of the toxicological laboratory of the Ministry of State Security (he recanted his confession in 1958) and from Broverman, deputy head of Abakumov's secretariat.

Riumin, Ignatiev's deputy, was fired by the latter at the end of 1952, probably for going too far in torturing people and not getting far enough in the "doctors' plot". The investigation department found itself at a loss, since it was now unable to proceed on the basis of the accusations prepared by Riumin. The Jewish doctors under investigation were accused of following the criminal orders of Abakumov to plan the stage-by-stage elimination of Soviet leaders by using poisonous substances received from the Ministry of State Security. But the testimony of the head of the toxicological

■ *Right:* Lavrenty Beria, here photographed in 1938, lost control of the secret service in 1946, which allowed Khrushchev and his supporters to take the first steps towards seizing power in the Soviet Union.

laboratory that allegedly supplied these substances was not confirmed by the confessions of the doctors, who did not even know such a laboratory existed.

The arrested officers were brutally beaten, placed in specially cooled chambers, and kept in handcuffs and fetters – and all this was taking place in the second half of the twentieth century. The records of the interrogations, if they did not contain the required confessions, were simply destroyed. This was to be typical of Khrushchev, and throughout his reign various documents were withdrawn from archives and destroyed on his orders, including those which showed that "The Architect of the Thaw" played a very bloody part in the Great Purge of the 1930s. Other documents destroyed reportedly contained information from various frontline officers and soldiers about the behaviour of his son, who, while serving as an officer, was said to have killed his orderly and, when sent to a penal battalion, defected to the Germans.

False rumours

Torture and intimidation finally made most of the suspects confess to crimes they had never committed. However, Abakumov, a strong man, and also General Eitingon and Colonel Matusov rejected all accusations. Two weeks after the arrest of Eitingon, Riumin arrested Eitingon's sister Sofia, who was a doctor, claiming that she was the link between the state security bodies and the "plotting doctors". This accusation was leaked, and rumours started to fill bars and squares that Jewish pharmacists were poisoning ordinary Russian people. That was tantamount to inciting a pogrom.

Eitingon's sister got 10 years for "wrong medical treatment" and her part in the "doctors' plot". Initially the sentence was eight years; but, unfortunately for her, prosecutor Daron was a Jew, and he, fearing accusations of showing sympathy to the defendants, insisted on increasing the term. As for General Eitingon and his associates, Khrushchev's henchmen were still

considering what sort of sentence they should get. But soon the situation changed.

On 5 March 1953 Stalin died, and Beria became head of the combined Ministries of the Interior and State Security. He immediately issued an order to close the absurd cases of the "Zionist plotters". Beria's triumphal return to the intelligence community meant that Eitingon was released, as were his sister and his colleagues. But that was not the end of the purge.

Killing the main witness

Stalin's death reopened old wounds. It is said Khrushchev could not forget that during the war Stalin had refused to exchange Leonid, Khrushchev's son from his first marriage, as well as his own son Yakov Dzhugashvili, both taken prisoners of war, for captured German generals, and thus sent them both to their deaths. There is another version of events, though, which was suppressed in Khrushchev's time. Leonid Khrushchev, a spoilt boy from his early years, got involved before the war in banditry, and was arrested and tried. Saved from jail, he was sent to an aviation school, and during the war was either shot down or landed his plane in German-occupied territory. He reportedly cooperated with the Nazis, and even made appeals on the radio to his compatriots to surrender. Kidnapped by a special unit of the Soviet secret service, he faced execution. Khrushchev asked Stalin for mercy, but the dictator rejected his plea.

No wonder Khrushchev hated the deceased leader and his loyal lieutenants. He also wanted the main post in the state, as did Malenkov. There was a tough, uncompromising power struggle, and Khrushchev's grouping was ultimately victorious. It consisted of party bureaucrats and unscrupulous schemers of the worst kind, apparatchiks who were ready to tear to pieces anyone who might jeopardize their comfortable positions.

Their device for obtaining power was simple: a military coup arranged by marshals and generals headed by Georgi

■ *Above:* **Nikita Khrushchev (front row, right), on a hunting trip. He hated Stalin for turning down his pleas for mercy regarding his traitorous son during World War II. This hatred extended to Stalin's loyal lieutenants.**

precious tableware, furs, paintings and other antiquities. There is a document to prove this: a statement entitled "On the transfer to the Administration Department of the Council of Ministers of USSR of the confiscated war booty, valuables and other objects unlawfully acquired and appropriated by Marshal of the Soviet Union G.K. Zhukov". It lists 323 valuable fur pelts, 3420m (11,220ft) of various types of cloth, 60 paintings from Potsdam Palace, furniture, tapestry and carpets, and hundreds of other valuables. A short while before the operation customs officials had stopped seven railway cars that were carrying furniture to Russia for Marshal Zhukov. He also robbed valuable books from libraries.

His close friend Lieutenant-General Kriukov acted similarly: while the battles still raged in Germany in 1945, he was collecting diamonds for his wife, the famous folk-singer Ruslanova. Incidentally, this ingenious general had a field hospital, one section of which became a brothel. The girls were decorated for good work with orders and medals. There were many other generals who behaved no less "courageously". General Ivan Serov, who incited the army generals against Beria and who became in Khrushchev's era first the head of state security and later the head of military intelligence, instructed his subordinate officers during World War II to bring him all valuables found on dead or captured German officers. Upon becoming MVD (Ministry of Internal Affairs) emissary in Germany, Serov exported valuables from Germany in military trains and even by military aircraft. When his henchman, General Sidnev, was caught red-handed after stealing dozens of valuable carpets, Sidnev told counter-intelligence officers that Serov had appropriated 30kg (66lb) of German gold, and most probably had shared it with Marshal Zhukov.

SMERSH also had General Batitsky on its blacklist. The future marshal of the Soviet Union frequently arranged orgies at the battle front. There were also rumours

Zhukov, the most popular military commander in the Soviet Union. Many historians believe that the World War II victories of Marshals Zhukov, Moskalenko and Konev were achieved not because of their military talents but by massing enormous forces and by the profligate sacrifice of their troops. A soldier's life had no value for them: ultimate victory was everything. But what is important here is the motives that drove the top brass of the Soviet armed forces to undertake a military coup.

The main reason was primitive: greed. While commanding their armies in Eastern Europe, they had shamelessly robbed palaces, museums, banks and jewellers. Army counter-intelligence reported the facts of this looting by the generals thousands of times. So when the war ended Stalin ordered the Ministry of State Security to start an investigation. Abakumov's officers secretly searched the Moscow apartment of Marshal Zhukov and his villa at Rublevo nearby. They found 17 gold watches and over 50 chests filled with that Batitsky had raped a very young girl, who then disappeared. In 1953, after Khrushchev's victory in the fight for the Kremlin, these SMERSH reports were simply removed from the archives and destroyed, according to counter-intelligence officer Pavel Korotkov.

The execution of Abakumov

This is why Minister of State Security Victor Abakumov, who previously led SMERSH and who investigated the case of the high-ranking criminals, was arrested in 1951, along with tens of his officers, on the instructions of Khrushchev, his associate Ignatiev and top army generals, and summarily shot – despite the fact that the death penalty had been abolished at this time. His arrest on Khrushchev's order was in a way symbolic: at the end of the Great Purge, in which Khrushchev had dirtied his hands, Abakumov was taking part in an investigation of illegal arrests in the Rostov *Oblast* (Province), which resulted in 60 percent of the arrested being set free.

Abakumov and his former SMERSH colleagues had been a great threat to the army generals: they knew something that the country, adoring its victors, was not supposed to know. Some of the army generals might have been put behind bars by Stalin (Kriukov, for instance), while Zhukov was demoted and sent to a provincial military district, but they did not want things to get worse now the "Big Master" was dead.

Nikita Khrushchev, whatever some Russian historians claim, was an ignorant and ultimately ineffectual figure, and neither the world nor Russia benefited from his reign. But he was an ingenious schemer and extraordinary opportunist. The Russians say that those who can, do, and those who can't, scheme. Schemers won after Stalin's death. Artfully spinning his web inside the Political Bureau, Khrushchev incited the old members of this body against Beria by assuring them that the latter was a renegade and revisionist. He

told Malenkov that Beria wanted to replace him as chairman of the Council of Ministers and was preparing a *coup d'état*. As for the marshals and generals, he warned them that Beria, as security supremo, would make them pay for their various "pranks" in Germany after World War II.

Khrushchev also wanted to get rid of Beria, as the main witness of his own crimes. He knew perfectly well, as did Brezhnev, Ignatiev and dozens of other apparatchiks who signed the execution lists during the Great Purge, that, since Beria had succeeded Yezhov in 1938, he knew everything about each of them. After killing thousands of innocent victims by signing shooting lists as a member of the *troika*, Khrushchev always dreamt of getting access to state security archives to destroy any evidence of these crimes. But that was possible only if he became the country's undisputed leader. To be that, he needed to destroy the obstacles to this aim: Beria and his state security generals.

"The Architect of the Thaw" was not fastidious about bribes, far from it. He promised some generals of lower rank who were needed to implement the coup that they would receive the gold star of the Hero of the Soviet Union. In fact, they merely got the Order of the Combat Red Banner in 1954, though they were also promoted to high posts in the military hierarchy.

Beria's arrest, on 27 June 1953, was like some coup in a banana republic. A group of

■ *Below:* The funeral of Stalin in Moscow on 9 March 1953. Prominent among the mourners is Khrushchev on the far right.

marshals and generals headed by Marshal Zhukov entered his study in the Kremlin with guns in their hands and took him to the military stockade where he was kept under permanent close surveillance, while all the soldiers under arrest in the stockade were at the same time set free. Almost simultaneously, about 10 top generals in state security were arrested including Kobulov, Dekanozov and Meshik. Beria's arrest was basically illegal; Chief Prosecutor Rudenko issued his arrest warrant on 8 July, almost two weeks later.

Zhukov knew that, in the absence of their top commanders, the MVD and state security officers and troops would follow the orders of their commanding officers to resist any incursions into the main buildings and prevent access to documents, which the generals were anxious to destroy immediately. The administrative troops of the Moscow Military District seemed insufficient to break the resistance of even the MVD local stations. So General Dorodnov, commander of the Kantemir Guards Tank Division stationed near Moscow, was ordered to assist, and soon tanks appeared on the Lenin Avenue in Moscow. Some fighting took place between the troops of the Moscow Military District and surrounded outposts of the MVD. The Kremlin was also surrounded by troops, with tanks and armoured personnel carriers in adjacent streets and yards.

In accordance with emergency plans, the officers of many counter-intelligence and interception units of the state security elements of the MVD moved to underground bunkers and barricaded themselves in. The skeletons of one such unit were discovered a decade later in the basement of a building destroyed by tank fire and then left in ruins: they had starved to death.

On 28 June Serov and Kruglov, Beria's assistants who had connived in his arrest, arrived at the stockade but were not let in. The generals were not taking any chances. Meanwhile, airborne units were brought in to take part in the arrest of 16 more commanders of Beria's MVD and state security units and organizations.

On 2 July the Plenary Session of the Central Committee took place, at which Beria was wholly discredited. He was accused of espionage for the British intelligence service, torture of prisoners, rapes and provocations, and of preparing a *coup d'état*. There were no facts and no evidence; still Malenkov, Khrushchev, Andrei Andreev (an old Bolshevik) and others called on the members of the Central Committee to support them. Two people who did owed much to Beria: the Azeri party leader Bagirov and state security general Merkulov. The latter, who joined the Khrushchev camp, was executed the same year, and the former three years later – Khrushchev did not trust the traitors who jumped on his bandwagon.

Accusations that Beria was a spy were ridiculed even by Zhukov supporters. Similarly, it was difficult to accuse the man of torture when, in 1938, he had officially forbidden it in the NKVD. As to the raping, here again the accusations were as false as they were hastily fabricated, and with the aid of threats and intimidation. To start with, the women who denounced Beria were not called to the trial. The prosecutor merely had statements, and the names meant nothing to anybody: most probably these were fakes or those of released crime suspects. But two names were real: that of the famous film actress Zoya Fedorova and a very young woman called Valentina Drozdova.

The innocent victims

Zoya Fedorova had a romance with Jackson Tate, an American intelligence officer in Moscow in the 1940s, and gave birth to a daughter, Victoria (who, after becoming a film actress herself, emigrated to the USA and played in a number of Hollywood productions). The handsome American and Zoya were soon forcefully separated, of course, but it would have been unnatural for an intelligence ace like Beria not to use such a contact. Zoya apparently worked for him. She, like other women spies, visited him at his residence in the centre of Moscow. But in 1947 she was accused of being a double agent and imprisoned. She got a 25-year sentence. Now, pressed by the new blackmailers, she signed a statement that she had been forced to cohabit with Beria. That bought her freedom: she was released in 1955. In 1981 she was killed by a "burglar", and Zoya's story was thus erased from the books.

The story of Valentina (Liallia) Drozdova is even more tragic. It seemed to start with a statement by this woman dated 11 July 1953 and addressed to Chief Prosecutor Rudenko. She wrote that after she had read an article in *Pravda* she decided to complain of her rape by Beria, who then forced her to become his mistress.

Her identity is now known: she was the woman Beria wanted to marry.

At the time he was arrested, Beria was 54 years old. For a man from western Georgia that is not aged, as people there tend to be healthy and long-lived. He had a wife and adult son when, at the age of 49, he met and fell in love with a young and beautiful Russian girl who lived just around the corner. He arranged for Liallia and her mother to live at one of the suburban state villas, where she was protected and looked after. Liallia soon became pregnant, and Beria arranged an abortion. Their unlawful romance had lasted four years when finally he told his wife about his affair, and decided he would have a divorce and a new family. Liallia proceeded to give birth to a child by Beria.

It can be imagined what sort of pressure was exerted on this unlucky girl, a lover and wife-to-be of one of the most powerful and feared men in the country and mother of his child, to make her state that he raped her after picking her up in the street. This must be remembered when some historians try to portray Khrushchev as the liberator of Russia from the evil of Beria.

■ *Below:* Marshal Zhukov, Hero of the Soviet Union, headed the group of senior Red Army commanders who arrested Beria on 27 June 1953.

Beria spent six months in a dark underground bunker, without any communication with the outside world and without his glasses. Other generals were placed in solitary confinement as well. Beria's son and wife were arrested and detained, and all the wives of the arrested generals and adult children were also taken to military prisons, in the best traditions of the OGPU. This put additional pressure on the defendants, whose will had to be broken at any cost, and they were warned in a straightforward manner that for the sake of their loved ones they should not try to communicate with the outside world.

Beria's trial

The trial took place on 23 December. During this circus none of the defendants was permitted to make a statement, and probably did not wish to since they knew the tribunal members for the high-ranking criminals they were: Marshal Konev, Marshal Moskalenko and General Batitsky. Chief Prosecutor Rudenko, well known not only for his participation in the Nuremberg trials (the trials of former Nazi leaders by the International Military Tribunal) but also for the trials during the Great Purge, played his usual role. Most of those sentenced to death were shot in the Moscow Butyrka prison within an hour-and-a-half of the trial ending. Batitsky volunteered to shoot Beria himself with his war trophy, a German Parabellum pistol. He was so fearful of what Beria could reveal that he was prepared to play executioner to silence him as soon as possible.

The myth of Lavrenty Pavlovich Beria as the most frightening man in the Soviet Union was created by Khrushchev and his henchmen. Beria was born in 1899 in a small village near Sukhumi, Georgia, to a peasant family and died Marshal of the Soviet Union, Hero of Socialist Labour and Laureate of the Stalin Prize. He joined the Russian Social Democratic Workers' Party at the age of 18 and was planted, on the instructions of Kirov, in the counter-intelligence service of then independent Azerbaijan. Later he organized an underground Bolshevik network in Georgia, which was also then independent. When the Red Army invaded Georgia in 1921, Beria promptly joined the *Cheka*, and was the chairman of the Georgian GPU and vice-chairman of the GPU of the Transcaucasian Federation from 1926.

Beria, an assessment

"He was an amazingly courageous man," Colonel Gorlin wrote in his memoirs. "I remember he was once leading an operation to catch an extremely dangerous gangster and his band – I think it was in 1923. He was the first to storm into the house through the window with two Nagant revolvers. He also was a man who loved truth; lies made him angry. Here are two examples. In 1927 Beria received a new office car. It was absolutely beautiful, and I have never seen anything of the kind. I was only 25 then, and was a rank-and-file officer, but I dreamt of having a ride in this car. So once, when it was very quiet in the office, I persuaded the driver to take me for a ride. It only took about 10 minutes, but we soon found out that Beria was looking for his car to go somewhere. I was brought before him, and he asked where I had been. I could have invented an operational emergency, but I confessed that I had simply wanted to have a ride. He laughed and let me go. The next day he called me after the working day and gave me a lift to my house. He could be tough, and he could be generous as well.

"Another story is that a junior officer of the GPU was arrested for allegedly spying for Turkey. His file was brought to Beria, and he called in the suspect. I was at that moment in Beria's study. When the man came in Beria said: 'If you tell me the truth, I won't even look at these papers. If you are guilty, by doing this you will save your life. If not, you tell me that now.' The man confessed he was selling information about Red Army troops in Georgia. Beria exploded: 'Couldn't you find a more decent intelligence service to work for, you cheap bastard?' But he saved the man's life as promised."

Between 1931 and 1938 Beria was First Secretary of the Central Committee of the Georgian Communist Party. In 1933, while Stalin was in Abkhasia, Beria saved his life by taking an assassin's bullet. In 1938, when the Great Purge was over, Beria was transferred to Moscow and appointed Deputy People's Commissar of Internal Affairs and the head of the Main Directorate of State Security. He was soon able to uncover a huge number of fabricated cases, and after the arrest of Yezhov he released over 450,000 innocent people from prisons and camps. This was never made public by Khrushchev.

On the eve of the German invasion in June 1941, Beria was appointed Deputy Chairman of the Council of People's Commissars. His job was to secretly build armament and ammunition depots, raw material dumps and weapon production lines beyond the Ural Mountains, and to make plans for the transfer of military plants in case the German thrust was successful. During the war he headed the unified Commissariat of Internal Affairs and State Security, was a member of the State Defence Committee and later supervised work on atomic and missile weaponry. Phenomenally industrious, after the war he was put in charge of the political and economic situation in Eastern Europe,

as well as advanced military technologies and intelligence services.

After Stalin's death, on the eighth anniversary of Victory Day, he announced an amnesty for over one million prisoners. He stopped the case against the Jewish doctors instigated by Khrushchev and Ignatiev (see above). He arrested Riumin, the accuser of Abakumov and of the so-called Zionist plotters; he released a group of generals imprisoned for deficiencies in anti-aircraft artillery and aircraft engines; he cut the personnel of the secret service; he advocated the ending of total police surveillance throughout the country; he stopped work on ambitious and unnecessary state projects; and he started negotiations with Yugoslav leaders about normalizing relations. He suggested the reunification of Germany provided it remained demilitarized, and an end to the imposition of Socialism there, and maybe in other Eastern European countries. He even made some suggestions to liberalize the agrarian sector in these countries – and possibly in the USSR – by slowly moving from collective farms to cooperation between free farmers. He called for a change in the international climate by enhancing trade between the major powers.

Had he not been killed by the dogmatists and schemers, the end of the Cold War might have come more than 30 years earlier.

The reason so much space has been allotted to Beria is that it is customary to

■ *Below:* Two accomplices in the plot to remove Beria. Colonel-General Kruglov (left) was Beria's deputy, while Chief Prosecutor Rudenko (right) issued the arrest warrant.

blame him for every tragedy and every broken life in Russia from the 1920s until his execution. But Beria was neither in charge of the state secret service nor in a top position in Moscow until 1938, and although he was the head of the NKVD until 1946, it was only a part of the secret service beginning from 1943, when the People's Commissariat of State Security and SMERSH were detached from the NKVD. After Stalin's death he was intelligence supremo for about four months only. The myth of his evil role in Russian society was created by Khrushchev to help his own rise to power, and since that time all historians have repeated the line produced by Khrushchev's public relations men, and embellished it with various details borrowed from graphic Russian feature stories which appeared in the Khrushchev years.

A web of lies

One such story was that Beria and his henchmen picked up beautiful women in the street and, threatening them with arrest, took them to safe houses where they were raped. The absurdity of such accusations was obvious even to the most entrenched of Beria's enemies, as in a police state like the Soviet Union, where special services spied not only on foreigners and common citizens but also on each other, such misdemeanours would have resulted in his immediate downfall. But whoever created this myth was a storyteller of genius because it was accepted and noisily discussed in Soviet society for decades.

Yet, the story is not totally ungrounded – it is just not connected to Beria. The creator of this myth used the *Cheka* archives to find a similar crime that was also noisily decried, but occurred 30 years earlier. The review of the operations of the Moscow Extraordinary Commission in 1920 contains information about the arrest of a band that cruised the centre of Moscow in cars and selected the most beautiful women in the street. They pretended to arrest them, and then took them to a suburban house

and gang-raped them. The gang consisted of about 20 people, all serving the Republic's Revolutionary Council and Main Military Engineering Directorate. In addition to the myth of Beria's sexual maraudings, Khrushchev and Serov spread rumours that he had raped the wives of a number of Georgian dignitaries. They knew how sensitive the people of the Caucasus are to their family honour and reasoned that Georgians, though normally sympathetic to their compatriots, would not defend him. It was also put about that Beria was an imperialist agent from an early age. This claim, even made by the chief prosecutor, about a man who organized a network abroad capable of stealing atomic secrets, was ridiculous, but it was one he had heard before.

The "Beria Band"

"I remember the party purge – cleaning the ranks of Communists in Georgia in 1930 when all organizations without any exceptions were involved," Colonel Gorlin remembered. "The Investigating Commission in Georgia was headed by an old Bolshevik called Kvantaliani. He dared to challenge Beria by asking him about his service in Azeri nationalist counter-intelligence in Baku in 1920. Beria, then GPU chief in Georgia, was furious. 'Every man in this country knows I was planted there on the order of Sergei Mironovich Kirov,' he answered coldly. 'This question is embarrassing and intended for simpletons – who I hope are difficult to find here.' He turned and left, while Kvantaliani tried to stop him shouting: 'Comrade Beria, where are you going? Please wait! Let's talk!' 'What's the point?' Beria grunted. He did not take such conferences seriously, especially after Kvantaliani's challenge."

The people whom Beria selected in the 1930s to be his associates were professionals, not orators or party functionaries. Most of these, generals and colonels in state security bodies and foreign intelligence, were arrested in the first hours of the Khrushchev coup, and later shot on the ridiculous grounds of being foreign spies and enemies of the Soviet people. In all 114 people were arrested as accomplices in the "Beria coup", showing how well-organized and elaborately planned the real coup had been; about 50 of them were to be shot. Very few were Georgians; the rest included Armenians, Jews, Ukrainians, Russians, Daghestanis, Ossetians, and even Poles among the "Beria Band".

Some of the generals and officers tried along with Beria, or soon after, were either relieved of their posts by him on the eve of his own arrest or were under investigation. Lieutenant-General Lavrenty Tzanava, for instance, was accused by Beria of killing, presumably on instructions from Khrushchev and Ignatiev, the famous Jewish theatrical notable and public figure Shlomo Mikhoels. Beria ordered Tzanava to be jailed but, as he awaited trial, overnight he switched from being Beria's suspect to being Beria's accomplice. He died in captivity. It was reported he had killed himself but not a single person believed this: he undoubtedly knew too much.

General Rukhadze

The story of another ethnic Georgian, General Rukhadze, is even more interesting. "I clashed with this man for the first time in early 1949," says Colonel Gorlin in his memoirs. "At that time I was in charge of all secret communications at the governmental level. Rukhadze was appointed Minister of State Security in Georgia in 1948. It was quite unexpected as he was not a very able man. But his profile was high, and his wife, a singer and actress, was a socialite. He was in military counter-intelligence during the war and was friendly with the future Marshal Grechko and the future KGB chief Serov: probably that's why he quickly got to the top.

"In early 1949 he called me and instructed me to connect his office to the First Circuit: that meant he could tap the telephone conversations of Beria's mother and other relatives who lived in Georgia,

and even Beria himself. I answered that I had no right to do such a thing and would not do it. Rukhadze was outraged. 'Then we shall not possibly work together,' he threatened. I retorted by expressing my readiness to submit my resignation the next morning – which I did. That later saved my life because, not being associated either with Rukhadze or with Beria in the early 1950s, I survived the purge, while most of my colleagues were arrested and shot or imprisoned."

Lies within lies

"Although I was now a pensioner, Rukhadze did not leave me alone. He knew that I worked with Beria in the late 1920s, and probably he was afraid I was still maintaining secret communications with him. Rukhadze wanted to keep me monitored, so he offered me the post of director of the Intourist Hotel in Tbilisi. I flatly refused, explaining that I had never had any experience in catering and hotel management. Several months later he called me again and offered me the post of director of a Georgian soccer team which frequently travelled abroad. I laughed at the offer since I knew nothing about professional soccer. Then I was called to the Republican Ministry of State Security in 1953. When I arrived (it was 11 a.m.) Rukhadze's secretary informed me that the minister had been summoned to see the First Secretary of the Georgian Communist Party, Boris Mgeladze, Malenkov's protégé. I waited until about 7 p.m. By that time I finished reading all the magazines in reception, and was extremely bored. 'If the minister wishes to talk to me, I shall be home,' I said heading for the door. I learnt what happened much later. When Rukhadze entered the study of Mgeladze, the latter's bodyguards twisted Rukhadze's arms, handcuffed him and took him to the military airfield to be delivered to Moscow. He was accused of fabricating the so-called Mingrelian Affair: Mingrelians were alleged to have conspired to get top positions in the Georgian Republic in order to create a nationalist enclave, organize bribery and set up a shadow economy.

■ *Above:* Marshal Konev, veteran World War II commander, sat on the panel of judges that decided the fate of Beria and his supporters.

Although there was undoubtedly some corruption in the top echelons in Georgia – as there was in all the republics of the Soviet Union – Rukhadze was definitely fabricating the whole case on instructions from Ignatiev. This was at the time that, under pressure from army generals, Ignatiev had Minister of State Security Abakumov arrested and became the minister himself. It is obvious to me that Khrushchev and Ignatiev were aiming at Beria, who was Mingrelian, and, as there are strong family ties in that small area of Georgia, they were trying to incriminate him in the 'Mingrelian Affair'.

"I think the main problem for the schemers was that the Mingrelian Affair coincided with the Jewish Affair in Moscow and the arrest of the alleged Zionists, including Raikhman and Eitingon. Raikhman was married to one of Malenkov's relatives, and so Malenkov decided to terminate these trumped-up charges, fabricated by Rukhadze in Georgia and Riumin in Moscow. Beria soon released their victims, and started the prosecution of the schemers themselves. After both were arrested and imprisoned there was little doubt he would find the people who were behind them, but Beria's own time was already up."

While in Lubianka prison, neither Rukhadze nor Riumin knew what was going on in the Kremlin. They were writing letters to Beria from prison asking him to pardon them, and included long lists of all the operations they took part in under the leadership of this "great man". Their investigators encouraged them: write more, say more. It never occurred to Riumin and Rukhadze that they were writing their own death sentences because Beria was already under arrest. These letters became important evidence for the people who wanted to get rid of dangerous witnesses. Both were finally executed. The tragicomic aspect to this is that Rukhadze was shot in 1955, together with about 15 people whom he had framed before his own arrest.

In 1954 the trial of Abakumov took place in Leningrad, a city particularly hostile to state security bodies, especially after the arrest and execution of Leningrad's young party functionaries in 1948, a purge for which it was claimed that Abakumov was responsible. His men did investigate the corrupt party and Soviet elections in Leningrad and reportedly advocated execution for the organizers, but it was definitely not in his powers to execute them.

"Now we know that the results of the voting in Leningrad in 1948 were really falsified, but the defendants played no part in that," wrote General of State Security Sudoplatov in his memoirs. "The Political Bureau as a whole, including Stalin, Malenkov, Khrushchev and Beria, unanimously voted that Abakumov should arrest and try the Leningrad group, but, whatever is written in the school party history textbooks and whatever Khrushchev wrote in his memoirs, Abakumov was not the initiator of this move." On the contrary, Malenkov and Khrushchev were the real initiators because they were afraid that younger and better-educated politicians like Nikolai Voznesensky, Stalin's favourite, could soon replace them in the Political Bureau. Once again, as in the 1930s, it was party bureaucrats who were killing people with the hands of the secret police. And once again, as in the early 1920s, the party mandarins and their henchmen demonstrated exceptional cruelty in treating the families of the accused. Abakumov's wife, a young woman not involved in any intrigues, was arrested and imprisoned with her two-month-old son, and spent three years in prison without trial.

Colonel-General Abakumov was sentenced to death, as were former chief of the state security investigation department Leonov, and two of Leonov's deputies, Komarov and Likhachev. Broverman, who agreed to "provide evidence", was sentenced to 25 years in the labour camps, and Chernov, one of the most talented officers, got 15 years for not being vigilant and not reporting his superior.

The testimony of one Turko, former secretary of the Leningrad *Oblast* Party Committee, shows the true quality of the trial evidence. He incriminated Abakumov as the destroyer of his friends and colleagues. Three years later, when Khrushchev was getting rid of his accomplice Malenkov, the same Turko testified that it was Malenkov who had forced him in 1948 to give false evidence against the young Communist leaders in Leningrad. He did not mention anything of the kind during the Abakumov trial. This example demonstrates how great was the desire of the army generals and Khrushchev to put an end for good to any witnesses that could expose them.

Death was probably a relief for Abakumov. He was monstrously tortured by Riumin, who wanted to link Abakumov to the "Doctors' Plot" at any cost, and spent three months in chains in a freezing cell. To the end he refused to accept his guilt and the existence of the Zionist plot. His courage and resilience made it impossible for the executioners to continue the case, as he was meant to be the leading figure in the "Doctors' Plot", and without his confession there was no case. As a result, all the defendants were released in the spring of 1953, but not Abakumov, since the enemy

■ *Left :* During Khrushchev's purge intelligence ace Zoya Rybkina was sent to work at the Gulag for supposedly being a Beria supporter.

of Khrushchev and Zhukov could not be set free. He followed Beria to the grave, and then his torturer Riumin followed soon after, ironically shot as an accomplice of Beria.

The bloody purge was sucking in more and more victims like a whirlpool. General of the Army and Hero of the Soviet Union Maslenninkov, Commander of MVD troops (he had been a front commander – equivalent to an army group – during World War II) and Beria's deputy, committed suicide: he was one of a select number of army generals who guarded his honour. General Sudoplatov, who headed the Special Operations (the 9th) Department, and his deputy Eitingon were imprisoned. Semen Semenov, the venerated Soviet agent who risked his life in America to steal atomic secrets for Russia, was expelled from the secret service without a pension, and for the rest of his life worked as a boilerman. Zoya Rybkina, the Russian intelligence services' legend, was sent to work in the Gulag.

But there were thousands of less famous or important individuals who were also shot, imprisoned or exiled, to silence any information that could damage Khrush-chev, the new ruler. Even pages of the interrogation reports that contained his name were removed from the files. The official statistics show that about 4000 secret service generals and officers fell in this, the Last Purge. Practically every general or officer who knew of the role played by Khrushchev and his supporters in the *troikas* in 1930s was either shot or imprisoned.

"The accusations varied enormously," remembered Colonel Gorlin. "If someone had followed Beria's orders, he had performed 'criminal acts' irrespective of their effects. If invited to a conference attended by Beria, he had taken part in 'the coup with the aim of overthrowing the legitimate authorities and assassinating the leaders of the party and state'. If one was a SMERSH officer, one had 'arrested innocent people'. And if there was nothing to be accused of? Then the investigators found a way to compromise you. For instance, to have bought confiscated furniture was a basis for relieving a man of his post without pension, for allegedly tarnishing his honour. And the fact that the generals who helped Khrushchev in his coup brought carloads of war booty from German palaces did not stop them from condemning men who risked their lives in the country and abroad."

Tidying up loose ends

"A retired officer of the archives, after treatment at the secret service hospital, suddenly started to experience awful headaches and vomiting, and after five weeks he died. The official conclusion was heart disease. But we later learned that when he – and some other officers – were prescribed mineral water baths the water contained thallium or another chemical substance. His problem was that, working at the archives, he knew which files were removed immediately after the arrest of Beria and other security chiefs, so that meant the end of him."

All that happened because a cabal of unscrupulous and greedy bureaucrats and generals were scared to be exposed as criminals. But they were also probably convinced that in the country where, starting from "Iron-Clad Felix", the law is used to repress political opponents and personal enemies, and where it is almost impossible to prove one's innocence after arrest, so it is better to scheme and strike first before anyone else does.

Coup benefits

The coup ultimately made Khrushchev the ruler of Russia. He abused the country's economy with his ambitious and ill-conceived projects until he was deposed in 1964, and almost provoked a nuclear war by locating Soviet missiles in Cuba. Yet, many Western historians claimed that under him despotism had been weakened, whether he wanted that or not, and that many talented intellectuals finally started to have some influence in the country. The last, however, was due to the efforts of Adjubei, his son-in-law and an able journalist.

Khrushchev's reward was absolute power for a decade. Georgi Malenkov, something of a figure of amusement, was part of the Khrushchev-Malenkov-Bulganin triumvirate for only a short time, before being sent to distant areas in 1955. Marshal Nikolai Bulganin, the vice-premier and minister of defence who contributed to the coup as much as his modest abilities allowed, became premier in 1955, but was demoted to colonel-general and sent into retirement for criticizing Khrushchev two years later. It is characteristic, however, that Khrushchev's accomplice had turned on him so soon.

Marshal Zhukov was reinstated as the top military commander in the USSR and became the minister of defence in 1955. But he was too popular for Khrushchev to let him be at the very top for long. Besides, they clashed in 1956 when Khrushchev instructed Zhukov to award his son Leonid the title of Hero of the Soviet Union posthumously. Zhukov flatly refused, saying that there could be no reward for a traitor. So in 1957 he was relieved of all his posts and sent into retirement.

Marshal Konev, who sentenced Beria to death, became commander in chief of Warsaw Pact (a military treaty and association of East European states, formed in 1955) forces, and Marshal Moskalenko, who was also a member of the tribunal, became the commander of Soviet Ground Forces, replacing Marshal Rokossovsky, an outstanding military commander who had refused to take part in the coup. General Batitsky, Beria's voluntary executioner, was promoted to be commander of the Moscow Military District, then to be deputy chief of the General Staff, and finally commander of the Air Defence Forces. At the peak of his career he was Marshal and Hero of the Soviet Union. He enjoyed life immensely until the end of his days.

A lifetime of honours

Lieutenant-General Brezhnev, Head of the Political Directorate of the Soviet Army, who reportedly was among the officers who rushed into Beria's office with guns in their hands, became secretary of the Communist Party of the Soviet Union (CPSU) Central Committee, then chairman of the Supreme Soviet (USSR Parliament) and finally replaced Khrushchev as general secretary. At the end of his life he was self-made Marshal of the Soviet Union, a Hero of the Soviet Union, four times Hero of Socialist Labour, and also decorated with more than 200 other Soviet awards. So for most of its military participants Khrushchev's coup proved to be extremely beneficial. Six months of shame and dishonesty – and a lifetime of honours and luxury.

The treason of the secret service mandarins was not as well rewarded. After Stalin's death Ignatiev was promoted to secretary of the Central Committee of the CPSU, but was soon removed because his role in the fabrication of the "Doctors' Plot" became known publicly. Malenkov saved him from prison and sent him to Bashkiria. Khrushchev was more radical: he relieved Ignatiev of all his posts and had him permanently monitored by local security bodies. Ignatiev vegetated until his death in 1983 at the age of 79, a totally broken man. His accomplice, Colonel-General Kruglov,

stayed in Beria's chair only until 1954. His friends considered him a decent man who made only one fatal mistake when Stalin died: teaming up with Serov, a confirmed and greedy traitor. An economist and expert in Gulag affairs, Kruglov only came to the fore during World War II, attached to SMERSH. He was not too bright but was a methodical organizer, being highly commended for the security measures he provided for the "Big Three" at Tehran, Yalta and Potsdam. He probably thought that Beria was out to destroy him. Kruglov did not stop – or could not stop – halfway when Beria and his team were eliminated, and had to follow Khrushchev's rules of the game, issuing orders for the arrest of his former friends and associates, while completely subjugated by Colonel-General Ivan Serov, who was initially his deputy.

The "grey man"

Serov in Russian means "of grey colour". This short man with an everlasting wry smile playing over his greyish face was really something of an *éminence grise* before the coup. After the coup, this man without any talents or adequate knowledge of modern espionage served at various times as the chief of the two most important Soviet intelligence bodies: the secret service and military intelligence. Truly it was a triumph of scheming over intellect.

Serov started his military career quite late, graduating from an artillery school in Leningrad at the age of 33. Before that, he was a *seksot* (informer). He arranged for himself, through his NKVD contacts, instruction at the intelligence department of the Frunze Military Academy, and was assigned on graduation to an NKVD unit. In 1939, when most of the Yezhov appointees were removed or imprisoned, there was a shortage of national security cadres in almost all the republics. Ukrainians were needed for posting to Kiev, and Serov played his manipulative game again. Though from the northern Russian province of Vologda, he declared that he was an ethnic

■ Above: General Ivan Serov, a loyal Khrushchev supporter who had honed his murderous talents in the Ukraine and Poland prior to Russia's entry into World War II.

Ukrainian. As a result, he found himself no less than Minister of Internal Affairs of the Ukrainian Soviet Socialist Republic.

At that time, Khrushchev was the first secretary of the Communist Party of the Ukraine. He needed men of Serov's calibre, the more unscrupulous the better. He ordered Serov to arrest even moderate nationalists, and when in 1939 Russian troops entered previously Polish territory in the western Ukraine, Khrushchev told him to kill or execute prominent figures there, including the Catholic clergy. In return he made Serov a member of the Central Committee of the Communist Party of the Ukraine. The top NKVD officers who visited the Ukraine in those years complained that Serov was not thorough enough in properly disposing of the bodies of people executed on his and Khrushchev's orders: sometimes they were buried in mass graves in monasteries and churchyards, and not in remote and inaccessible sites. Serov had assumed that the skulls with the bullet holes would never be found, but they were, albeit many decades later.

As his boss was climbing the hierarchy ladder, so did Serov. On the eve of the German invasion, when Stalin decided to have two commissariats in charge of security and internal affairs rather than one, on the recommendation of Khrushchev Serov was

transferred to Moscow and appointed the First Deputy People's Commissar of State Security under Merkulov. From this moment onwards he was usually entrusted with the most appalling state security jobs, like the liquidation of the Volga Germans and the deportation of Chechens, Ingushi, Kalmyks, Crimean Tartars and other national minorities. During the deportation of all the Ingushi peoples from the North Caucasus, when weeping women and children were pushed onto crowded railroad cars, the brave General Serov, warmed by good wine at the station restaurant, ordered some young Ingushi to perform folk dances.

In March 1957 Serov appeared in London to discuss security measures for the forthcoming visit of Nikolai Bulganin and Nikita Khrushchev to Great Britain. In those years memories of Serov's victims were still vivid in Western Europe, where some survivors of his concentration camps and deportations had found refuge. They appealed to the media, and the British press duly informed its readers that Soviet Russia's "Ivan the Terrible" had stepped onto British soil. The campaign in the British press was so virulent that Serov was recalled.

A year later he migrated to military intelligence, where he was much more powerful and unchecked than he had ever been in the secret service. His downfall came when he was deeply involved in one of the most scandalous affairs in the history of Soviet military intelligence: the treason of Colonel Penkovsky; who supplied American and British intelligence services with important information about Soviet missiles, rocket fuel, new artillery equipment and many other secrets. Serov had favoured this man, who was eventually executed. As for Serov, he was simply forced to leave the highest level of the Soviet nomenklatura.

But nothing he did while in its ranks was as important as what he had done in March 1954. It was then that he became the head of the organization which in the end had a longer reach and more intricate mechanics than any of its predecessors.

CHAPTER 8

SCENES FROM THE COLD WAR

In the 1950s the KGB enjoyed a number of successes in penetrating Western intelligence agencies and recruiting spies.

The advent of the KGB (*Komitet Gosudarstvennoi Bezopasnosti* – State Security Committee), formed by a state decree in March 1954, was received in the Soviet Union with caution rather than optimism. The citizens of the first Socialist country in the world had already seen several reformations of the secret service, and on each occasion they hoped it would cease to be a feared repressive body, and every time their optimism had been swiftly punctured by new repressions. As so many speeches had been made by Khrushchev and Malenkov about the "return to Socialist legality", the younger generation of intellectuals hoped that the new body would be at least slightly different. But those who had experienced the deportations, arrests and exiles organized in the past by the newly appointed KGB chairman, Serov, did not expect any significant changes from him.

Khrushchev regarded Serov's KGB first and foremost as the main tool with which to consolidate his personal power. That is why the first KGB task was the destruction of documents that might jeopardize his rule or compromise his position. In the Lubianka secret service headquarters in Moscow, at least a dozen bags of documents were collected and carried to unknown destinations, most probably to be destroyed. In Kiev the number of

■ *Left:* **A photograph from Soviet files of a Russian soldier killed by Hungarian nationalists during the uprising in 1956.**

files destroyed was smaller, as many had been burnt when the Germans approached the city during World War II. Many more, however, were withdrawn from the Leningrad and Moscow secret service centres and from the republican headquarters in Georgia. In 1956, the copies of some documents that were kept in the archives of the Council of Ministers were also doctored by Serov's subordinate Ivanov, and the names of Marshal Zhukov and Ivan Serov were obliterated under a thick layer of black ink. When the so-called Commission for Checking the Reasons for Sentencing was formed on Khrushchev's instructions, it consisted of Aristov, Rudenko and Serov, i.e. people who had themselves carried out repressions. The commission was used to incriminate Khrushchev's political opponents. At the end of his life Malenkov, exiled and humiliated by Khrushchev, wrote a letter to the then chairman of the KGB, Yuri Andropov, in which he revealed how these criminal operations, including the withdrawal of important documents, had been performed.

There were three other elements that Serov introduced into the life of the KGB. The first was favouritism of a special kind: a readiness to accommodate and promote

in his agency the sons and nephews of party apparatchiks and generals. The KGB offered high pay in a poor country, especially for officers posted abroad. Dynasties of security officers were favoured in Russia, and Communist mandarins were always ready to appoint their relatives to key positions, but the nepotism was never as great as in Khrushchev's times.

The second feature was the provision of special luxuries for the KGB élite. Since the downfall of Yagoda, most senior secret service officers had led model lives, as if modest intellectuals. Khrushchev's era opened the floodgates, as special shops were created and comfortable villas were built in the suburbs to accommodate KGB generals, close to those of the party bureaucrats. The KGB élite became the best-paid and the most envied segment of the Soviet nomenklatura.

The third feature was making lying the official policy of the KGB. It was Serov who, as early as August 1955, issued Directive No 108 cc (top secret) to be circulated among the chiefs of the KGB in Soviet republics and *oblasts* (provinces). This document specified the procedure for replying to the thousands of queries from Soviet citizens who, following Khrushchev's

■ *Right:* Armed Hungarian nationalists on the streets of Budapest in 1956. Future KGB chief Yuri Andropov was at the time Soviet ambassador to Hungary.

demagoguery about "restoring Socialist legality", wanted to know what had happened to their relatives arrested and tried by the ill-famed *troikas* of the 1930s. Serov instructed that, instead of admitting that people had been executed, the KGB should inform them orally that their relatives had died in a camp about 10 years after their sentence, due to some imaginary illness, most commonly heart disease. Local registrars were to issue the corresponding death certificates on request. "Return to legality" in Serov's version meant that at least 50,000 people in the Soviet Union received fake papers that camouflaged the tragic fate of their loved ones. These replies were received, not only by the relatives of a Lett or a Daghestani who had refused to cooperate

with the camp administration, so was re-tried by a *troika* and shot outside the camp, but also by the relatives of such famous and tragic figures as Artur Artusov, the intelligence ace (see Chapter 3).

The new head of the secret service felt invulnerable from his first day in office, since Khrushchev and Malenkov, the top party leaders, and the marshals were all in his debt. Serov boasted of his long and close friendship with Khrushchev and of serving under Zhukov in Germany, when he was the marshal's deputy in charge of security. He knew a lot about the top party officials, especially about their failures and bluffs, and could use this knowledge to harm them. From day one in office he was helping Khrushchev and Malenkov to

■ *Above:* When the Soviets crushed the Hungarian revolt thousands of Hungarians were sent to the Gulag.

commit new crimes. To reduce any possibility of even a minor revolt among the military, they arrested and imprisoned Stalin's younger son, Vassily. Although Stalin knew that his elder son, Yakov, would never make it alive from the Nazi concentration camp in which he was held and his grief was enormous, he let Vassily, his beloved child, graduate from aviation school and become a frontline pilot. Vassily was daring, sometimes even foolishly courageous; he simply could not afford to behave otherwise. He progressed quickly: colonel at 20, a major-general at 24 and a lieutenant-general at 27. He commanded an aviation corps, and later became the commander of the air force in the Moscow Military District. Flamboyant and universally adored, he drank a lot after his father died and his friends were persecuted by Khrushchev and Malenkov. In 1953 he was arrested, accused of power abuse and improper behaviour. Vassily was initially kept in solitary confinement at the ill-famed Vladimir Central Prison, where his fellow inmates were mostly secret service officers and generals fortunate enough to be imprisoned by the new rulers rather than shot like Beria. Vassily got eight years and was transferred to the Lefortovo prison, where he was permanently watched by the military and KGB. After being released, he was sent into exile in the Tartar capital of Kazan. According to the official version, he died there of alcoholism, and was buried in the city cemetery under the name of Dzhugashvili (his father's real name). But the truth is different. He was found in a desolate street with a fatal dagger wound to his heart. It remains a mystery whether this was Serov's work or not.

The Hungarian revolt

In 1956 Hungary erupted. That was not the first rising in the "Socialist camp": there was one in Berlin and the Eastern Zone of Germany, i.e. the Soviet occupation area, in 1953, but the Russians swiftly crushed it with their troops and tanks. In Hungary the situation was much more serious for the Communists. Resentful of Soviet control, on 23 October 1956 students, workers and others revolted in Budapest against the Communist government, demanding among other things the reinstatement of former premier Imre Nagy. To make matters worse for Moscow, the Hungarian Army joined the demonstrations.

A bloody victory

The popular movement was not monolithic; part of it was driven by the forces that had supported the extinct pro-Fascist regime, while the other part was seeking genuine democracy. Serov was duly sent there. He acted in Hungary as he would have acted anywhere in Soviet territory: he applied brute force. The reaction of the Hungarians was to resort to arms. Hundreds of local secret-police officers and sergeants were executed by the rebels or imprisoned. When Soviet tanks entered Budapest on 24 October, the rebels used schoolgirls to greet them with flowers, and once close to the tanks, to throw Molotov cocktails at them. That provoked an even harsher response from the Russians, and more bloodshed. The rebels were well armed: they had more than 180,000 handguns, about 3000 machine guns and dozens of artillery pieces and mortars. Soviet forces withdrew from Budapest at the end of October, but on 4 November occupied the city using 200,000 troops and 2500 tanks and armoured personnel carriers.

The Russians won, but a deep scar remained. It was over Hungary that Serov for the first time clashed with an experienced party apparatchik called Yuri Andropov, the future KGB chief and later the general secretary of the Communist Party of the Soviet Union (CPSU) Central Committee. Serov forbade Andropov, then ambassador to Hungary, to evacuate the families of Soviet diplomats and accused him of "negotiating with the enemy". In fact, these negotiations were a trap, and some Hungarian leaders who arrived at the

■ *Above:* Soviet tanks in Budapest after the crushing of the uprising. Soviet ambassador Andropov did good work luring some rebel leaders to his residence.

Serov and the local military district commander urged that Ministry of Internal Affairs (MVD) and army troops be sent to bayonet demonstrators gathered around a monument in the park, and that sparked a popular rebellion. Special troops and tanks were used, and hundreds of people, mostly students, were killed in the streets. Many arrests followed, and the first KGB chairman showed his "humanity" by pressing magistrates to review some cases and increase prison terms.

Georgia was not the only republic where popular discontent was smothered by brute force. Similar operations involving security forces and the army also took place in the Central Asian republics. The secret service also launched a massive operation in the Baltic region to eradicate guerrilla bases both in small farmsteads and in the forests of Estonia and, to a lesser extent, Latvia and Lithuania. The guerrilla detachments, called "forest brothers", consisted of the former security and police officers from the period when the Baltic republics were independent, people who served in Nazi units during the German occupation, and young nationalists.

These detachments had superbly camouflaged dugouts and tunnels, and enjoyed the support of émigré organizations in Sweden and Finland, and also in Great Britain and the USA. The supplies they received included silenced weapons, radio equipment, booklets and substantial sums of money, and although the groups were scattered and not numerous, their attacks on Soviet administrators and *militsia* (police) drew substantial security forces into the area. Although most of the guerrilla detachments were found and destroyed in the early 1950s, some survived until the early 1960s.

As to the hunting-down of nationalists abroad, there was little change in the pattern of operations. When generals Sudoplatov and Eitingon were arrested and imprisoned for their "complicity with Beria's crimes" their unit in charge of special operations, assassinations included, was

Soviet Embassy for them were seized and later executed.

Another country where Serov "distinguished" himself was Georgia. The people of this small republic, considering their compatriot Stalin a kind of national hero, refused to dismantle his monuments following directions from Moscow so to do in 1956, and mass rallies started in Tbilisi.

disbanded. However, it was soon resurrected, and when the KGB appeared this unit was called the 13th Section. The difference between the killings done abroad in Stalin's time and those during Khrushchev's regime was only that Stalin normally took personal responsibility for the decision to eliminate a political enemy, while Khrushchev presented the case to the Presidium of the Central Committee and made it look like a unanimous collegial decision.

As in the 1930s, when he displayed vocal hatred for Ukrainian nationalists, Khrushchev was once again eager to exterminate all important figures in the Ukrainian émigré nationalist movement, first and foremost Georgi Okolovich, leader of the People's Labour Union (NTS), Doctor Lev Rebet, the standard-bearer among émigré intellectuals, and Stefan Bandera, leader of the Ukrainian right radicals and Organization of Ukrainian Nationalists (OUN). Until about 1950 there were still some nationalist guerrilla detachments in various distant regions of the Ukraine, called *banderovtsy* (Bandera followers), which used armoured personnel carriers and machine guns to kill local secret service personnel and party functionaries every week. Bandera himself was unscrupulous in ordering terrorist acts in the Ukraine or in Eastern Europe against

people and targets of any sort. But there was something in Khrushchev's speeches and his actions that resembled a personal vendetta, which made some secret service officers in the Ukraine comment sarcastically that maybe he had been rejected by the nationalists when he was young, so had been taking his revenge on them ever since.

In 1952 the chief of the Ministry of State Security (MGB) Ignatiev tried, on Khrushchev's instructions, to arrange the kidnapping of Okolovich. It failed, and in early 1954 Kruglov, the new security boss, ordered a trained assassin, Captain Nikolai Khokhlov, to kill Okolovich. He was to use a special silent electric pistol firing both poisonous and dumdum bullets. Instead of killing his victim, though, Khokhlov revealed the plot to Okolovich and defected to the Americans. The reason for this move was said to be that Khokhlov was connected to former MGB minister Abakumov, who by that time was already in jail, and so was afraid that, whether he killed Okolovich or not, he would end up in prison himself. Khokhlov exposed two other Soviet agents, who were arrested by the Americans. An object of much publicity in the West, Khokhlov became ill three-and-a-half years later in Frankfurt, and it was found that he had been poisoned with irradiated thallium. He survived only thanks to urgent measures

■ Right: Central Committee Secretary Alexander Shelepin replaced Serov as head of the KGB in 1958.

■ Far right: Yuri Andropov, party apparatchik and ambassador to Hungary between 1954 and 1957. He became head of the KGB in 1967.

■ *Above:* Senator Joseph McCarthy, chairman of the House Un-American Activities Committee, whose Communist witch-hunts in the 1950s hindered Soviet espionage in the United States.

assassinations. His widely publicized trial and the public outrage at KGB killings in a sovereign state made the Kremlin reconsider such "special operations". Khrushchev and his associates recognized how damaging these acts were to international relations. These were the last international terrorist operations instigated and organized by Serov along the lines pioneered by the OGPU and NKVD. All the paraphernalia created at special laboratories, like single-shot lipstick cases, umbrellas discharging cyanide needles and heart-paralyzing cigarettes, now became relics of the past, aside from those used to liquidate KGB defectors.

In his own "apparat", Serov was promoting those generals and officers who were always prepared to falsify a case. Generals Krainov, Betin and Fedotov, who were under his patronage, were notorious for the enormous number they fabricated. Serov was always very assured of himself. But he had not appreciated properly the real strength of the "apparat", the party bureaucracy, and its ability to use and then dispose of unscrupulous people it had earlier nourished and promoted when the need arose. Serov was rude and arrogant with his subordinates, and now he became rude with the apparatchiks as well. For their part they disliked him as a symbol of deportations and violations of the law, at a time when they were trying to distance themselves from Stalin's era.

A chance to remove control of the archives and the secret service from this unpleasant and dangerous man who knew too much came in 1958 when Mironov, director of the KGB Leningrad Department and a man truly seeking to reform the secret service, sent Khrushchev his programme of preventive measures to counter anti-Soviet sentiments and actions, i.e. so that it would not be necessary to rely on punishment alone. Khrushchev consulted Serov, who was outraged. Firstly, he did not like what he saw as Mironov's insubordination; secondly, he could not comprehend the idea of

taken by American physicians and then to long-term intensive treatment.

When Serov became head of the KGB, the instructions from Khrushchev to terminate Lev Rebet and Stefan Bandera were still standing, and another assassin called Bogdan Stashynsky was assigned to do the job. Rebet was killed in October 1957, and Bandera in October 1959. Stashynsky used prussic acid for both assassinations: one dose discharged from a vial and another by air gun. Awarded the Order of the Red Banner for the operation, Stashynsky later returned to West Germany. In 1961 he defected to the Americans with his East German wife and confessed to the preventive measures simply because he was basically an executioner, unable to plan or anticipate. So Khrushchev asked Central Committee secretary Alexander Shelepin to comment on and develop this programme, and his report was so liked by party officials that he was appointed chief of the KGB instead of Ivan Serov, who was sent to direct military intelligence. Serov retained his high salary and benefits in his new position on the order of Khrushchev.

His activity there is outside the scope of this book, but to complete the picture it is worth telling one more story linked to him. Internal investigations and matters pertaining to deported peoples were still processed by the MVD, not the KGB. Some documents found in the MVD archives made Nikolai Dudorov, the MVD minister and an energetic and hard-working man, launch investigations about deportations conducted by Serov, and appalling facts came to the surface about hundreds of people who died or were killed during these forced movements. Reports on the findings were prepared, but suddenly Dudorov discontinued further investigation. His son had been found on a staircase with his back broken, paralyzed for life. Dudorov had another child, a daughter, and he decided not to take any more chances. Although there was no visible connection to Serov, veteran security officers speculated that no one within the KGB would carry out such a task, and only GRU (Main Intelligence Directorate – military counterpart of the KGB) assassins, blindly following orders and not even knowing the name of the victim, could do that to an innocent boy.

The Canberra affair

The destruction of Beria and his appointees had sent shockwaves not merely throughout the entire intelligence community in Russia, but also far beyond Russia's frontiers among the intelligence officers who had been posted abroad by them. This led to quite unexpected incidents, one of which took place in Australia.

In 1951 a new third secretary, Vladimir Petrov, arrived at the Soviet Embassy in Canberra with his good-looking, blonde spouse Evdokia, who was not going to take a job but was going to be the perfect Russian housewife. The interesting point is that almost everything in the previous sentence is untrue. Nominally a diplomat, Petrov (real name, Proletarsky) was a colonel in state security in charge of clandestine operations in Australia, and his wife Evdokia Kartseva, a career spy and an accomplished linguist (she spoke English, Swedish and Japanese), was to help him navigate through the local diplomatic community. Her previous husband, an NKVD officer, died in the Gulag after being arrested for conspiratorial activities in 1937, but she, also an NKVD operative codenamed Tamara, stayed afloat and married Proletarsky in 1940. They were a professional spy couple, and performed their intelligence missions in an exemplary manner.

The Petrovs defect

But there was one problem: Vladimir Petrov had been highly valued and promoted by Lavrenty Beria. After Beria's downfall Petrov knew perfectly well what would happen to him, in the classic tradition of the Soviet secret service, upon his return to Russia; he did not expect anything less than death in a remote camp. So he decided to defect and ask for asylum. He met officers of the Australian Security and Intelligence Organization and got their assurances that asylum would be granted. Because he was pressed for time, or because he suspected Evdokia of reporting on her first husband – or for one of many other possible reasons – Petrov did not inform her about his defection, and she was grabbed by MGB security heavyweights from the Russian Embassy and taken to the airport for the flight to Russia.

Having worked for the NKVD throughout the years of the Great Purge and World War II, Evdokia knew what would be the fate of a defected spy's wife. There were no Aeroflot flights to Moscow

in those days, and her minders hustled her, sedated and desperate, minus one shoe, onto a BOAC plane. By that time the story of the Petrovs was already widely known, and hundreds of onlookers screamed abuse at her escorts at the airport. On the aircraft Evdokia managed to alert a stewardess, and when it landed at Darwin police officers came aboard and clashed with her minders, demanding they be disarmed. In the ensuing chaos, Evdokia escaped and was soon reunited with her husband. For decades afterwards they lived a safe and

secluded life in the Melbourne area, as Sven and Maria Anna Allyson.

It must be remembered that the mid-1950s was the most chilling period of the Cold War, with the McCarthy witch-hunt in America against Communists, left-wing trade unionists and all manner of "un-American" activities (Senator Joseph McCarthy made unsubstantiated allegations that Communists had infiltrated the US State Department; in 1953 he became chairman of the House Committee on Un-American Activities). The Kremlin might

■ *Above:* **Khrushchev at the United Nations General Assembly in October 1960. At this time his KGB was involved in both espionage abroad and suppressing freedom of speech within the Soviet Empire itself.**

have been trying to change public opinion in the West after the death of Stalin and execution of Beria, but it was also attempting to stop all anti-Soviet and anti-Communist movements in Eastern Europe. Both the West and the USSR used huge human and technical resources during this battle. The Soviet Union, in addition to resources required for espionage and surveillance abroad, needed an enormous machine for domestic suppression and counter-intelligence.

Espionage activities

Khrushchev inherited from Stalin an intelligence "apparat" which was slightly battered at the top, yet nicely oiled and tuned nevertheless. As before, many Kremlin decisions taken in the international sphere were based on intelligence. From 1945, when Soviet Pioneers (Communist boy scouts) presented a nicely carved Great Seal of the United States to the American ambassador in Moscow to mark the joint victory over Germany, the Kremlin had no problems in getting accurate information about messages sent by him and successive ambassadors to Washington, since the Great Seal contained a voice-activated radio device. This was revealed in 1952, but the Russians replaced it with many others during the construction of the new US Embassy building in 1953. About 40 were discovered in 1964, when Soviet defector Nosenko showed the Americans on a diagram the location of the bugs they were not able to find with metal detectors. These were placed in bamboo tubes built into the walls behind the radiators.

When the Berlin crisis of 1961 took place (when the East German authorities built the Berlin Wall to stop the drain on their manpower), the KGB obtained, through a French officer in NATO (North Atlantic Treat Organization, established in 1949), a copy of the contingency plan for the defence of the three Western sectors of the city. Although it showed a firm resolution to protect the sectors by all means necessary, it

stated that if the East Germans were to erect some sort of barrier separating their zone from the others, the Allies would not interfere. As a result, the Berlin Wall was built, and remained a symbol of Communist isolationism for three decades.

Political information was important, but the swift development of electronics, computer technology, avionics and other areas affecting military equipment, especially fighter aircraft, missiles and helicopters, meant information about these topics was equally vital. Before Khrushchev ordered the scrapping of attack bombers and destroyers around 1960, on the assumption that a future war would be fought solely with missiles, the Soviet secret service, unwilling to rely on the resources of military intelligence, paid particular attention to American and British technical achievements. A Soviet master spy known as Rudolf Abel was sent to the United States in 1948, and remained there as head of an illegal network gathering technical intelligence for about 13 years.

Abel's real name was William Fisher, born in Newcastle-upon-Tyne in 1903, the son of a German father and Russian mother, both political émigrés. Named after Shakespeare, William went to university, but in 1920 his father took the family to Russia. William served in the Red Army as a radio-telegraph operator, but the OGPU simply could not overlook a young man who spoke perfect English, German and French, and he was recruited by the Foreign Department (INO) of the OGPU in 1927. He was sent to Norway and Great Britain before World War II as a radio operator, and there is little doubt he was in that period cooperating with the "Cambridge Five". During the war he worked under Sudoplatov and Eitingon in frontline intelligence. He was probably the best technical spy the USSR ever had. He was an expert in radio, electronics, chemistry and nuclear physics. He spoke several languages, painted professionally and was considered a good photographer.

Fisher (codename Mark) settled in Brooklyn in New York in 1948 as the artist and photographer Emil Goldfus. His main mission in that period was to set up a parallel network capable of receiving and re-transmitting information on weapons plutonium and other important atomic projects, as the Federal Bureau of Investigation (FBI) was on the trail of some existing Soviet espionage networks. He became the main recipient of the packages carried by Lona Cohen, and was also getting super-secret information about the formation of the Central Intelligence Agency (CIA) from an agent whose codename was Gerbert, a career officer in the US intelligence community. After the Cohens had to flee as a result of the Rosenbergs' arrest, Fisher set up bypass channels for the inbound information, but he needed an experienced link agent and radio operator. Soon the required person joined him: Reino Hayhannen (codename Vic).

■ *Left:* East German tanks in East Berlin in 1961. Khrushchev was keen for the other half of the city to be de-militarized of Western troops.

■ *Below:* Building the Berlin Wall. It was constructed to stop the flow of skilled workers, professionals and intellectuals to the West, whose loss threatened to destroy the economic viability of East Germany.

In June 1957 a Soviet mole in the CIA reported that MGB Lieutenant-Colonel Reino Hayhannen, while in transit in Paris, had visited the American Embassy and asked for political asylum. Soviet intelligence historians insist that Vic was drinking too much, pocketed US $5000 issued for agents and ignored his main functions, which made Fisher send him back home. But it seems there were other grounds as well. Hayhannen had been assigned to the intelligence service with Beria's blessing, and some of his friends were arrested and sent to the Gulag in 1953 and even in 1954. He certainly did not want to join them there.

Fisher was immediately informed about Vic's defection and was supposed to move to Florida and then to Mexico, to pick up a reserve passport and return to Europe. However, he was arrested in a New York hotel after he had visited his studio in Brooklyn to destroy incriminating evidence. While being arrested, he managed to drop a microdot message concealed in his tie pin (a microdot is in essence an A4 sheet reduced to miniscule size by a special technique). He also destroyed some other spy paraphernalia, including his cipher pad, but the fact that he was careless enough to have all this equipment in his studio was sufficient for the KGB and the Soviet Government not to award him later the title of Hero of the Soviet Union for his 13-year American saga. He got the Order of Lenin instead.

Fisher was tried and sentenced to 30 years in prison, although he could have expected the death sentence. In 1962, he was exchanged for the American pilot Francis Gary Powers, whose U-2 high-altitude spy plane was shot down in 1960 near the city of Sverdlovsk in the Urals region. Although both sides celebrated the deal, they realized that the people exchanged were of totally different calibres. Fisher did not cooperate with his interrogators, and did not disclose either his real name or his mission, while Powers talked a lot. As for Hayhannen, he died

soon after the trial when his car crashed into a trailer. As he was drunk, it was assumed to be a road traffic accident.

Another Soviet master spy of the period, Konon Molody (codename Ben), was sent to Great Britain illegally under the name of Gordon Lonsdale to collect information about the biggest naval research centre in the world, which was also one of the most secret: the British Admiralty's Underwater Detection Establishment at Portland. Moscow was interested in Britain's research and experiments on submarines, the friend-or-foe identification system, and modern armament electronics. Lonsdale's contact was Harry Houghton, a clerical officer at the Portland base, who had been recruited by the Soviet secret service for money while serving as a clerical officer at the British Embassy in Warsaw. Most of the secret information came from Houghton's lover Ethel "Bunty"

■ *Below:* William Fisher, alias Rudolf Abel (centre), following his arrest in New York by the FBI. He was lucky not to receive the death sentence for his espionage activities, and even luckier to be exchanged for Gary Powers in 1962.

Gee, a clerk at Portland who had access to the secret library and archives. As she was doing a lot of copying of classified material, she was able to reproduce and smuggle some files out of the premises. The Soviets boasted that, thanks to the Portland Spy Ring, they knew as much about Her Majesty's submarine fleet as did the British Admiralty.

Konon Molody

Konon's biography was as unusual as that of Abel. Born in 1922 in Moscow into the family of the physicist and sci-fi novelist Trofim Molody, he lost his father when he was only seven. In 1931 his mother's sister, who lived in California, visited him and offered to take Konon to the USA. Somehow permission was granted, but the Americans then would not let in the child of a Soviet employee. A relative then approached his friend Yagoda, an OGPU high-flyer and future *narkom*, and the latter instructed the church where Konon was baptized to forge a new birth certificate, according to which Konon was the son of his other aunt who lived in Estonia. Konon went to America and stayed there until 1938. He was recruited into the Red Army in 1940 and won three orders and a score of medals.

After the war he entered the Military Institute of Foreign Languages and studied Chinese. But with his American accent and schooling he was perfect material for the secret service. Additional training followed and, after several months of establishing his background in Canada, he arrived in London in March 1955. His cover there was that of a wealthy businessman. Initially the Soviet secret service supported his businesses, but later he became a very prosperous entrepreneur and owner of four profitable enterprises. His main businesses were foodstuffs and cigarette machines. To illustrate how well he was doing, every time he covertly went to Moscow he had to pay several thousand pounds sterling as his individual party fees.

The link agents and radio operators, who worked hand-in-glove with Molody,

were none other than Morris and Lona Cohen, posing as antiquarian book dealers Peter and Helen Kroger living in Ruislip, less than an hour's drive from central London. Molody delivered the documents to them, which the Krogers microfilmed and used drops to transfer to secret service officer Vasily Dozhdalev, stationed at the Soviet Embassy *residentura*. They also produced microdots for posting to the Moscow centre, or used a high-speed (250 words per minute) radio transmitter.

Smashing the Portland Spy Ring

The Portland Spy Ring ceased to exist because of the betrayal and defection of Michael Golenevsky, head of the British department of the Polish security service. He told the CIA about an English sergeant who had been recruited by the Russians in Poland. MI5 was tipped off, and soon found Houghton. All the ring members were arrested and sentenced to long prison terms. Molody got 25 years and was placed in a high-security prison where he met George Blake, another Soviet spy, Communist and double agent sentenced to 42 years for treason. The situation looked hopeless for both, but Molody promised Blake that they would both be present in 1967 at the military display commemorating the 50th anniversary of the October Revolution in Red Square in front of the Kremlin. His words were prophetic. Konon Molody was exchanged for British businessman Greville Wynne, sentenced to eight years for being a main link between the GRU traitor Oleg Penkovsky and US and British intelligence. The KGB was sure it was making another good deal by exchanging their master spy for an obscure semi-professional. Later, however, they believed that Greville Wynne had been one of the British top agents, a figure the equal of Molody. As for George Blake, he had a miraculous escape from prison in 1967 and successfully made it, with the aid of KGB officers, to Moscow. The Krogers were exchanged in 1969 for Gerald Brooke, a British lecturer arrested by the Russians and sentenced to five years in prison for espionage in 1965.

In the last years of his life Konon Molody was very critical of his superiors for jeopardizing his mission by putting him in contact with an agent who had previously served in a Soviet bloc country, i.e. Houghton. He was also unhappy about the regime he found on his return to Moscow. He died in 1970 at the age of 48, reportedly after suffering a stroke while camping with his friends and family in a forest about 200km (125 miles) from Moscow. According to a Soviet mole in MI6, the British were still trying to keep an eye on Molody even though he was effectively in retirement, and the news of his death reached London the same day he died.

Pure luck

Intelligence is often like gambling, where so much depends on a streak of good luck. After the exposure of Kim Philby and other members of the "Cambridge Five", the Soviet secret service had two almost unbelievable streaks of luck in the 1950s and 1960s. One of them was made possible by the double agent George Blake. He was head of a section in MI6, and was thus one of the most trusted and well-informed members of the Western intelligence community.

Blake was Dutch by birth. While working in the British Embassy in Seoul during the Korean War (1950–53), he was captured by the North Koreans and successfully brainwashed by the Russians. The KGB knew him as agent Diomed and considered him invaluable. In December 1953 a secret conference of MI6 and the CIA was held in London, at which a decision was taken to dig tunnels under the Soviet communication lines that linked Moscow and Berlin, and tap them. About two weeks later the 1st Chief Directorate of the KGB received the minutes of the conference, supplied by George Blake.

The American tapping system was used by the Russians to disseminate a whole series of disinformation campaigns, and in

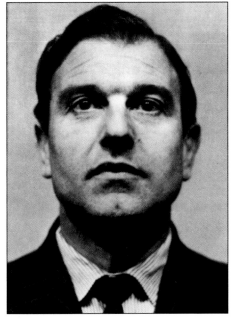

■ *Above:* Soviet troops in a Berlin tunnel. The KGB used these tunnels to great effect in the 1950s.

■ *Left:* The Soviet spy George Blake. He was head of a section in MI6, and was thus one of the most trusted and well-informed members of the Western intelligence community.

fact Operation Tunnel was the most efficient Soviet disinformation operation in the entire Cold War period. The most important element of this operation was that the Russians had feedback, since Blake provided them with reports on how the disinformation was received. To protect him, some real information was also passed back to the West. This, however, did not ultimately save him. The Polish traitor Michael Golenevsky, the man who exposed Molody, also revealed Blake.

Another outstanding Soviet intelligence bonanza took place some 10 years later. The main character in the story was Sergeant Robert Lee Johnson. This military clerk who had worked in Berlin since early 1950 was tired of the US Army, offended by lack of promotion and inclined to try his luck in the Socialist world. He applied to the Soviet authorities in East Berlin for asylum, but a KGB officer persuaded him to stay in the US armed forces and help the "cause of peace" by supplying the Soviet Union with classified information. In return, the KGB promised him help from unidentified sources and money. They were not happy with Johnson's drinking bouts, though.

Under the guidance of Vladimir Krivoshei, an officer from the local KGB *residentura*, Johnson photographed some classified material in the intelligence section of the Berlin Command. Later, on his own initiative, he recruited his close friend, Sergeant James Allen Mintkenbaugh, who was covertly transported to Russia where he received intelligence training. After leaving the army in 1956 he found a job in California, still spying for the KGB. He was used extensively by the Russians in the following years, operating in Virginia, Florida and Canada on their instructions and performing various intelligence jobs.

As for Johnson, he left the army in 1956 as well, but Moscow got him to rejoin. He was stationed as a guard at a California missile site, and succeeded in getting some specifications of the Nike Hercules missile, and even samples of its fuel. But then he was transferred to an American base at Port d'Orleans in France, into an ordnance battalion of no importance to the KGB, so he was encouraged to apply for a transfer. He finally managed to move to the US Armed Forces Courier Center at Orly Field.

When the Russians learned of this they were stunned, as it was an intelligence target they had been looking to penetrate for a long time. The most important documents from the Pentagon and NATO were processed through it, and both military and diplomatic papers from the United States for American military and naval commands in Europe were sorted and re-routed there. The cipher keys from the National Security Agency (NSA) and even operational and mobilization plans of

NATO states passed through the centre. The centre was basically a concrete bunker with a single door and no windows. Inside, there was an office for sorting the mail and a secure vault with two steel doors, each with sophisticated locking systems. There was a permanent guard inside the office, and nobody was ever permitted to enter the vault alone.

A classic operation

Robert Lee Johnson first became a guard in the centre, and then a duty clerk who could stay in the vault at the weekend, when there were few deliveries. Johnson succeeded in making a mould of one key and then found the combination for another lock. The Soviet secret service manufactured a special portable X-ray machine that, attached to the second steel door, could reveal the key combination of its lock.

As French counter-intelligence was quite effective in its surveillance of Russian officers in diplomatic and trade missions, every withdrawal from the American vault was supported by several Russian agents in separate cars. There were diversionary activities as well, and cover from a professional hit-and-run squad on standby. The pattern of withdrawals was the same. After opening the vault, Johnson stuffed the papers into an Air France shoulder bag, left his post at the dead of night and drove to a deserted byway near Orly. He was met there by a KGB officer and exchanged bags with him, getting an identical bag with food and drinks in it. Johnson returned to his office, while the KGB officer hurried to the Soviet Embassy where special experts were flown in from Russia to delicately remove seals, open envelopes and photograph the papers. After restoring seals and envelopes to their original condition, the KGB exchanged the bags with Johnson at another rendezvous near Orly.

The KGB and Johnson had seven such exchanges, but then the former realized how dangerous it would be to go on, after Johnson nearly got caught. After taking the documents to the Soviet agent and

returning to his office, he drank too much and fell asleep. The Russian who brought the papers back to the rendezvous point after they had been copied in the embassy saw the deadline was approaching, and made a desperate attempt to save the operation, driving into the Orly compound and putting the bag containing them into Johnson's car. Johnson woke up minutes before his shift was due to end, ran to the car in despair and saw the bag. He replaced the papers in the vault and had just locked the last steel door when his replacement appeared. The KGB decided not to take any more chances, happy with what they had got – items like the operational plan of the American supreme command in Europe in the event of nuclear war between NATO and the Warsaw Pact, and the so-called Handbook of Nuclear Yield Requirements, which showed potential targets in the USSR, other Warsaw Pact countries, and also Egypt, Iran, Syria and Iraq. When published, these papers provoked public outrage in many countries.

Johnson was later transferred to the Pentagon, where there might have been even greater opportunities, but his wife, who had some form of mental disorder, started telling doctors and nurses in the military hospital about her husband being a traitor and meeting Russian agents. Besides, by that time the Americans had their own streak of luck: the defection of an important Soviet intelligence officer, Yury Nosenko. Although the FBI and CIA did not believe him to begin with, in due course Johnson and Mintkenbaugh were arrested, tried and imprisoned. Johnson was killed by his son Robert, a Vietnam War veteran, during a visit to his father at a Federal penitentiary in 1972.

The sparks of the new opposition

Thousands of books have been written about Khrushchev's dismantling of Stalin's monstrous regime and how he cleaned out the top echelon of his evil lieutenants, yet Stalin never sent tanks and infantry to kill unarmed people in the street as did his

■ *Above:* Soviet master spy Konon Molody (codename Ben), who in the 1950s was sent to Great Britain under the name of Gordon Lonsdale to collect top-secret military intelligence. He was captured by the British but then exchanged for Greville Wynne.

successor. In Hungary in 1956 there was at least armed resistance to Communist rule, but there were many other places where popular movements were crushed by brute force simply because they threatened to topple Khrushchev. He was not only a worthless economist and a poor administrator, he was also almost as cruel as Trotsky and Tukhachevsky in suppressing popular unrest.

Massacre at Novocherkassk

On 1 June 1962 a new decree was issued about increased prices for meat and butter. Russians were not accustomed to price rises and in Stalin's era prices were actually reduced, though insignificantly, seven times. But the real problem was that prices went up at the moment when pay rates at the metallurgic and forging departments of the Novocherkassk electric locomotive works

went down by 30 percent. The workers staged a rally, and operations stalled. General Manager Kurochkin appeared with his retinue, and when asked by the workers, "How can we live now?", answered arrogantly: "Well, you guzzled meat pies, now you will guzzle liver pies." By midday the whole works was on strike, an unheard-of illicit event in the USSR. Some 30 workers, "the instigators", were arrested, the city erupted, and tanks and troops moved in.

The next day a protest march moved towards the city centre. There were hundreds of children and women among the demonstrators, many carrying portraits of Lenin. It did not save them. The troops were there to shoot, and if they did not do so from the start, it was because their commanding officer committed suicide rather than give the order to open fire. But those who replaced him did. The first salvo killed mostly children sitting in the trees on branches, watching the demonstration. Others swept the lines of unarmed people, killing more than 70. The troops were commanded by General Pliev, a "war hero", and used dumdum bullets with devastating effect. Hundreds were taken to hospital, and there were pools of blood in the street. The regime had shot at its own people indiscriminately. The rallies and demonstrations were finally dispersed the day after, and two of Khrushchev's close associates, Anastas Mikoyan and Kozlov, arrived to bring the situation under control. There were no regrets expressed by Mikoyan, who claimed that it had been the enemies of the people who had organized the bloodshed and, since dumdum bullets were not in service with the Soviet Army, these bullets must have been used "by the enemies". It would have been farcical were it not so tragic.

Now the KGB entered with all its resources. The wounded disappeared, and their relatives were swiftly exiled. All the people spotted and/or photographed in the demonstration vanished as well. The "instigators" were taken to the Vladimir Central Prison. In the two trials that followed, 9 men were executed and 2 women were sentenced to 15 years in prison; they all were sentenced as criminals, not as political opponents of the regime, as mass rallies were classified as banditry. The most amazing feature of the story is that very few people in Russia knew about it, and even fewer abroad. That was the greatest achievement of the then chairman of the KGB Vladimir Semichastny, and Minister of Defence Marshal Malinovsky.

The killing of invalids

Another crime of Khrushchev and his henchmen may well be the strange, almost simultaneous deaths of about 4000 invalids in 1954–55. These people, very severely wounded and maimed during the war, were assembled on Stalin's orders in about 10 distant hospital camps. The intention was not to sadden too many with the sight of these poor invalids, and also to stimulate enterprise in those rural areas where the population had been depleted during the war and where virtually no businesses could be profitable. Soon after Stalin's death the mortality rate in the camps suddenly grew out of all proportion. Colonel Gorlin commented in his memoirs: "I had no doubts that the invalids were exterminated. That was the gratitude of the Motherland for their desperate resistance to Fascism. Most of them were officers and people who had been awarded high combat orders, and, according to my friend who was in charge of organizing one of the hospitals for them, initially they had had good accommodation, nursing and food. I have no idea what methods were used by Khrushchev's killers to finish them off, medical maltreatment or slow poisoning, but in late 1957 I received information from at least two independent sources that some of the hospital camps were closed because all their occupants had died. That was probably Khrushchev's idea of how to get 'unnecessary expenses' completely off the book."

Lies, corruption and unscrupulousness became the main features of party life during Khrushchev's time and permeated all of society, including the KGB. There always had been defectors from its ranks, but most of them were escaping, like Orlov, from the Great Purge in the 1930s or, like Petrov, from the Last Purge of the early 1950s. The 1960s brought about an entirely new type of defector, one who was not forced to flee but who went of his or her own free will. They called themselves "conscientious opponents of the regime", and many of them were, since the tyranny of the Communist regime created by Lenin and developed into an overwhelmingly repressive police state by Stalin had, since the beginning of the Khrushchev era, a layer of the worst type of corruption and élitism at the top.

Major Anatoly Golitsyn

Major Anatoly Golitsyn was an apparently typical defector of the new type. He had worked in Finland under the cover of vice-consul at the Soviet Embassy. He defected with his wife and daughter by going straight to the residence of the CIA station chief in Helsinki, Frank Friberg, whose address he had managed to acquire from KGB sources. A pompous, second-rate operative, Golitsyn had a quality highly respected in Khrushchev's times: he spoke with assurance and persuasion and looked respectable. His limited abilities were not enough to get him to the top, hence his peripheral jobs in "quiet" countries like Finland and Austria, but he was over-ambitious and arrogant. The CIA took him more seriously than he merited and agreed to fly him and his family to the USA via Stockholm. His claim was that he was disillusioned with the "Soviet reality", but the CIA also knew another reason for Golitsyn's defection: he was at war with the *resident*, the head of the KGB station in Helsinki, and knew perfectly well he would be fired upon his return to Russia. He chose a comfortable life in America rather than exile in Siberia.

Although the KGB never admitted it, they were deeply grateful to Golitsyn. He at the CIA. After Nosenko's defection, the KGB kept wondering for a decade why their networks had not crumbled immediately and why they had time to save most of their spies and local agents.

There were hundreds of other non-returnees: sailors stayed in foreign ports, engineers applied for asylum while on business trips, and intelligence officers defected, despite the watchful eyes and the endless checks of the KGB. There were sons and daughters of the ruling élite among these "traitors of the Motherland", as they were called, because they knew the real value of the regime, a haven for corrupt bureaucrats and criminals. There were also thousands of young people who believed Khrushchev's speeches about "real democracy" and "true legality". Many were the sons and daughters of those imprisoned in all the purges, from 1934 to 1953, who now expected not only the proper rehabilitation of their parents but also compensation for their ruined lives and guarantees that similar repressions would never happen again. Once their fathers and mothers were rehabilitated, they also wanted them to go back and live in their flats and villas, occupied by the bureaucrats and lackeys of the regime. There were confrontations and endless court sessions about these issues.

Artists and writers were other turbulent groups who believed Khrushchev's assurances that the time had come to let in fresh winds. In 1959, *Syntaxis*, the first samizdat (banned or dissident literature) magazine, appeared in the USSR, featuring the writings of underground poets and novelists and edited by Alexander Ginzburg, but it lasted only three issues. An exhibition of nonconformist artists took place in the main Central Exhibition Hall in Moscow, right in front of the Kremlin, and Khrushchev ranted at the work of these abstract painters and sculptors. As a result of these first stirrings of freedom of speech and creation, the KGB started to flex its muscles in this area.

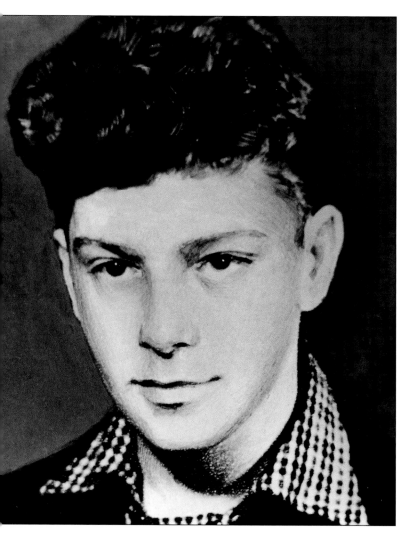

■ **Above:**
Alexander Ginzburg, the editor of the samizdat magazine *Syntaxis*. Its dissident contents ensured it lasted a mere three issues before it was banned.

never knew many secrets, and so improvised fantastic stories for his new bosses. He became a trusted consultant and advisor to James Jesus Angleton, head of the counter-intelligence section at the CIA, and it was due to him that the CIA was plunged into an unprecedented witch-hunt, looked for Russian plants where there could not possibly be any, and rejected or fired the people who could have been useful and important in the years to come. Golitsyn introduced into the CIA counter-intelligence department the tainted atmosphere of Khrushchev's KGB, and ruined many reputations and careers. It was due to his accusations that Yury Nosenko, a Russian defector much hated and feared by the KGB, was not trusted or even listened to properly

CHAPTER 9

THE STAGNANT YEARS

During the 1960s and 1970s the KGB had difficulty suppressing dissent within the Soviet Union and Warsaw Pact.

Khrushchev's agricultural and industrial projects were disastrous for the Soviet Union, as were his blunders in foreign policy and internal affairs. The Cuban missile crisis, the Novocherkassk Massacre, Penkovsky's case, the legion of defectors, the shortage of bread in almost all of the country, including even military schools and KGB units, and growing dissent seriously alarmed the party mandarins. There was no risk of them getting fewer benefits than before, of course, and they did not care that the lives of soldiers, workers, office employees and collective farmers were getting more miserable by the day. They were simply afraid that the people of the Soviet Union, so tolerant, so patient and long-suffering, might suddenly be unable to take some last straw, and the subsequent wave of popular rebellion would flush away the party élite and the whole regime.

In October 1964, Nikita Khrushchev returned from his Black Sea villa to Moscow together with Anastas Mikoyan, the chairman of the Supreme Soviet (the USSR's mock-up parliament). They were met at the airport by Chairman of the KGB Vladimir Semichastny, and the convoy went straight to the Kremlin where a group of top party figures known as the Presidium of the Central Committee (as the Political Bureau was called under Khrushchev)

■ *Left:* A Czech youth attempts to stop a Soviet tank following the Warsaw Pact invasion of Czechoslovakia in August 1968.

and its secretaries were already waiting for Khrushchev. They had conspired to depose him, and KGB chairman Semichastny was part of the plot. A relatively young apparatchik (he was only 40) and the former First Secretary of the *Komsomol* (Young Communist League), he was brought by Khrushchev from the Ukraine and placed at the top of the secret service as a bureaucrat personally loyal to him.

Khrushchev's removal

Later that night, both Leonid Brezhnev and Khrushchev appreciated the deadly efficiency of the KGB chief. All Khrushchev's guards at his Kremlin apartment, suburban villa, Moscow city mansion and office, and all the drivers, also KGB men, had been replaced by Semichastny with his trusted officers, so that the leader was actually under house arrest. The meeting continued the next day. The speeches were devastating for the first secretary. He snarled at his opponents and even threatened them, but he was doomed. Meanwhile, Semichastny's office was flooded by telephone calls from almost all the *oblast* (province) party secretaries and Central Committee members because they knew that, under the Soviet system, all the strings were in the hands of the KGB. They remembered how Molotov and other adversaries of Khrushchev were removed, and they feared for themselves.

The calls clearly showed how far removed from any conception of the democratic process the Soviet apparatchiks were. Some urged Semichastny to take action to relieve Khrushchev, who was besieged at the meeting of the Central Committee Presidium, and some demanded that he immediately arrest Brezhnev and other opponents of Khrushchev. The KGB boss, however, reported all important calls and changes in the situation to Brezhnev, who told him that Khrushchev was losing and would have to go. A Central Committee Plenary Session fired him the next day.

Semichastny's active part in the coup was immediately rewarded by promotion to

■ *Above:* Leonid Brezhnev (far left), chairman of the Presidium of the Supreme Soviet, the coalition that deposed Khrushchev in October 1964.

the rank of general, although he had never served in the army or secret service. But Brezhnev, who spent almost all his life in party organizations and political bodies, was a typical Soviet-style court intriguer, not trusting anybody unless he could control that person. There was nothing in Semichastny's life that could be used as leverage by his superiors to exert pressure on him. His participation in the resultant coup and knowledge of all its internal workings worried Brezhnev. The new general secretary manifested an insatiable appetite for total control from his very first days in the office, and it cannot have come

at least three decades. The times of grey tunics and ascetism were over. Khrushchev and his family showed the apparatchiks that Soviet Socialism could accommodate luxury as easily as California high society. But it was Brezhnev who encouraged unlimited hedonism and favouritism of the worst kind, totally neglecting the interests of all those people who were below the ruling stratum of bureaucrats and party functionaries. The Soviet Union survived and developed due to the hard work and sacrifice of honest and industrious people, and in spite of the inefficiency and retarding interference of the top echelon.

The age of corruption

The role of the KGB in the life of the country changed, too. KGB professionals watched silently as the totally useless offspring of party mandarins took key positions in intelligence units, jeopardizing the very existence of their colleagues. Military counter-intelligence officers learnt that reporting on generals who instructed procurement officers to supply their households at the expense of miserably fed soldiers could cost them promotions. Corruption in the departments engaged in foreign trade was out of all proportion, but since these were controlled in many cases by the friends or relatives of the top echelon, the KGB officers who monitored them knew that their reports would not change anything at all.

as a surprise to the chief of the KGB that less than a year after deposing Khrushchev, Brezhnev suggested he leave the KGB and become a member of the "top detachment", i.e. the inner circle of the party or state bureaucracy. Semichastny could pick from a position as Central Committee secretary, a deputy chairman of the Council of Ministers, or a sinecure abroad. But he knew that career bureaucrats hate upstarts unused to their ways and refused. That was a setback for Brezhnev, and the beginning of the rift between him and his supporter.

Changes were taking place in the life of the country that would define its future for

Once a party functionary or a bureaucrat entered the top nomenklatura in this period, he knew that, unless he confronted the Political Bureau and the party machine openly, he would make a good living for the rest of his life. If a top apparatchik failed in one position he would be moved sideways, to another department or another region. The apparatchiks knew that as long as they loudly supported the leader, they would be untouchable. There was a new system of law in the USSR, the so-called "telephone law". A telephone call from the top echelon could protect one from criminal prosecution or destroy another who dared to raise his voice against injustice.

As the chief of the KGB, Semichastny received reports from the special guards assigned to protect Brezhnev and other Political Bureau members and many other dignitaries, so he knew every detail of their lives. The daughter of the general secretary, Galina Brezhnev, was a spoilt and arrogant woman with a lot of unsavoury connections. She was using the "telephone law" even before her father became the country's leader, but now there were no limits to her ambitions. She intervened, through her father and his assistants, in the criminal investigations of a number of her acquaintances who had grossly violated the

law, and demanded that the KGB drop the cases. After Semichastny had tried on several occasions to dissuade Brezhnev from being involved in such interventions, he was doomed.

A pretext for his dismissal was found. Svetlana Alliluyeva, Stalin's daughter, was impetuous and unbalanced, capable of sudden affections. While a mature woman and mother of two, for example, she fell in love with an Indian who worked at a Moscow publishing house as an interpreter. When he died she decided to go to India to scatter his ashes in the Ganges, as Hindu tradition prescribed, and got permission to do so from Alexey Kosygin, the then Soviet premier. She never came back, and soon her

■ *Below:* The trial of underground writers Andrei Sinyavsky (right) and Yuly Daniel (left) in 1966. They were imprisoned for "anti-Soviet propaganda", but their cases hastened the removal of Semichastny as head of the KGB.

■ *Right:* Svetlana Alliluyeva, Stalin's daughter, who visited India on the pretext of scattering her dead lover's ashes in the Ganges. She never returned, which infuriated the party apparatchiks.

book *Twenty Letters to a Friend* appeared in the West. That prompted some apparatchiks to declare that the whole story about the Indian ritual was just a hoax, and Semichastny was accused of mishandling the affair.

Semichastny's downfall

There were possibly two other reasons for Semichastny's downfall. Firstly, Shchelokov, the newly appointed head of the Ministry for the Protection of Public Order – the Interior Ministry – may also have insisted on removing him because the KGB had thick files on him and his family. Secondly, the Political Bureau may not have been happy with the way Semichastny handled the case of Andrei Sinyavsky and Yuly Daniel, two Russian underground writers who were published abroad under the pen names Abram Terz and Nikolai Arzhak. Their articles and short stories had been smuggled out of the country since about 1956 by a French scientist, Hélène Pelletier-Samojska. Arrested in 1965, Sinyavsky and Daniel got prison sentences for "anti-Soviet propaganda", but the party élite did not fail to notice that the KGB had first spotted them carrying the coffin at the 1960 funeral of Boris Pasternak's (the author of *Doctor Zhivago*), had known they were writing nonconformist stories and poetry since 1961, and had done nothing about them for several years. Besides, the 1965 sentences and the press attack on the underground writers were not considered harsh enough by the party bureaucrats, once similar cases were revealed and became the subjects of public discussion.

In May 1967, Semichastny was removed from his position and sent to the Ukraine as deputy chairman of the Council of Ministers of the Republic. The previous KGB chief, Shelepin, was assigned to direct the All-Union Central Council of Trade Unions, and ended his life in relative obscurity. A new boss came to the Lubianka – a 43-year-old party functionary called Yuri Andropov. A *Komsomol* apparatchik in Stalin's times, he was appointed Soviet ambassador to Hungary in 1953 and was instrumental in organizing the crushing of the Hungarian rebellion in 1956. From 1957 he was head of the Department of Socialist Countries in the Communist Party of the Soviet Union (CPSU) Central Committee, and in fact directed ideological and intelligence work in all the Soviet bloc outside the USSR.

There were three reasons for Brezhnev's choice. The first was Andropov's party apparat experience, which was valuable for his boss: he was, so to speak, "one of their own". The second was his strong long-term connections with the state security bodies. But perhaps the most important reason as far as Brezhnev was concerned was that he had a detailed report about Andropov's enormous zeal in condemning and eliminating the Leningrad and Petrozavodsk party organizations on instructions from Malenkov and Khrushchev in 1949. That was a lever to control the new KGB chief. Later he was made a member of the Political Bureau of the CPSU Central Committee so as to render him even more compliant. A dogmatic Communist but an intelligent administrator, Andropov planned to use his powers to restore the KGB to its former glory, which implied that it would target the lower levels of Russian society, the source of dissent.

While the party theorists creatively developed Lenin's ideas of "imminent world revolution" and proudly paraded the dozens of leaders of Communist and workers' parties that gathered in Moscow for each CPSU Congress, Russia remained a poor country. The effects of Khrushchev's disastrous economic experiments were still being felt; Premier Kosygin was desperately trying to make ends meet. The living standards of the common people were very low, and almost all goods were scarce. The ruling élite had access to special supplies of food (for about 18,000 families in Moscow scarce items sold at ridiculously low prices were delivered to their doorsteps), built superb apartment blocks for themselves and

their relatives, used special clinics and resorts, had an opportunity to travel abroad, and were assigned building plots in particularly beautiful countryside where they could build summer houses for next to nothing. Many of the families of senior bureaucrats resold goods purchased from special tax-free distributors at a large profit. There were also many thousands of parasites around them feeding off the scraps.

What had been inconceivable under Stalin, and done more or less secretly under Khrushchev, became quasi-legal in the

■ Above:
Semichastny was replaced as head of the KGB by Yuri Andropov (third from left), who was determined to restore the organization to its former glory.

■ *Left:* Minister of Culture Elena Furtseva (left), who was caught building a suburban villa for herself, using construction materials issued for the restoration of the Bolshoi Theatre in Moscow.

Brezhnev era. Corruption reached farcical levels. Minister of Culture Elena Furtseva, for example, was caught building a suburban villa for herself, using construction materials issued for the restoration of the Bolshoi Theatre in Moscow. Some top bureaucrats of the Ministry of Fishing organized the illegal export of caviar disguised as tinned herring and earned millions, but the heist was accidentally disclosed. The deputy minister was executed, while the minister, Brezhnev's friend, was simply sent into retirement. Huge thefts were organized by some managers of the Moscow city trade directorate and by the bureaucrats of the Ministry of Trade, and a number of them were arrested, while some were prudently killed by persons unknown before they could be arrested. The most extraordinary case was that of the First Secretary of the Krasnodar Regional Party Committee,

■ *Above:* Israeli troops during the 1967 Six-Day War. Israel's victory increased the desire of many Soviet Jews to leave the USSR, which alarmed the KGB as many were scientists.

Sergei Medunov, and his deputies, who were in fact the leaders of organized criminal gangs. They used criminals to deal with honest people, including the investigators and even the KGB officers who were after them.

From the top party echelon, the epidemic of corruption spread to the Interior Ministry. The people who set the tune there were the minister himself, Colonel-General Shchelokov, and his deputy Churbanov, Brezhnev's son-in-law. Shchelokov appropriated huge sums and antiques confiscated from criminals, while his son and daughter-in-law were engaged in laundering misappropriated funds by buying rare oil paintings. As for Churbanov, he was more interested in jewels since his wife, Galina Brezhnev, collected them. She was also engaged in buying jewellery cheap and then selling it at a huge profit. Information about her behaviour came to the KGB from all directions, but the agency was unable to do anything about it.

KGB deputy chairman Colonel-General Tzvigun was a loyal Brezhnev supporter, but when he tried to rein in Galina, he was attacked by the members of the Political Bureau so fiercely that he committed suicide. Some KGB officers took the decision to quit rather than be witnesses or involuntary accomplices to these crimes. Many others became as unscrupulous as their bosses. With their loyalty evaporating in the face of the moral degradation and decomposition of society, more than 20 intelligence officers defected.

A defector's fate

One of the most notorious defections in the 1960s was that of Lieutenant-Colonel of the KGB Yury Nosenko, deputy chief of the 2nd Chief Directorate (Counter-Intelligence) of the KGB. Although he physically defected in early 1964, he had been a Central Intelligence Agency (CIA) agent from the middle of 1962. That was a spectacular catch for the Americans, not only because

for the first time they had an agent at the top of the counter-intelligence service, but also because Nosenko was the son of a top-level state bureaucrat, the Minister of Shipbuilding, who held the rank of admiral, was a friend of Khrushchev, and was privy to many secrets of the Soviet élite.

Born in 1927, Yury, like most children or grandchildren of top Soviet bureaucrats, graduated from the prestigious Moscow State Institute of International Relations. To boost his career his father arranged for him to serve in naval intelligence, and three years later he was transferred to the 2nd Chief Directorate. There his area was surveillance of American diplomats and journalists in Moscow, and looking for ways of recruiting them. Then he served for two years in the 7th Directorate in charge of the surveillance of foreigners, where he specialized in the blackmail and recruitment of tourists, academics, students, United Nations (UN) officials and businessmen. It was here that he developed a taste for the high life and began to like to associate with Westerners. Returning to the 2nd Chief Directorate, he was soon promoted, but more important still he became a confidant and after-hours companion to General Gribanov, head of the directorate. As a result, personal favours followed that opened up enormous opportunities for Nosenko.

Nosenko's treachery

In 1962 he was selected to head the counter-intelligence team that was sent to watch the Soviet delegation at the disarmament conference in Geneva. During this three-month assignment, Nosenko used his professional skills to select an American diplomat whom he thought might be an undercover intelligence officer. He asked him for a small loan to settle some debts which, he said, would be repaid in the form of some intelligence information for the CIA. He made up the story, of course, but a line through to the CIA was now opened. The latter's Soviet Division was euphoric, as here was a man who could reveal not only the state secrets of its adversary but also much about the private life of many Soviet high-flyers.

Nosenko's information proved to be enormously important to the CIA. According to English television journalist and intelligence historian Tom Mangold, he gave a detailed description of Soviet surveillance on the US Embassy in Geneva, the patterns of Soviet security at their own embassy in that city, and the Soviet personnel in Geneva who were the best candidates for recruitment. He gave CIA officers the name of a top Swiss police officer who worked for the KGB. Nosenko also provided clues as to the identity of a KGB spy in the British Admiralty, which later led to the arrest by MI5 of William John Vassal, and, as mentioned previously, he disclosed Robert Lee Johnson, the US sergeant who had penetrated the Orly courier centre vaults.

Another batch of extremely important information supplied by Nosenko concerned the US Embassy in Moscow. He informed the CIA that the Russians had had a spy there as early as 1952: a code clerk supplying them with the codes which the KGB then used to transcribe important messages. Nosenko also warned the Americans that the man, who had been codenamed Andrei by the KGB, was later transferred to the National Security Agency (NSA) and might still be active. He revealed the exact location of 53 microphones planted by the Russians during the construction of the embassy, and disclosed the technique used by the KGB to apply a special dust on outbound mail which made it possible to positively identify the sender as being from the American Embassy, for example, if such letters arrived at homes of people suspected of carrying out espionage for the Americans, as well as secret enterprises or intelligence bodies. Another type of dust was applied by the maids in the embassy to the carpets, so that embassy staff, picking some of it up on their shoes, could be traced to secret drops by specially trained dogs.

The most ironic twist of the Nosenko story is that, although some information provided by him, when checked, proved real, the head of the counter-intelligence service of the CIA, James Jesus Angleton, was sure that his defection was a hoax and that he was a KGB plant, basing his conclusion almost entirely on the advice of defector Anatoly Golitsyn. In January 1964 Nosenko was again sent to Switzerland, for the second round of the disarmament talks, and decided that he would never go back to

■ *Above:* A Soviet tank, surrounded by crowds, in Prague, 22 August 1968. The Warsaw Pact sent 600,000 troops into Czechoslovakia to ensure it remained in the Soviet sphere of influence.

Russia. He planned to disclose to the CIA the name of an alternate member of the CPSU Political Bureau who could be forced to spy for NATO by sexual blackmail; to identify a high-ranking American officer who had spied for the Russians in West Germany and the USA; to reveal a NATO official who had handed over to the KGB some secret codes; and to list Western businessmen, connected to important government bodies in their countries, who were in fact KGB agents. But the CIA was more confident than ever that he was a KGB plant, and two months after his defection he was arrested by the Americans. He was kept under conditions much inferior to those in US prisons, fed only small amounts of very poor food, forbidden human contact, allowed no television or reading matter, denied cigarettes, and interrogated in a hostile and violent manner, while the FBI was still effectively denied access to him. The Angleton people went so far as to allege that Nosenko was not Nosenko but was someone else, although a professional psychologist who spent hundreds of hours talking to him was convinced he had been telling the truth.

Nosenko spent 1277 days incarcerated by the CIA, without any trial. The last two years and two months were especially hard, because he was locked in a 3m (10ft) square concrete, windowless cell. He was even deprived of blankets, pillows and linen, and the bulb overhead was lit 24 hours a day. The food was awful. When he tried to go on a hunger strike and lost almost 18.2kg (40lb), he was warned he would be force-fed. It was only in 1968 that the CIA came to the conclusion, based on a new polygraph test and eight-month interrogation session by security officers rather than those of the Soviet Division, that Nosenko had not been a KGB plant, and the process of his exoneration slowly started. The FBI was permitted to interview him, which resulted in the starting and the renewal of a number of counter-intelligence cases. Some of the suspects, to the FBI's regret, were already beyond their reach because of the time wasted. In March 1969 Nosenko was officially employed by the CIA as a "KGB independent consultant" with a steady income and legal protection, but it was not until 1975 that he was acknowledged in the CIA as a man who meant much more to the West than both Angleton and Golitsyn.

Nosenko's value

Although the CIA was sure that no information about Nosenko had been leaked, the KGB learned of his incarceration eight months after he was made incommunicado, and students at Soviet intelligence schools were told on many occasions how the USA had treated him. Another result of the Nosenko case was that the leaders of the KGB advocated more stringent rules of selection for KGB sinecures, especially for those officers to be sent abroad.

The first years of Andropov's regime in the KGB were very turbulent. Only three weeks after his appointment the so-called Six-Day War of 1967 erupted in the Middle East. Israel's rout of Egypt, Jordan and Syria was perceived by the majority of Jews in the Soviet Union as a proof of the steadfastness, military talent and technical ingenuity of the people of Israel, and made them think of joining the land of their forefathers. This in turn naturally enhanced the anti-Semitic feelings among some parts of the establishment, which had supported the Arab cause, and this in turn strengthened the desire of thousands of Soviet Jews to emigrate to Israel. Since so many Jewish scientists and engineers worked in the Soviet armaments industry, the KGB was very concerned.

The dissidents

The number of dissidents in the country was also growing. Those who demanded "real de-Stalinization" were naïve, not realizing that a substantial part of the establishment were in fact Stalin accomplices. No justice was possible while Khrushchev, Brezhnev and their ilk were at the very top of the party and bureaucratic machine. It was only natural that they ordered the KGB to perform surveillance on the leaders of every dissident group, at home or abroad.

Then there were young people who, learning of the lifestyle of boys and girls in the West, could not help wondering why they did not have similar opportunities. They wanted to have more money and fun, and were engaged in the clandestine production of jazz and pop records, the illegal sale of foreign second-hand clothes, and even of foreign currency. The music black market started, curiously enough, with the so-called "music on the ribs", i.e. records made out of old X-ray films. Later the market in magnetic tapes flourished. The Khrushchev government had tried to shut down the foreign currency black market by sentencing a group of dealers to death. As in many other cases, he was here violating the constitution, as they had

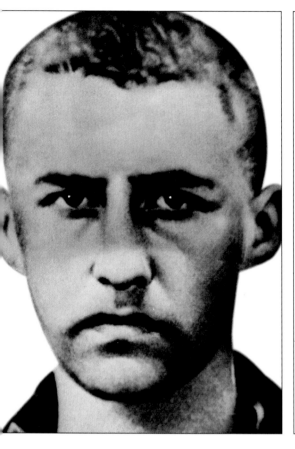

already been arrested by the KGB when the new law prescribing the death sentence for that offence was passed. Laws could not be retroactive, but still prisoners were informed that they would be shot.

Later, in Brezhnev's time, the KGB had little interest in currency speculation because the élite itself was deeply involved in it, albeit in the form of so-called "certificates". These were coupons which had the buying power of hard currency. When a Soviet citizen returned from abroad, he had to hand over all remaining hard currency and received these coupons instead, which he could use at special stores selling foreign goods or Soviet-made cars (also in short supply in those days). Needless to say, all the KGB apparat engaged in intelligence and counter-intelligence work abroad saved currency to exchange for "certificates" later on.

The dissidents represented a very small fraction of society, although quite an active

one. But what was new was the interest of the Western public in them, and also the interest of the Western secret services. It started with the concerns of international Jewish organizations and the world press for dissident Jews subjected to repression by the KGB and the Soviet judicial system for their beliefs and their activities in the protection of human rights, but it soon escalated. As dissent itself developed into the rejection of not only the Stalinist heritage but also the international, internal, economic and ethnic policies of the Soviet regime, support for the dissidents increased in many Western countries. A major boost to dissent was given by the Soviet invasion of Czechoslovakia in 1968, as it showed that no real reformation was possible within the entire Socialist bloc until the political dogmatists were removed from the Kremlin itself. Around 600,000 Warsaw Pact troops and hundreds of tanks invaded Czechoslovakia in August 1968 in response to

■ *Above:* Two of the many dissidents in the Soviet Union in the 1960s: the poet and publisher Yuri Galanskov (left) and Alexei Dobrovolsky. Leading dissidents were placed under KGB surveillance and often arrested for their activities.

liberal policies introduced by Czech leader Alexander Dubček.

There were several outstanding figures in the dissident movement, the most popular being Alexander Ginzburg, Anatoly Shcharansky, Yuri Orlov, Petr Grigorenko and Andrei Sakharov. Ginzburg, a champion of an independent press and a samizdat publisher, was arrested many times, imprisoned or kept for long periods without trial. In March 1979 the writer Alexander Solzhenitsyn, exiled by the Soviet Government, appointed Ginzburg to distribute part of his earnings from his books published in the West. Ginzburg was one of the main sources of information in the free press of how the KGB dealt with nonconformist writers and artists in the USSR, Jews demanding the right to emigrate to Israel, and Lithuanian Catholics and Crimean Tartars.

The Ginzburg case

After the Soviet Union signed the agreements drawn up at the European Security Conference in Helsinki in 1975 (the so-called Helsinki Accords were primarily an effort to reduce tension between the Soviet and Western blocs by securing their common acceptance of the post-World War II status quo in Europe; the main interest of the USSR was in gaining implicit recognition of its post-war hegemony in Eastern Europe through guarantees of the inviolability of frontiers and noninterference in the internal affairs of states in return for commitments on respect for human rights, freedom to travel, and the free flow of information across borders), Ginzburg was among the organizers of an unregistered group of enthusiasts who intended to check how the USSR fulfilled the human rights obligations that it had signed up to. The group was rounded up by the KGB, and Ginzburg took refuge in the residence of Andrei Sakharov, by then the leading dissident in the Soviet Union. The Ginzburg case finally became so important

that Brezhnev personally issued an order to the KGB chief to put an end to the dissident's activity. Ginzburg was put to trial and sentenced to eight years in a labour camp, but US president Jimmy Carter soon arranged an exchange of two Russian spies for five Russian dissidents, including Ginzburg. The latter was forced to emigrate, despite his protests, and lived at first in London and later in Paris. He repeatedly demanded that the KGB return the manuscripts of the very first editions of his samizdat poetry journal confiscated in 1962. He received them back 33 years later, to his astonishment finding that the KGB had carefully preserved everything.

Notable dissidents

In 1978 Anatoly Shcharansky, another leading Russian dissident and a founder member of the Helsinki Monitoring Group, had been accused of a much more serious crime: spying for the CIA. He was sentenced to 13 years in prison and labour camps for "treason and anti-Soviet propaganda". As he had been trying to emigrate to Israel, international Jewish organizations applied to the American administration, and Shcharansky's case became in a way the touchstone of Soviet-American relations. Shcharansky was freed after eight years in jail and escorted by the KGB to the West. He later became an important politician in Israel.

As for Andrei Sakharov, this internationally acclaimed scientist who had taken part in Soviet nuclear efforts since the 1940s joined the human and civil rights campaigners in 1972, and had been the undisputed leader of liberal intellectuals for about two decades.

Sakharov urged the party leaders to abolish the death penalty and free all political prisoners. A figure of enormous status and integrity, he attracted many talented intellectuals, and it was in part his stature that brought such people as the great cellist Mstislav Rostropovich into the human rights campaign. As he had called

■ *Above:* The writer Alexander Solzhenitsyn (centre) was exiled from the Soviet Union in March 1974 for disclosing the brutality of the Soviet regime. His Soviet citizenship was officially restored in 1990 and he returned to Russia in 1994.

■ *Left:* The cellist
Mstislav
Rostropovich, who
in 1970 made clear
his support of the
writer Solzhenitsyn
and invoked the
wrath of the Soviet
Government.

on the Soviet Government to renounce Marxism as a disproved theory, he became an enemy of the state and an object of KGB harassment. In 1975 he received the Nobel Peace Prize, which was a major setback for Brezhnev's government, and he was naturally denied a visa to go to Oslo to receive it. When he spoke out against the Russian invasion of Afghanistan in 1979, he became even more hated by the élite. In January 1980 Sakharov and his wife were arrested by the KGB and exiled to Gorky, an industrial city east of Moscow which was closed to foreigners. He was released from exile and returned to Moscow in 1986 on the instructions of then Soviet leader Mikhail Gorbachev.

Andrei Sakharov and other human rights campaigners had repeatedly urged the Soviet Government to discontinue sending protesters and political opponents of the regime to various mental institutions, a practice that became quite widespread in the late 1960s and 1970s. One of the best-known cases was that of Major-General Petr Grigorenko, a highly decorated war veteran. He had been arrested for the first time in 1969 for protesting at the beating of Crimean Tartars when they demonstrated in Tashkent. He was also known to have disagreed with the Soviet invasion of Czechoslovakia. Thereafter he was often kept at mental institutions for "inspection and diagnosing", and so were dozens of other civil rights activists. There were about 10 special KGB hospitals in the country, and many mental sections of prisons or MVD hospitals were directly or indirectly controlled by the KGB. These institutions were used to inflict psychological pressure on dissidents, subjecting some of them to intensive drug treatment to discourage further acts of dissent.

Overt disobedience might be extremely rare in the army and the secret service, but one incident shook the military establishment, as it showed clearly how deep and well-grounded discontent was in the armed forces, and how difficult it would be for the corrupt government to deal with it.

■ *Below:* The Soviet anti-submarine vessel *Storozhevoi*, which was the centre of a mutiny in November 1975.

■ *Left:* Captain 3rd Rank Valery Sablin, the leader of the *Storozhevoi* mutiny. His rather naïve assumptions that he could spark a wholesale reform of the Soviet state guaranteed him a death sentence.

The affair involved a large anti-submarine ship called the *Storozhevoi*. As in the case of Novocherkassk, the news of this mutiny on board a modern ship was immediately suppressed by the KGB and military commanders, and all the materials about it were classified top secret and kept in the archives of the party's general secretary.

The man who started the mutiny was Captain 3rd Rank (equivalent to lieutenant-commander) Valery Sablin. One of the most brilliant officers in the navy, a son and a grandson of naval officers, he became a gunnery expert after attending to the Leningrad High Naval School, and then entered the Military Political Academy in Moscow. It was here that he decided to struggle against the incompetence, corruption and degradation of the Brezhnev regime. After graduating with excellent marks he was assigned to the *Storozhevoi* as deputy captain in charge of political affairs. But instead of praising the regime and its leader, he spent two years propagating his own idea that the ruling élite and its Political Bureau had no legitimate right to govern, that freedom of speech and thought were being eradicated in the country, that the governing bodies were riddled with bribery, favouritism and arrogance, and that the only cure for this was root-and-branch reform of the state system and replacement of an election system which made the people a faceless mass.

In November 1975, there was a naval parade in Riga to commemorate the 58th anniversary of the October Revolution, and the warships were moored in line. On 8 November Sablin addressed all the crewmen, explaining to them his programme of action, and almost all pledged loyalty to him. He intended to moor near Leningrad and demand that a member of the Political Bureau come to the ship for an open discussion with the sailors, and that this discussion should be televised to the entire country. Most officers and warrant-officers refused to follow him, and were locked in specially assigned quarters. The captain of

the ship was also locked up, but separately. At 23:10 hours the *Storozhevoi* weighed anchor and dashed out of the harbour. Minutes later an officer who had managed to escape from the ship reported the mutiny on board. The fleet headquarters and the KGB were informed, and the *Storozhevoi* was immediately followed by the patrol boats of the KGB, ready to open fire.

The commander of the Baltic Fleet, Vice-Admiral Kosov, ordered his ships to apprehend the *Storozhevoi* and bring it back to Riga. In addition to ships with marines and special detachments on board, Kosov sent a squadron of 12 fighter-bombers. Soon after, another air force regiment was alerted on instructions of Defence Minister

■ *Above:* Defence Minister Marshal Grechko speedily crushed the *Storozhevoi* mutiny.

■ *Right:* Italian film star Claudia Cardinale, one of the many acquaintances of the Soviet spy Leonid Kolosov.

Marshal Grechko. The *Storozhevoi* was warned that unless it stopped, the rocket-carrying planes would destroy it. In reply Sablin sent an open radio message: "We have not betrayed our Motherland, and we are not adventurers looking for publicity at any cost. It is vitally important to openly raise a number of questions about the political, social and economic development of our country, about the future of our people, questions that require collective, truly popular discussion without any pressure from state and party bodies. But we also are aware of the danger of being physically or morally destroyed by the appropriate bodies of the state or hired individuals. Therefore we apply for the support of all honest people in our country and abroad. And if on the designated day, at 21:30 [hours] Moscow time, there is not a representative of our ship on the screen of your television, we ask you not to go to work tomorrow and continue your strike until the government retreats from its harsh violation of freedom of speech and until you can watch us. Back us up, comrades!" The ship's radio operator was probably more realistic in his evaluation of the situation, because he added at the end, on his own behalf: "Farewell, brothers!"

When the KGB crews threatened to open fire, Sablin used a loudspeaker system to explain his intentions, and amazingly no shots were fired. But the air force pilots, under pressure from their commanders, made dozens of runs over the ship, dropping bombs near the bow and stern (they later won decorations for exemplary shooting and bombing). The ship's steering mechanism was damaged, while a group of sailors, terrified by how things had developed, released the captain and armed themselves. Sablin was wounded, and the ship was stopped, surrounded by other ships and boarded by the marines. The mutiny was over.

Making the mutiny disappear

The crew was immediately brought to Riga where KGB investigators started questioning them. The ship was repaired, re-classed, renamed and its number was changed. Most of the crew was replaced, and then the ship was transferred to the Pacific Fleet. The officers of the KGB's 3rd Chief Directorate and their local colleagues collected the logs from all the ships that had been near the *Storozhevoi* during her capture, and soon returned them without the pages covering 8 and 9 November 1975. The KGB also did its best to spread its version of the mutiny in the Soviet Navy. It implied that Sablin was a traitor who incited the crew with the aim of hijacking the ship to Sweden. They compared him to one Artamonov, commander of a destroyer in the Baltic, who, while his ship was moored in Poland, defected to Sweden with his Polish lover, using his captain's launch, and finally surfaced in the United States. So Sablin was condemned and despised by the officers of the Baltic Fleet.

Sablin was accused of an attempt to hand over a modern ship, on the secret list, to the West, a treasonable charge which he strongly rejected. The absurdity of it was plain since he had had so many better opportunities to do just that, for instance while his ship was in Cuba, far from the Baltic Fleet and close to the USA. In fact he had been sentenced to death long before the

trial. A top-secret memorandum signed by Chairman of the KGB Andropov, Minister of Defence Marshal Grechko, Attorney General Rudenko and Chairman of the Supreme Court Smirnov and addressed to the Political Bureau had labelled Sablin's action as treason about five months before he was sentenced. Twelve members of the Political Bureau signed this memorandum, condemning him to death.

Sablin's appeal was rejected, and he was executed. His confidant and supporter, a sailor called Alexander Shein, was sentenced to eight years. Twelve more people, including two young officers, were found guilty of collaborating with Sablin, and they were discharged and exiled or sent to penal units. Before execution, Sablin was granted two meetings: a five-minute one with his wife and little son, and a fifteen-minute one with Leonid Brezhnev. It seems the leader of the country tried to figure out what had made a talented career officer "resort to crime", but Sablin answered coolly: "Whatever I say, it will be a dialogue of a blind man with a deaf man."

A spy by correspondence

Chairman of the KGB Andropov was much more sophisticated than General Secretary Brezhnev, much better informed and more far-sighted. Evaluating the situation within the country he realized that the popular movement for democracy could be checked by the combined efforts of the KGB, the Ministry of Interior and the armed forces. But there were two particular threats to his department which he had to stem himself: the appointment of worthless individuals at the behest of important state figures, and inadequate funds for intelligence operations. His plan was to make the KGB the preserve of incorruptible top-class professionals, dedicated to their job and much better paid than millions of their compatriots. As far as the big picture was concerned, hardly any of them might believe in the construction of a Communist society in the not-so-distant future, but the

cause they would be serving was the protection of their state and its people. Able young individuals were recruited to the KGB on this basis, although the "Communist cause" and "Socialist values" were still much talked about and political indoctrination was still an inseparable part of KGB training. Besides, the times demanded more technical and scientific specialists within the KGB, so new departments were established with better-educated staff. As for funding, while Andropov and his deputies demanded that new foreign spies be recruited primarily on ideological grounds, he instructed the heads of the chief directorates that, once a valuable source of information was found, no penny pinching was permissible.

His plans were delivered a major blow in September 1971, when 105 Soviet intelligence officers were banished from Great Britain, most of them KGB operatives of various departments. They were exposed by yet another important defector called Oleg Lialin, who was nominally assigned to Department V in charge of sabotage and "special operations", but who was also in charge of setting up a

■ *Above:* A young Andrei Gromyko, who later became Minister of Foreign His family was close to the defector Arkadi Shevchenko.

contingency counter-intelligence operation in London. Like Nosenko, who became a KGB officer only due to his father's influence, Lialin was a product of favouritism. While Nosenko's defection was disastrous only for the top brass of the 2nd Directorate and did not affect much of the rest of the unit, Lialin's sent waves through the entire exterior intelligence system and resulted in the recall by the KGB of many successful spies from various countries. The list of the recalled included Valery Kostikov (Mexico), Ivan Evdotiev (Federal Republic of Germany), Anatoli Baronin (Nigeria), Leonid Litvak (Greece), Boris Sazonov (France), and Lev Shingalev (Colombia). According to American sources, about 30 officers were recalled in total.

Leonid Kolosov

Leonid Kolosov was a typical victim of this mess, a top-class spy who operated in Italy under the cover of being the *Izvestia* correspondent and who many years later became a popular Soviet novelist and playwright. Amiable and good-looking, Kolosov was a *bon viveur* and a fluent speaker of Italian and French. In Italy he met hundreds of celebrities like the tenor Mario del Monaco and film star Claudia Cardinale, and his articles and essays were universally loved by *Izvestia* readers. Yet he was also an efficient spy who recruited dozens of people, including Mauro de Mauro, a correspondent of the Sicilian newspaper *Ora*, and who supplied information about secret American bases in Sicily, the Italian armed forces and the private lives of a number of Italian politicians linked to the Mafia. Kolosov was unfortunate enough to have been a student at the KGB school at the same time as Lialin, and was "in the cold" for six years after Lialin's defection, until Andropov let him be posted again as an *Izvestia* correspondent, this time to Yugoslavia, where he was active until 1982. As for Lialin, he died in Great Britain after quite a comfortable life, duly appreciated by NATO's intelligence and counter-intelligence services.

Yet another shock was experienced by the Soviet secret service in 1979 when Stanislav Levchenko defected in Tokyo. He was officially the correspondent of the Soviet weekly *Novoie Vremia* (*New Times*). Not a very bright intelligence officer and a mediocre journalist, he had also joined the Soviet intelligence service thanks to his contacts in high places. When his term was about to end, he found a CIA representative in Tokyo who arranged for his transfer to the USA. As he disclosed all the Soviet and local agents he knew in Japan, the KGB network in that country was almost entirely devastated, and in 1981 he was sentenced by the Military Collegium of the Supreme Court of the USSR to death *in absentia*. He settled in the USA and worked on the staff of *Novoie Russkoie Slovo*, a Russian-language newspaper half-full of émigré items and half-full of American propaganda; he also wrote novels and articles about secret services.

A bitter betrayal

A worse nightmare was the defection of Arkadi Shevchenko in April 1978. He held the position of deputy general secretary of the United Nations, controlling in part the military bodies of the UN. Although Shevchenko was not working for the KGB, he was part of strategic intelligence and one of the most trusted persons among the Soviet élite. His family was close to that of Andrei Gromyko, Minister of Foreign Affairs and a member of the Political Bureau, and Shevchenko's wife, Lina, took the wives and daughters of all top state and party figures shopping and entertained them when they visited New York. The worst side of Shevchenko's defection was that he must have known a lot about Soviet networks not only in the United States but also in other countries and, being close to the ruling élite, was privy to many secrets about the lives of Russian dignitaries. No wonder some intelligence officers of the older generation grimly commented that after his defection there would be no state secrets left in the USSR not known to the CIA.

CHAPTER 10

AN EMPIRE CALLED THE KGB

The break-up of the Soviet Union in 1991 presented a fresh set of challenges to the KGB and its former officer, Vladimir Putin.

Yuri Andropov was the head of the Soviet secret service longer than anybody before him – over 15 years – and his regime was the "Golden Age" of the KGB. At a very early stage he succeeded, through his connections in the Central Committee of the Communist Party of the Soviet Union (CPSU), in making party leaders respect the KGB's top professionals and seriously evaluate their reports. He managed to recruit a number of talented journalists and linguists, as well as electronic engineers and physicists, and gave them good salaries and regular promotions. He ensured that enough funds were allotted to the KGB, especially in the provinces where the shortage of food and cheap clothes was chronic. He widened the chain of special food and clothes distributors for KGB officers and Border Troops. But most importantly, he proved to the Central Committee that his agency could deal with dissent. Soviet dissidents, depending on how persistent and resilient they proved to be, were imprisoned, deported, exchanged for Soviet spies, placed in mental hospitals or exiled.

In 1973 Andropov became a member of the Political Bureau of the Central Committee, which enhanced his status in the country and was also appreciated by his subordinates. He renewed his effort in defence of the Socialist bastions, but was clever enough to realize

■ **Left:** Border Troops on patrol in the 1980s. From 1957 all Border Troops were under the jurisdiction of the KGB.

that it would be unwise and unrealistic, at the end of the twentieth century and with the mass media penetrating all barriers, to subject the intellectuals of the country to the political conditions of the Stalinist era, with total repression of free speech and continuous brainwashing. So he instructed his counter-intelligence officers that dealt with internal problems to take it easy when a case had no implication for the country's security. Subversive jokes about the political leaders or nonconformist poems were not considered worthy of prison sentences, as they had been under Lenin and Stalin, unless their author was the holder of a serious government job, in which case he could be fired, or deprived of his party card if a CPSU member. Normally there was simply an interview with a well-dressed and cold-voiced KGB officer, who warned of the possible consequences if such talk was not stopped. There were even cases where military counter-intelligence officers of the KGB saved army officers guilty of some form of anti-government propaganda from dishonourable discharge by advising their commanders not to take drastic measures, and think instead of a lesser punishment. Such behaviour added to the KGB's popularity and showed it in a lenient light, which was particularly important against the background of the persecution of organized dissidents.

The KGB empire

The KGB was a huge agglomeration of forces, offices, troops, enterprises, facilities and weapons. In the 1950s its personnel, both in and out of uniform, ran to at least 750,000, but later it was significantly reduced. From the beginning of the 1980s to the moment the Soviet Union disintegrated in 1991, it had about 480,000 people under its control. About 10,000, including all technical specialists, worked in intelligence, and about 24,000 were counter-intelligence personnel. From 1957, the KGB was responsible for the Border Troops and Naval Frontier Forces in charge of the Soviet state frontiers – 63,000km (39,375 miles) – which were previously a part of the OGPU, then the NKVD, and finally the MVD. They numbered about 250,000 uniformed personnel, both on land and at sea, and were a good reserve for the KGB, especially in peripheral republics. As the officers and men of the Border Troops received special training in surveillance, investigation and even intelligence, some of them later migrated to other KGB directorates and training centres.

KGB offices

As well as its all-Union headquarters in Moscow, the KGB also had 14 Republican headquarters (Russia did not have any). There were KGB directorates in every *oblast* (province), and autonomous republics and cities had, depending on their size, either KGB departments or sections. There were also sections in the army, big enterprises, ministries, research institutes, and even radio and television centres. The KGB had its own scientific and research institutes, too, with the best communications and computation equipment, radio-electronic and analytical centres, and education establishments, including the KGB school, considered one of the world's best intelligence training centres. This school was created as early as October 1938 and called the Special Purpose School (Russian acronym, ShON). Its name was changed several times later. When the Cold War started, its structure and curriculum were substantially remodelled, with new subjects added to the latter. There were also upgrade courses and intelligence "villas" where, in the quiet of suburbia, final training was provided for agents being posted abroad by the master spies and the foreigners in service with the KGB.

There were several KGB centres and housing directorates in Moscow whose personnel were not in communication with each other. The 1st Chief Directorate of the KGB was primarily in charge of worldwide espionage, but was also engaged in propaganda and disinformation operations.

The 2nd Chief Directorate was in charge of internal security and counter-intelligence, and in later years, to a certain extent, in fighting drugs and countering organized crime. The 3rd Chief Directorate was effectively a military counter-intelligence service and, unlike their colleagues in the first two directorates, its officers wore uniforms and cooperated closely with local military commanders. Special units of this directorate monitored military intelligence and interior troops, while some of its top-secret elements conducted surveillance of Soviet military personnel stationed abroad.

In addition to these bodies, there were directorates in charge of ideological operations and the suppression of dissent, exterior surveillance, communications, economic security, electronic surveillance and counter-measures, transportation and government protection, financial and administrative components, archives, and training centres for spies and surveillance officers. There were KGB censors in the media, especially for international radio and television programmes, and sections in charge of arts and literature in the KGB department of cultural affairs. Every

■ *Above:* Leonid Brezhnev held power in the USSR until his death in 1982. His rule was notable for the spread of corruption and cronyism within the Soviet bureaucracy.

important article dealing with international problems was initialled by censors.

It was a vast empire, but at various times the leaders of the USSR placed some army units under KGB control as well. Such units, most of them paratroopers, received special linguistic and tactical training and were used at home and abroad. However, the budget of the KGB as a whole, Border Troops included, was about 15 times smaller than the funds made available to the US intelligence community. This was not only due to the low salaries in the USSR, but also because Andropov had managed to create a cost-efficient system by the late 1970s. Its communication facilities and computer equipment, for instance, were vastly superior to those in the rest of the country.

Reliable subordinates

Andropov was careful when appointing his deputies, and then completely trusted the people he chose. Two of them, Viktor Chebrikov and Vladimir Kriuchkov, held the post of KGB chairman in succession after him. In 1967 he put them in key positions, although neither were intelligence professionals: one had graduated from the Dnepropetrovsk Metallurgical Institute and the other from the Senior Diplomatic School of the Ministry of Foreign Affairs. His subordinates suspected that Chebrikov was planted in the KGB by the so-called "Dnepropetrovsk Mafia" to watch Andropov, i.e. the Brezhnev-Chernenko group who had lived and worked in that Ukrainian city. But Andropov knew that Chebrikov was, like Kriuchkov, modest and hard-working. He had also seen Kriuchkov under pressure, in Hungary, where he had worked for Andropov during the Hungarian Revolution in 1956. He let them bring to the KGB a handful of trusted associates, chiefly experts on various international problems.

Although Andropov managed to make the Political Bureau consult the KGB before taking hasty decisions in international affairs, as had happened many times in Khrushchev's era, there were at least two occasions when the KGB was totally disregarded, with grave consequences for the USSR. The first took place in 1970 after Nasser's death when the Kremlin leaders decided to support the new Egyptian leader, President Anwar al-Sadat, despite the fact that both the legal and illegal *residenturas* reported that they anticipated he would lean towards the Americans rather than the Russians. Neither Brezhnev nor Nikolai Podgorny, chairman of the Supreme Soviet, agreed with those reports, and the Political Bureau was assured that the Kremlin still could influence the situation in Egypt. It soon learned this was not the case at all. Sadat expelled Russian advisors and began wide-ranging military cooperation with the United States.

Disaster in Afghanistan

The second was much more tragic and costly for the Russians. In 1978, the KGB exterior intelligence cell in Kabul was instructed by the Kremlin to support leftist forces to ensure the removal of President Daoud of Afghanistan. In 1979 the Political Bureau, deeply concerned by the deteriorating situation in Afghanistan, where a moderate Socialist leader, Nur Taraki, was toppled by the radical Hafizullah Amin, sent troops to install yet another Soviet puppet, Babrak Karmal, brought back from exile. The KGB top brass was strongly against the move, as the agents in the field reported anti-Communist sentiment in virtually every part of the country. But the Political Bureau was influenced by the apparatchiks of the Central Committee International Department, who were talking about the danger of Islamic radicals penetrating Soviet Central Asia, and also by the generals who declared they needed a pro-Soviet Afghanistan to secure the southern flank of their forces in that area. Instead of trying to solve the Afghan problem by political and diplomatic means, the Kremlin used brute force again.

Special forces were dispatched to Afghanistan about two weeks before a massive invasion by Soviet troops. They consisted of a 30-strong platoon of the anti-terrorist unit Alfa, the so-called Group Thunder (*Grom* in Russian), plus Group Zenith, which included a number of KGB intelligence officers and hit-squads. They were supported by military intelligence special forces, airborne troops and the so-called Muslim Battalion, a 500-strong volunteer unit of the Soviet Army. At the end of December 1979 Andropov gave these units the order to storm the palace of Hafizullah Amin. While making a telephone call to the man in charge of the assault, Yuri Drozdov, he specifically underlined that the decision to use the special forces and begin the massive invasion was that of his superiors from the

■ *Above:* Alexander Shelepin with Anwar al-Sadat of Egypt (right). The KGB informed the Political Bureau that Sadat was pro-American, advice that the Kremlin ignored.

Political Bureau, and even named all its members who were responsible for the action. These special forces took the presidential palace of Taj-Bek in 43 minutes, with about 10 killed and 50 wounded. Another group of KGB officers, supported by two platoons of army airborne troops, stormed the Afghan intelligence and counter-intelligence services building, losing just one man. Although the losses in these operations were not high, heavy resistance to the Soviet invasion proper resulted in enormous loss of life on both sides, especially among the civilian population of Afghanistan.

In January 1980 the head of KGB exterior intelligence, Vladimir Kriuchkov, and his top officers reported to the Central Committee that it was necessary to seriously consider, in view of the complexity of the situation in Afghanistan, an immediate withdrawal of Soviet forces from the country.

Moscow sent more troops and more weapons instead. The Russian occupation lasted a decade and made the problems of the country much more complex than they had been under the monarchy. However, almost immediately the KGB drew a lesson from the initial period of the war and the inability of regular troops to combat insurgency. The first special-purpose unit sent to Afghanistan for this task was badly battered by the mujahedin, the Afghan resistance forces, and the KGB's 1st Chief Directorate therefore formed a new unit, much better trained and equipped. This unit was trained to cooperate with Soviet illegal spies in operations of the utmost complexity in any country. It was later called *Vympel* (Russian for "streamer") and operated in Afghanistan until 1989, losing dozens of men. It was trained in various countries, learning jungle tricks in Vietnam and marksmanship in Nicaragua.

■ *Below:* **Babrak Kamal, leader of the People's Democratic Party of Afghanistan, who was installed by the Soviets as leader of Afghanistan in December 1979.**

Andropov could have stayed on as the head of the KGB indefinitely, but Leonid Brezhnev died in 1982 after an 18-year reign, and Andropov, with his stature and connections in the corridors of power, was the best candidate to succeed him. In May 1982 General Vitaly Fedorchuk became the chairman of the KGB, an appointment universally considered a victory for Brezhnev's outgoing clan, but he only lasted half a year and was then transferred to control the Ministry of Internal Affairs. General of the Army Chebrikov, vice-chairman of the KGB from 1968, became the new boss of the Soviet secret service. His position was rock-solid, since he had the full-hearted support of General Secretary Andropov.

The facade of Andropov's KGB might have seemed unassailable, but there were deep cracks inside Russian Socialism. What started out as popular discontent in

■ *Above:* President Daud of Afghanistan sought to lessen the country's dependence on the Soviet Union. On 27 April 1978 he was killed in a KGB-organized coup.

■ *Left:* Soviet forces in Afghanistan during Moscow's armed intervention in the country in December 1979. The KGB, aware of the dangers of Islamic radicalism spreading to Soviet Central Asia, was against the invasion.

Khrushchev's era and was aggravated by the lawlessness and corruption of the decadent Brezhnev regime, finally became a universal rejection of Communist rule and the élite's hypocrisy. Dissent was growing and receiving greater acknowledgement in the West. In the era of Stalin or Khrushchev, when the people were totally oppressed and isolated from the outside world, it was enough for the Political Bureau and secret service to arrest the main dissidents and enforce an information blackout about their activities, but in the 1980s it required an entirely different approach. The main reason was the growing championship of the dissidents' cause by Western democracies and – a new phenomenon – Communist and workers' parties throughout Europe. Realizing that the absence of human rights in the USSR undermined their position in their own countries, they appealed to the Soviet leaders, asking them to discontinue the repression of dissidents, permit Jewish emigration to Israel, and make at least cosmetic changes to the regime. Knowing this to be the case, the relatives of arrested dissidents applied to the leaders of these parties in the West on many occasions.

The winds of change

The new realities made the Political Bureau and KGB act with care in almost every case involving well-known dissidents and on every appeal they received. In some cases, when the KGB reported such matters to the Political Bureau, the latter took the decision to simply ignore the appeals from political figures or international organizations. That happened, for example, when the Austrian Chancellor Bruno Kraisky sent a letter to the Soviet leadership urging it to liberate the Russian dissident Yuri Orlov, or when 376 US congressmen appealed to Andropov in 1983 to let 2000 Soviet Jews emigrate to Israel. But in most cases the Soviet rulers reacted negatively. For example, when the KGB and the Ministry of Foreign Affairs reported to the Political Bureau about the

steps taken by Amnesty International over human rights abuses in the Soviet Union, the Central Committee departments received an order to print a number of articles in the Soviet press, accusing Amnesty of subversive activities in Socialist countries. When the president of the Soviet Academy of Sciences received a letter from 118 members of the French Academy who showed concern for interned or incarcerated Soviet scientists, including Sakharov and Shcharansky, the Soviet leadership, instead of answering, ordered the publication of an article on the role of scientists in Socialist states.

■ *Below:* Well-armed mujahedin (guerrillas) in Afghanistan. The KGB formed a new unit to battle the Afghan resistance, called *Vympel*.

■ *Left:* KGB chairman Viktor Chebrikov, who in September 1986 offered to set free all those incarcerated on political grounds provided they "discontinued hostile activity".

The dissidents, particularly the leading ones who had become known in the West and those who had emigrated, were instrumental in informing Western public opinion about the state of freedom in the Soviet Union. The books and articles of Solzhenitsyn, Aksenov and Kuznetsov made a great impression on the reading public in Western Europe and America, and were secretly disseminated throughout almost all the Soviet republics. However, as the regime had already showed on many occasions that it would crush any open demonstration of public discontent, the majority of the population was totally indifferent to them.

All the above had a serious effect on moral and political sentiment in government bodies, the KGB included. As a result, the number of KGB defectors increased rapidly, falling into three categories. The first, represented mainly by those who had found their way into the KGB due to the "telephone law" (see Chapter 9), were unscrupulous and greedy characters who defected just because they thought they would have a luxurious life in the West. The second group consisted of officers who despised the regime and their superiors, and chose to defect as a form of rejecting the Soviet way of life. The last group were Jews who were recruited by American and Israeli intelligence services. They observed anti-Semitism in the KGB, the armed forces and the country as a whole and decided that they wanted no more of a regime that encouraged it. It is important to mention that officially there were very few Jews in the KGB (their CVs would have categorized them as Russians and Ukrainians and almost never as Jews as, from Khrushchev's era onwards, the official policy of the KGB was to erect barriers to prevent Jews from serving in the KGB or entering a military academy).

Colonel Oleg Gordievsky

The biggest group of defectors was from the exterior intelligence. In 1982 Major Vladimir Kuzichkin defected in Iran and surfaced in Great Britain, while another officer, Anatoli Bogaty, defected in Morocco and found his way to the USA. In 1985, Colonel Oleg Gordievsky, acting KGB *resident* in Great Britain, defected, although he had been working for British intelligence for quite some time previous to this date. In the same year Vitali Yurchenko, a colonel in the exterior counter-intelligence, defected in the USA. In 1986, Colonel Victor Gundarev defected while posted in Greece. Lieutenant-Colonels of the 1st Chief Directorate Leonid Poleshchuk, Gennady Varennik, Boris Yuzhin and Vladimir Fomenko, plus Majors Sergei Vorontsov, Michail Butkov and Sergei Motorin, also defected. An immediate effect, especially with regard to the treason of Oleg Gordievsky, was that about 60 officers of the exterior intelligence were either arrested in various countries or banished, and at least 20 important local agents in these countries were also arrested and imprisoned. The 1st Chief Directorate was completely demoralized, and its operations in such countries as Great Britain and the United States ground to a halt due to the disclosures made by Oleg Gordievsky.

A crushing blow was also delivered to the KGB by the defection of three important figures in the scientific and technical intelligence service: Sergei Illarionov, Vladimir Konoplev and

Vladimir Vetrov. From them NATO discovered what interested the Soviet Union most of all in both military and civilian technology, and its targets in the field of economic espionage. But probably the most devastating blow for the technical branches of the KGB was the leakage of information via two officers from the 8th Chief Directorate of the KGB: Major Vladimir Sheimov and Lieutenant Victor Makarov.

The 8th Chief Directorate, once created for government communications and radio interception, was by the middle of the 1980s probably the most important component in the KGB system. In addition to internal telecommunications, operating secure high-frequency government networks and analyzing foreign radio signals, it was also designing codes, message

■ *Above:* KGB Colonel Oleg Gordievsky, who defected to the British in 1985 – one of a number of damaging defections the KGB suffered in the 1980s.

inscription and "hacking" into the computer systems of Western bodies ranging from banks to intelligence services. Vladimir Sheimov was a cryptologist and computer master who was involved in "hacking" into government and military computer systems. After he contacted the Central Intelligence Agency (CIA), Sheimov and his family were transported to the United States. His defection revealed to the CIA and National Security Agency (NSA) many secrets about Russian intrusions into their secure installations and webs. He was so important to the Americans that he had been promised a million dollars if he defected, but he was apparently unable to get that much. He then migrated to the commercial sector, which was looking for protection against hackers and cyber-spies, and was successful in creating an anti-hacking system that prevented any intrusions. His colleague Victor Makarov, who spied for MI6, was arrested and imprisoned for 10 years. He was pardoned in 1992 and secretly travelled through Latvia and Finland to Great Britain, where he received a modest pension.

Dissatisfied defectors

Another defector who made it to Great Britain, Michail Butkov, achieved a certain notoriety. A KGB intelligence officer in Norway, he decided to run away with his lover, an Aeroflot employee. He knew a lot about KGB operations in Scandinavia, and she had some information about the military intelligence unit there, so they were sure they would be highly valuable in Great Britain. But he merely received a lump sum of £100,000 and an annual pension of £14,000. The couple considered that too little for the lifestyle they sought in Great Britain, and decided to turn to crime. Using the letterheads of a Reading business centre, they distributed invitations to attend courses at a California-based commercial management school, sending them to 700 addresses in Russia and the Ukraine. It was a time when thousands of "new Russians"

were ready to pay for good capitalist management training, and there were about 1500 replies. The entrepreneurial defector and his lady amassed US $2.4 million and planned to flee to Andorra, but were arrested and imprisoned in Great Britain.

Some of the defectors returned to Russia. Anatoly Semenov, who defected while a cipher clerk at the Soviet Embassy in Niger in 1976, returned to Russia in 1981. Colonel Vitali Yurchenko also returned from the USA, and his story is still unclear. He was the second-in-command in the Soviet *residentura* in 1985. He claimed he had been kidnapped by the Americans, but managed to flee from the guards attached to him while he was shopping in a supermarket, got to the Soviet Embassy and was returned to Moscow. His superiors and colleagues were sure he had defected of his own free will, and did not trust him at all.

The lot of double agents

There were some KGB officers who pretended to change sides on the instructions of their government. As a rule, they came to regret this. Colonel Maksimov was ordered to let Canadian intelligence recruit him. Afterwards he was suspected by the KGB of real collaboration, but was finally left alone. Another KGB officer suspected of treason was Martynov, an undercover agent in the Soviet *residentura* in Washington. He was arrested and imprisoned in the USA after Oleg Gordievsky defected to Great Britain and exposed him. Martynov spent about 18 months incarcerated and was kept incommunicado by counter-intelligence officers. He succeeded, however, in fleeing from a safe house where he had been kept with his wife and two children by the Americans, and made it to the Soviet intelligence *residentura*. When back in Russia, he was exiled to a small provincial town where he was intensively interrogated by KGB counter-intelligence aces, who thought he might have been recruited by his captors. After 10 years of this, assured that he was not a traitor, the KGB finally reinstated him, gave him back his rank and medals, and even backdated his salary, including that due to him in foreign currency.

But the obvious *cause célèbre* among the KGB defectors was Oleg Kalugin. In his prime he was one of the youngest and probably the most successful officers of the 1st Chief Directorate. Born in 1935, he was lucky enough to be sent by the KGB to the United States for a year, to Columbia University posing as a graduate of Leningrad University. While there he met and befriended another odious figure, Alexander Yakovlev, sent to Columbia by the Central Committee of the CPSU, who later showed that he could easily change his political allegiance in no time at all. In the Khrushchev and Brezhnev eras there was no chance that anyone could be sent to study abroad unless there was backing from on high, or a huge bribe was paid to a party or government official, and there is little doubt that neither Kalugin nor Yakovlev were exceptions. Former colleagues of Kalugin in the 1st Chief Directorate believed that in the 1950s he ha been a friend of Khrushchev's daughter, and in the 1970s of Brezhnev's son-in-law, Churbanov.

Kalugin in the USA

The biggest boost to Kalugin's career, however, owed nothing to friends in high places but everything to pure luck. For some unknown reason, an American citizen of Kuban Cossack origin called Anatoly Kotlobay approached the 24-year-old Kalugin while he was working as a guide at a Soviet exhibition in New York, and after several meetings informed him that he was, despite his wartime collaboration with the Germans, basically a Socialist, and wanted to hand over to Russia secrets about America's solid propellant for rockets. Kotlobay became a Russian agent, codenamed Cook, and Kalugin got his first state decoration, the Sign of Merit.

After some additional training in the USSR, Kalugin was sent back to the USA to work for political intelligence. In the Soviet Union such postings have always been considered sinecures. For about 10 years Kalugin circulated among journalists, diplomats and adventurers who fed on the leftovers of political celebrities. His work afforded contacts with many women, and Kalugin was handsome enough to use the opportunities offered. Kalugin was commended for his achievements and recommended for promotion. At the age of 35 he suddenly migrated to the department of counter-intelligence of the 1st Chief Directorate, as second-in-command, and three years later became head of counter-intelligence. He was made a major-general of the KGB at the age of 40, the youngest senior officer in exterior intelligence.

This posting was against the rules and regulations of intelligence. Transfer of an intelligence operative to counter-intelligence was taboo. Besides, he was inexperienced in counter-intelligence operations. Despite a number of defections from the KGB, Kalugin's department did not reveal a single traitor throughout almost 10 years when he was in charge. But he was a planner and supervisor of an operation that went disastrously wrong and left many still unanswered questions: the kidnapping of a Soviet agent known as Lark.

Lark's real name was Nikolai Artamonov. In 1959, when a 33-year-old captain 3rd rank and a Russian destroyer commander,

■ *Right:* Soviet super-mole Aldrich Ames. Before he and his wife were arrested in 1994, they had received over US $2.7 million from the Russians for spying.

■ *Below:* The Russian Embassy in Washington, which Ames visited on a number of occasions to deliver top-secret information relating to CIA operations and spies.

he fled from the Polish port of Gdynia with his lover Eva Gura. They made it to Sweden in the commander's launch, and were transported by the CIA to the USA where they were given asylum and later citizenship. He worked for US military intelligence, but the Russian secret service managed to approach him in 1966 and he agreed to cooperate. Though Lark supplied the KGB

residentura in America with extremely valuable information from 1966 to 1971, Kalugin and his people suspected him of being a double agent and decided to kidnap him. Whether this suspicion was well-founded will never be known. In 1975 Artamonov came to Vienna for a meeting with a Soviet agent but instead was captured, drugged and carried across the border. He died *en route*. The KGB claimed the death resulted from a drugs overdose.

At the end of 1978 Kalugin was suspected of espionage for the USA, and in 1979 he was appointed second-in-command in the Leningrad Directorate of the KGB. He spent his time there recruiting a number of people who were to be accused of various sorts of intrigues and machinations in the 1980s, and who later controlled dubious business ventures in Leningrad. Former KGB operatives insisted that it was no coincidence that in the early 1980s, after Kalugin had moved from counter-intelligence, the Russians succeeded in exposing 26 foreign agents in their country, including some in the intelligence community and one already retired.

The rewards of incompetence

In 1987 Kalugin was returned to the acting reserves of the KGB in Moscow, and worked first as security chief at the Academy of Sciences and later at the Ministry of Electronic Industries. He was retired as soon as he reached 55. At the beginning of the 1990s Kalugin migrated to Boris Yeltsin's camp and started to criticize the regime and the KGB. The latter retaliated by depriving him of his major-general's rank and state awards. But he had a powerful friend in the establishment, Alexander Yakovlev, who had been his colleague at Columbia University and who became a very powerful member of the Political Bureau under Gorbachev. When Vadim Bakatin became the chairman of the KGB for three months in 1991, Kalugin was restored to the rank of major-general by Gorbachev on the latter's and Yakovlev's recommendation, becoming Gorbachev's advisor. After unsuccessfully trying his luck as a politician in newly democratic Russia, he emigrated to the USA in 1994. There he wrote a book about his experiences in the KGB and made guided tours in Washington to the spots where the secret KGB drops and meeting places were located in the "good old times". He also became a businessman, heading a Russo-American joint venture, and helped edit some espionage publications.

Kalugin's revelations led to the arrest of several Americans who were suspected of being Russian agents. One of them was retired Colonel George Troffimov. Russian by origin, he was accused of having been recruited by the KGB and of supplying it with important information. Another was an NSA serviceman, Robert Lipka, who received a long prison term. There is a strong belief among some KGB veterans that Kalugin was an important CIA agent for a long time, maybe from the late 1960s, and that he was "conserved" by the CIA. They believe that his role in the rounding-up of Soviet agents in the USA by the FBI, and maybe in some other countries, was much greater than is generally imagined. But most people in Russia think Kalugin was just an opportunist who decided to use his KGB past to ensure a decent income in the USA after his former employer ceased to exist.

The Soviet super-mole

While Soviet defectors and moles regularly supplied the Americans with Russian secrets, a similar process occasionally took place in the reverse direction. In 1985 alone, 14 American officials were arrested for espionage. It seemed almost inexplicable to American intelligence historians why a high-ranking American intelligence officer could start working for the Russians in 1985, and yet Aldrich Ames, Head of S/E (the Soviet and Eastern Europe Operations Division in the CIA) did so for nearly nine years. Ames admitted that he had supplied the KGB with the names of virtually every American and foreign operative in the Soviet Union known to him. It was a major disaster comparable to those in the KGB and GRU (Soviet military intelligence) that were triggered by Dmitri Poliakov or Oleg Gordievsky.

There are different opinions as to what actually pushed Ames into treason. The traditional version is that he had substantial debts (from US $35,000 to US $50,000), so he decided to sell what was at hand.

Certainly Ames received about $1.5 million from the KGB for the information he supplied. He could also have been subject to the so-called Leman Syndrome (after a Russian pre-war spy in the German Gestapo), i.e. an agent recruited in return for financial reward seeking a moral justification for his actions and finding it in the adoption of the ideology of the recruiting side. For instance, Colonel Penkovsky of the GRU declared during his trial in Moscow that he was a political enemy of the judges and did not accept the validity of the court. Before he became a British-American spy on his own initiative, his record in the Soviet armed forces was quite exemplary.

Ames was also an "initiative spy". He knew many Russians who worked in America and contacted them on many occasions beginning from 1980 onwards, talking about politics and especially the problems of disarmament and international cooperation. His permanent contacts in New York included Sergei Divilkovsky, an efficient and able councillor of the Soviet representative at the United Nations who was, unofficially, the representative of the Department of International Information

■ *Above:* Mikhail Gorbachev (right), the general secretary of the Communist Party of the Soviet Union (CPSU) between 1985 and 1991 and president of the Soviet Union between 1990 and 1991.

of the CPSU Central Committee. His mission as such was to talk to influential Americans and people from other countries in order to get the information required as a guide for Soviet international propaganda, as well as for political decisions. Divilkovsky claimed he got the impression that Ames could be useful to Soviet intelligence, and he immediately informed the New York KGB supervisor about him. However, it was Ames himself who made the first step. In April 1985 he brought an envelope to the Soviet Embassy in Washington which contained, as well as some publications, another, smaller envelope. It contained information about two KGB officers recruited by the CIA and a request for $50,000 for future services. He later disclosed to the Soviets about 10 more valuable American agents.

The motives of Ames

Interrogated by an FBI officer after his arrest in 1994, Ames was asked which he would choose if he were to start anew, and Ames replied "the KGB". Talking to a *Washington Post* journalist he again stressed that he had been ready to collaborate with Soviet intelligence because of his beliefs. In fact, his hostility towards right-wing politicians and some important CIA officials had earlier made him a kind of dissident within the US intelligence establishment. As for the abundant payments, KGB officers and the emissaries of Soviet political and strategic intelligence who cooperated with Ames stick to their version that he asked for just $50,000 when he brought the first batch of the information, while the rest was later provided on the initiative of the KGB itself. He was stunned and pleased by the golden rain, and enjoyed his lifestyle immensely; but money, they say, was not the main motivation at a later stage of his "KGB career".

Born in 1941, Aldrich Ames joined the CIA on the recommendation of his father, a CIA officer. He married a girl who also worked at the CIA and who was obliged to quit, according to regulations. In 1980 he was sent to Mexico but his wife refused to follow him. There he met his new love, a young and very beautiful woman who was a Colombian cultural attaché. Ames took her to the USA, but the subsequent divorce was costly and his debts were mounting. Besides, he thought that neither he nor his father had been properly appreciated by the CIA, and when he had a chance to look into his father's file and discovered that he was not valued at all, that disillusioned him still further. He spent the early 1980s in New York working with Soviet diplomats, but in 1985, when already a Soviet agent, he was again posted to the main CIA headquarters at Langley and soon knew every detail of the operations against the KGB in all continents. He worked in Rome from 1986 to 1989, where the KGB received from him bags of secret papers on a regular basis. When he returned to Langley, he frequently made reports and memos on KGB operations for his superiors, so the KGB not only knew about all CIA moves from him but also had the chance to shape through him the CIA's perception of Soviet intelligence. Ames had unlimited access to the top-secret database, which he used to supply the most valuable information to the Soviets, and that later prompted American humourists to comment that, from 1989 to the moment of his arrest, the KGB had a free subscription to CIA Online.

The price of treachery

There was some kind of poetic justice in the fact that among the CIA agents disclosed by Ames to the KGB there were two people who resembled himself. One was Adolf Tolkachev, an engineer in a top-secret research laboratory who sold the Americans the secret of the Russian "friend-or-foe" identification system and received over US $2 million for this. The other was Major-General of the GRU Dmitri Poliakov, who had first contacted the CIA on his own initiative and during the following 25 years

■ *Below:* Boris Yeltsin (bottom of photograph, with white hair and raised hand) was victorious in the elections for the presidency of the Russian republic in June 1991.

disclosed 19 Soviet undercover agents, more than 150 foreign agents of the GRU, and had revealed the connection of about 1500 military officers with the Soviet intelligence services. He also supplied the CIA with some information about Soviet strategic rockets. The KGB had reports of Poliakov's espionage activities, which probably had come from another mole in the USA, Robert Hanssen (see below), but it was Ames who completed the jigsaw. Both spies were arrested and executed in the 1980s. Had they survived undiscovered a little longer, they might well be alive today.

The investigation of Aldrich Ames started in 1990, and he was finally arrested in 1994 and sentenced to life imprisonment. The official CIA version is that he recklessly failed to conceal that his revenues were well above his salary. He had, for instance, three Jaguar cars and his lifestyle was that of a millionaire. But former KGB officers claim he was betrayed by a CIA mole in the Russian Government or party apparat, most

probably in Gorbachev's circle. In fact, there must have been a danger of Ames disclosing this person too, because from about 1988 he was not only revealing ordinary spies recruited by the CIA in the field but also agents who were at the centre of the Communist élite. He also knew about all sorts of payments transferred by the CIA to the bank accounts of its high-echelon collaborators in Russia, and this information was also accumulating in KGB headquarters. From this point of view, Ames's arrest was beneficial not only to the CIA but also to some figures in the Russian Government.

The Ames clone in Russian intelligence or government circles was probably responsible for the arrest of another important Soviet mole, FBI agent Robert Hanssen. In the late 1970s Hanssen spied for the GRU, and his information also helped

the Russians reveal Dmitri Poliakov. When his wife discovered he had been spying, he stopped it for five years. When he resumed selling Federal Bureau of Investigation (FBI) secrets, it was to the KGB. This time he had access to more intelligence secrets and security matters, and could even give away the basic contingency programme in the event of nuclear war, the so-called US Continuity of Government Plan. This led KGB historians to declare that Hanssen as a spy was no less important to the USSR than Kim Philby or Aldrich Ames. Knowing the FBI and CIA methods and aware of their frequent penetrations of Soviet intelligence, Hanssen ensured that the KGB did not know his identity, but was he arrested in February 2001 after the Americans had received enough evidence from their moles in the Soviet Government to identify him.

■ *Above:* Tanks roll into Moscow in August 1991 during the short-lived coup by Communist hard-liners against Gorbachev's reforms.

■ *Right:* The will of the people – a barricade manned by pro-Yeltsin and pro-Gorbachev supporters in Moscow in 1991. Many KGB officers supported the demonstrators.

Ames's colleagues claimed there was no chance he could be ever released, and "life" also means life in Hanssen's case. Both will die in prison. The post-Soviet Russian regime proved to be milder at about this time, when President Yeltsin pardoned 12 Soviet traitors who had worked for the CIA or defected.

Yuri Andropov, Communist Party leader, former KGB boss and collector of Glenn Miller records and modern novels, died on 9 February 1984, officially after a long struggle with kidney disease, and was replaced within hours of his burial by the oldest man ever to come to rule the land, 72-year-old Brezhnev protégé Konstantin Chernenko. The new general secretary was not a healthy man, either. He had emphysema and talked with obvious difficulty, but the "old guards" were happy when he was elected by the Political Bureau since he had been a close friend of Brezhnev; indeed, he had once been his garage manager and later his staff administrator. Of very limited abilities and with a negligible power base, he could be fully controlled by Brezhnev's family and former associates.

The death of Andropov is still a mystery. He had kidney problems for sure, but there were rumours in Moscow that he had been shot twice by the wife of former Minister of Internal Affairs Shchelokov, in revenge for ruining her husband's career and destroying her wealth. She probably reckoned that once Andropov was dead and Chernenko took over, she would be pardoned by the new leader from the "Dnepropetrovsk Mafia". The small-calibre bullets allegedly pierced Andropov's kidney. If these rumours are true, Andropov's death is one of the greatest cover-ups the KGB ever perpetrated. Some retired KGB officers speculated that Andropov ordered a total news blackout about the assassination attempt for the sake of his country – his idea of patriotism in action.

Chernenko himself died a year later, and the new leader was Michail Gorbachev, only 54 and considered a reformer. A graduate of the law faculty of Moscow University and the youngest member of the Political Bureau, he had been considered Andropov's heir apparent by many from the very beginning. Gorbachev started the process of *Perestroika*, that is, "reformation" or "rebuilding" of society. His intentions

■ *Above:* Vladimir Kriuchkov was appointed head of the KGB in 1989. He became intelligence supremo at a time when the Soviet Union was beginning to disintegrate.

were noble and just, and he was genuinely trying to get rid of the worst features of the Bolshevik past: first and foremost, the total lack of democracy typical of single-party systems. But Gorbachev was amazingly inconsistent, continually oscillating between dogmatic hard-liners like Yegor Ligachev and infantile adventurers like Boris Yeltsin. He was far too radical for the Communist mandarins and insufficiently determined for the true reformers. On the one hand, he instructed the KGB to look into the release of political prisoners, and in September 1986 KGB chairman Chebrikov offered to set free all those incarcerated on political grounds provided they "discontinued hostile activity". That was after the April Plenary Session of the Central Committee had promised more political freedom and greater democracy in the USSR. Some of them were indeed released. However, on the other hand

Gorbachev agreed to the deprivation of citizenship and deportation abroad of a number of consistent dissidents, and to press attacks on those who intended to disclose the real role of the KGB and the party in all sorts of purges and repressions during previous decades.

In 1989 Chebrikov retired from the KGB and was replaced by Vladimir Kriuchkov, head of KGB intelligence. Officially Chebrikov retired for reasons of health, but his subordinates believed that their boss had a highly developed instinct for self-preservation and saw rough times ahead. If so, his instinct was right. In April 1989, there were demonstrations in Georgia demanding justice and democratization and a greater independence for the republic. The leader of the Georgian Communists and the commander of the Transcaucasian Military District, alarmed by the scale of the separatist movement, sent soldiers to disperse demonstrations. The troops attacked students in the first rows with sapper shovels, killing dozens and wounding hundreds. Georgia was deeply shocked by the brutality of the "elder brother" with whom she had a common religion and had shared a common history for 200 years. Nine months later the Russians used special forces in Azerbaijan when ethnic troubles started, and again many people were killed and wounded. There were political, ethnic and religious troubles in many other areas of the USSR as well. The Communist empire was crumbling, and its disintegration now seemed unavoidable.

A nation in transition

It was truly a transitional period in the life of the USSR, when the country's political leadership was divided into groupings. One opted for greater freedom and democracy, sought after by the majority of the population, while the second was sure that, as soon as the steel bonds of the KGB and armed forces were removed, the Soviet Union would quickly fall apart. This group rejected any radical reforms. A third, the "realists", was of the opinion that reformation was needed, but that it should be based on a solid political and economic foundation. They suggested economic reforms to start with, privatization of small enterprises and the building of mixed government and share-holding management, and thus a smooth transition to a capitalist economy. They totally rejected separatism and radical reformism.

Needless to say, the latter group included most of the KGB top brass. They knew the inability of the Communist Party to maintain any form of an "iron curtain" in the age of computers, satellite television and electronic communications. They saw and could compare the Western economies with that of their own country, and realized the weaknesses of the state-regulated industries. But they also wished to retain their power and the state system that ensured that power, and thus their own role in society.

The KGB also knew that any transitional period could create chaos, which would be taken advantage of by criminals and terrorists of all sorts. As guardians of state secrets and vulnerable sites, the KGB showed genuine concern for atomic enterprises and the like that could be targets for any terrorist activity, such as the theft of nuclear materials and equipment. But the KGB was also trying to scare the reformist camp by highlighting the danger from subversive and terrorist operations, in case reforms went too far and the state was weakened. It showed alarming documentaries to the members of the Central Committee, or used its *Vympel* raid unit to show how simple it would be for foreign special forces or a professionally trained terrorist gang to seize sensitive sites. The *Vympel* had a secret exercise in the Kremlin and the Soviet president's suburban villa and, despite the 200-strong presidential guard, managed to penetrate both with ease. The *Vympel* also demonstrated how simple it would be to seize an atomic power station by a swift helicopter landing on top of the atomic reactor.

The *Vympel* unit

The apogee of the *Vympel* unit's demonstrations was the seizure of the works that assembled nuclear warheads in the secret city called Arzamas-16. To show that no defence could work against a unit of professionals, *Vympel* informed the local authorities, police and counter-intelligence units of the impending raid. Two divisions of Interior Troops were alerted, and a top-security regime was enforced. The first group of the *Vympel* raiders established drops and secret stores. The second group reconnoitred to find access routes to the nuclear works. Some from this group drank litres of vodka with talkative locals, getting valuable information about the target. *Vympel* officers also settled in a monastery miles from the city pretending to be pilgrims, while others flirted with local girls and stayed overnight at their homes to avoid having to register at an hotel. When all the preparations were complete, the storm group arrived, and it took them just three hours to finish the operation.

In August 1991, a group of senior figures made a desperate attempt to prevent the disintegration of the Soviet Union and the dismantling of the Socialist regime. The so-called State Committee for the Extraordinary Situation was formed, and included Soviet vice-president Gennady Yanayev, Prime Minister Valentin Pavlov, KGB chairman Vladimir Kriuchkov, Interior Minister Boris Pugo, Defence Minister Dmitri Yazov and other important officials. They were supported by a number of the KGB's top generals. The summer residence of President Gorbachev in Faros, on the Black Sea, was surrounded by Border Troops subordinate to the KGB, while naval components of the same force blockaded the area from the sea.

Popular resistance led by reformers resulted in clashes in Moscow with army and police detachments, but many army and KGB officers were openly sympathetic with the crowds raising barricades against tanks and troops. KGB special forces

refused to take part in any actions at all. The coup failed: seven members of the committee were arrested and one, Boris Pugo, committed suicide. Realizing the danger of another, more effective coup, Gorbachev appointed Vadim Bakatin, a mediocre bureaucrat from the Ministry of Interior Affairs, to be head of the KGB. Bakatin succeeded in dismantling the mammoth ministry in two-and-a-half months. The KGB ceased to exist. Its place was taken by the Exterior Intelligence Service, the Federal Security Service, and the Communications and Information Service, while the Border Troops were also detached to a separate directorate.

But was this really the end of the KGB? Some officers became star figures later. Russian Minister of Defence Sergei Ivanov was the first ex-KGB officer to head the Russian armed forces, historically a post held only by marshals. In 2000 Lieutenant-General Sergei Lebedev was appointed the head of the Exterior Intelligence Service (SVR). A specialist in German-speaking countries and the USA, he was known for his exceptional memory and industriousness. Before this appointment Lebedev served as official representative of the SVR in Washington, so it is not difficult to appreciate why the Russian president chose him. He wanted a man who symbolized cooperation rather than confrontation, and the idea that the great powers should join forces against common enemies.

Many KGB generals and officers who left the service became managers in security companies. Almost every bank and large-size corporation in Russia hired a former KGB officer to oversee security matters, and these men maintain contact with their former colleagues in similar enterprises and in the state security bodies, ensuring that the company is well informed, protected and safe. Their language skills and knowledge of various countries also led new Russian capitalist ventures to hire former KGB officers for overseas postings. In addition, many KGB engineers worked for

■ *Below:* Ex-KGB officer Sergei Ivanov was appointed minister of defence in Putin's government, historically a post only held by marshals.

big multinationals throughout the former territories of the Soviet Union, especially in telecommunications.

But the highest civilian position in Russia is, of course, that of Russian president, and on 7 May 2000 it was filled by an ex-lieutenant-colonel of the KGB, Vladimir Putin (born in 1952). His family connections with the service go back to his grandfather, who was a cook appointed by the secret service to Lenin's dacha in Gorky, and later to one of Stalin's dachas near Moscow. During World War II his father volunteered for the Destroyer Battalion in the so-called Neva Foothold during the epic siege of Leningrad (1941–44). Putin served in the KGB in Germany and learned to speak German and English. He had been well educated and was well suited for higher office.

Although there were some fears that a former KGB officer would somehow revive ill-famed secret service practices, there were other, more common-sense reactions from enlightened establishments in various Western countries, where politicians were fed up with dealing with former Communist Party mandarins or amateurish upstarts. They would rather talk to a man who had gained extensive knowledge of the Western way of life and mentality, who was well educated and who was prepared, by all his previous experience, to look into complex subjects and be attentive to details. However, a new, capitalist and democratic Russia depends not only on President Putin and his successors, but also on the politicians of the West dealing generously with Russian problems. A common effort can ensure that the bad old times are never repeated.

■ *Above:* Vladimir Putin, former officer in the KGB, became president of Russia in 2000. His aim to end corruption and create a strongly regulated free-market economy in Russia faces many hazards.

APPENDIX

POWER IN THE SOVIET UNION

From 1918 until 1991, the Communist Party of the Soviet Union (CPSU) was the ruling party in the Soviet Union. The constitution and law were both subordinate to the CPSU and its leadership, and though constitutionally the Soviet Government and CPSU were separate bodies, in reality all government high officials were also party members.

The basic unit of the CPSU was the primary party organization, also called a "cell". At the party's peak size in the early 1980s (19 million members) there were 390,000 primary party organizations (cells), distributed among factories, government offices, schools and collective farms. Above the primary party organizations were district, city, regional and republic committees.

The supreme body in the CPSU was the party congress, which normally met every five years and was attended by several thousand delegates. The party congress elected the 300 or so members of the Central Committee of the CPSU, which met at least twice a year to carry out the work of the party in between congresses. The Central Committee elected the members of the Politburo and Secretariat. In the mid-1930s Stalin had most of the Central Committee

executed to guarantee his complete control over the party.

The Politburo – around 24 members – was the supreme policy making body in the country and exercised power over every aspect of public policy, both domestic and foreign. It was based in Moscow.

The first Politburo was created in late October 1917. Due to his control over the party machine the general secretary became the Politburo's most influential member. Following Lenin's death in 1924 Stalin became general secretary, and had complete control over it and the party, and thus the country.

The chairman of the Politburo was the general secretary of the party, and its members always included the minister of defence, the leader of the KGB, and the heads of the most important republic or urban party organizations. The Politburo was abolished and replaced by the Presidium of the Central Committee in 1952, which stressed "collective leadership" and actually removed Khrushchev from power in 1966.

The Secretariat appointed individuals to execute policy at lower levels, controlled all government bodies and carried out the party's paperwork.

GLOSSARY

Abwehr: *Amt Ausland/Abwehr im Oberkommando der Wehrmacht.* The Foreign Bureau/-Defence of the Armed Forces High Command. German Nazi military intelligence, formed in 1938.

AMTORG: Soviet Government Trading Commission. It was used extensively by the Soviets for KGB operations.

Apparatchik: Russian colloquial expression for a person of the party apparatus, sometimes used in a derogatory sense.

Bolshevik: Meaning "One of the Majority" in Russian. A member of a wing of the Russian Social-Democratic Workers' Party, which, led by Lenin, seized control of the government in Russia (October 1917) and became the dominant political power in the country.

Cheka: Also *Vecheka* (*Vserossiiskaia chrezvychainaia komissiia po bor'be s kontrrevoliutsiei i sabotazhem – VChK*). The All-Russian Extraordinary Commission for Combating Counter-Revolution and Sabotage. The Soviet political police created by the Bolsheviks in 1917.

Chon: *Chasti osobogo naznachenia.* Special Purpose Units. Punitive squads formed from units of the People's Commissariat of Internal Affairs and the Red Army in the 1920s.

CIA: Central Intelligence Agency. The main US intelligence and counter-intelligence agency.

Collectivization: A policy adopted by the Soviet Government, pursued most intensively between 1929 and 1933, to transform traditional agriculture in the Soviet Union and to reduce the economic power of the *kulaks* (prosperous peasants). Under collectivization the peasantry were forced to give up their individual farms and join large collective farms (*kolkhozy*). The process was ultimately undertaken in conjunction with the campaign to industrialize the Soviet Union rapidly.

Comintern: Association of national Communist parties, founded in 1919. Though its stated purpose was the promotion of world revolution, the Comintern functioned chiefly as an organ of Soviet control over the international Communist movement.

Communist Party of the Soviet Union: The major political party of Russia and the Soviet Union from the Russian Revolution of October 1917 to the dissolution of the Soviet Union in 1991.

FBI: Federal Bureau of Investigation. The largest investigative agency of the United States Government. The bureau's many responsibilities in the internal security field include matters pertaining to counter-espionage, espionage, sabotage, sedition and related internal-security matters. In connection with these duties, the bureau is responsible for correlating information on internal security matters and disseminating it to other interested federal agencies.

Gestapo: *Geheime Staatspolizei.* Nazi secret police which ruthlessly eliminated opposition to the Nazis within Germany and its occupied territories, and which was responsible for the round-up of Jews for deportation to extermination camps .

GPU: *Gosudarstvennoe politicheskoe upravlenie.* Soviet State Political Administration. The security police successor to the *Cheka* between 1922 and 1923.

GRU: *Glavnoye Razvedyvatelnoye Upravleniye.* Central Intelligence Office, the chief intelligence directorate of the Soviet Army general staff.

Gulag: *Glavnoye Upravleniye Ispravitelno-trudovykh Lagerey.* Chief Administration of Corrective Labour Camps. The system of Soviet labour camps and accompanying detention and transit camps and prisons that from the 1920s to the mid-1950s housed the political prisoners and criminals of the Soviet Union.

INO: *Inostrannyi otdel.* The Foreign Department of the Soviet Chief Political Administration of the People's Commissariat of Internal Affairs.

Izvestia: In full, *Izvestiya Sovetov Deputatov Trudyashchikhsya SSSR, News of the Councils of Working People's Deputies of the USSR.* Russian daily newspaper published in Moscow by the Presidium of the Supreme Soviet of the USSR. It was the official national publication of the Soviet Government until 1991.

KGB: *Komitet Gosudarstvennoy Bezopasnosti.* State Security Committee. Political police and security agency that was also the primary intelligence and counter-intelligence entity of the Soviet Union from 1954 to 1991.

Komsomol: Abbreviation of *Vsesoyuzny Leninsky Kommunistichesky Soyuz Molodyozhi*).

All-Union Leninist Communist League of Youth, a political organ for spreading Communist teachings and preparing future members of the Communist Party.

Kulak: A successful, independent farmer of the period before collectivization. The term was eventually applied to any peasant who opposed collectivization.

Los Alamos: The Los Alamos National Laboratory, New Mexico. In 1942 Los Alamos was chosen by the US Government (because of its comparative isolation and natural facilities) as the location for the Atomic Research Laboratory, then known as the Manhattan Project, which developed the first atomic, bomb.

Menshevik: "One of the Minority" in Russian. A member of the non-Leninist wing of the Russian Social Democratic Workers' Party, which evolved into a separate political organization.

MGB: *Ministerstvo gosudarstvennoi bezopasnosti.* Ministry of State Security. The main security police organization between 1946 and 1953.

MI5: Military Intelligence 5, also called the Security Service. British counter-intelligence agency.

MI6: Military Intelligence 6, also called the Secret Intelligence Service. British intelligence and espionage agency.

MVD: *Ministerstvo vnutrennikh del.* Soviet Ministry for Internal Affairs.

NATO: North Atlantic Treaty Organization. The military alliance established by the North Atlantic Treaty (also called the Washington Treaty) of 4 April 1949, which sought to create a counterweight to Soviet armies stationed in Central and Eastern Europe after World War II.

New Economic Policy: The economic policy of the government of the Soviet Union from 1921 to 1928, representing a temporary retreat from its previous policy of extreme centralization and doctrinaire Socialism.

NKGB: *Narodnyi komissariat gosudarstvennoi bezopasnosti.* People's Commissariat of State Security. Functioned in 1941 and again between 1943 and 1946.

NKVD: *Narodnyy komissariat vnutrennikh del.* People's Commissariat for Internal Affairs. The Soviet secret police from 1934 to 1943.

NSA: National Security Agency. Intelligence agency within the US Department of Defense responsible for cryptographic and communications intelligence and security.

Oak Ridge: Oak Ridge National Laboratory, a reactor technology school located in Tennessee, USA. In 1950 it became the Oak Ridge School of Reactor Technology (ORSORT).

OGPU: *Ob'edinennoe gosudarstvennoe politicheskoe upravlenie.* Unified State Political Administration. The Soviet security police from 1923 to 1934; successor to the GPU.

Okhrana: The Russian security police under Alexander III (1881-94).

People's Commissar: One of the leading group of Soviet government administrators.

Political Bureau: Also called Politburo. The supreme policy making body of the Communist Party of the Soviet Union. The Political Bureau until July 1990 exercised supreme control over the Soviet Government.

Pravda: "Truth" in Russian. Former daily newspaper, published in Moscow and distributed nationwide, that was the official organ of the Communist Party of the Soviet Union from 1918 to 1991. Founded in 1912 in St. Petersburg as a workers' daily.

proletariat: In Marxist terms, the class of wage workers who were engaged in industrial production and whose chief source of income was derived from the sale of their labour power.

Red Army: *Krasnaya Armiya.* Soviet army created by the Communists after 1917. The name Red Army was abandoned in 1946.

ROA: *Russkaia Osvoboditelnaia Armiia.* Russian Liberation Army. Force raised by the Nazis in November 1944 from prisoners of war. Headed by the captured Red Army general Andrei Vlasov.

SMERSH: *smert shpionam*, meaning "death to spies". An NKVD branch (later a ministry) responsible for maintaining security within the armed forces and watching for potential traitors within the military and intelligence services.

Socialist Revolutionary Party: Russian political party that represented the main alternative to the Social-Democratic Workers' Party during the last years of Romanov rule. The party was suppressed by Lenin after the Bolshevik victory in the Civil War.

soviet: A council that was the primary unit of government in the Union of Soviet Socialist Republics, and that officially performed both legislative and executive functions at the all-union, republic, province, city, district and village levels.

SS: Abbreviation of *Schutzstaffel* (in German: "Protective Echelon"). Black-uniformed élite troops of the Nazi Party.

Warsaw Pact: Warsaw Treaty of Friendship, Cooperation And Mutual Assistance (14 May 14 1955–1 July 1991). Treaty that establishing a mutual-defence organization composed originally of the Soviet Union and Albania, Bulgaria, Czechoslovakia, East Germany, Hungary, Poland and Romania.

BIBLIOGRAPHY

Works in English:

Banyard, Peter, *Hitler and His Henchmen. World War II Special*, Orbis Publishing Limited: London, 1976.

Barron, John, *KGB: The Secret Work of Soviet Secret Agents*, Hodder & Stoughton: London, 1974.

Beck, F., and Godin, W., *Russian Purge and Extraction of Confession*, Hurst & Blackett Ltd.: London, 1951.

Kennedy, Ludovic, *The Portland Spy Case*, in *Great Cases of Scotland Yard, Volume I*, The Reader's Digest Association: London, 1993.

Davies, Joseph E., *Mission to Moscow. United States Ambassador to the Soviet Union from 1936 to 1938*, Victor Gollancz Limited: London, 1943.

Don Levin, Isaac, *Stalin*, Private Lives Library: London, 1931.

Levitsky, Boris, *The Uses of Terror: The Soviet Secret Service 1917–1970*, Sidgwick & Jackson: London, 1971

Littlepage, John, and Demaree, Bess, *In Search of Soviet Gold*, George E.Harrap & Co.: London, 1939

Lockhart, Sir Robert Bruce, *Memoirs of a British Agent*, Penguin Books, Harmondsworth: Middlesex, 1932.

Lorimer, Frank, *The Population of the Soviet Union: History and Prospects*, League of Nations: Geneva, 1946

Mangold, Tom, *Cold Warrior. James Jesus Angleton: The CIA Master Spy Hunter*, Simon & Schuster: London, 1991

Pearson, Michael, *The Sealed Train*, Macmillan Limited: London and Basingstoke, 1975.

Piekalkiewicz, Janusz, *Secret Agents, Spies & Saboteurs. Famous Undercover Missions of World War II*, David & Charles: Newton Abbot, 1974.

Sayers, Michael, and Kahn, Albert E., *The Great Conspiracy Against Russia*, Collet's Holdings Ltd.: London, 1946

Scholmer, Joseph, *Vorkuta*, (translated from the German), Weidenfeld and Nicholson: London, 1954.

Solzhenitsyn, Alexander, *The Gulag Archipelago 1918–1956. An Experiment in Lirerary Investigation, I–II*, Book Club Associates: London, 1974.

Freedman, Robert (ed.), *Soviet Jewry in the Decisive Decade, Duke Press Policy Studies*, Duke University Press: Durham, South Carolina, 1984.

The Earl of Avon, *The Eden Memoirs: Facing the Dictators*, Cassel: London, 1962.

Reddaway, P. (ed.), *Uncensored Russia: The Human Rights Movement. The Annotated Text of the Unofficial Moscow Journal 'A Chronicle of Current Events'*, Cape: London, 1972.

Webb, Sidney, and Webb, Beatrice, *Soviet Communism: A New Civilization?*, printed by the authors for the members of the Labour Party, 1935.

Wright, Peter, *Spy Catcher. The Candid Autobiography of a Senior Intelligence Officer*, William Heinemann: Australia, Richmond, 1987

Works in Russian:

Beria, Sergo, *Moi otets Lavrentii Beria,* Sovremennik: Moskva, 1994.

Chekisty, *Sbornik doukumentov,* Molodaia Gvardia: Moskva, 1970.

Dolgopolov, Nikolai, *Pravda polkovnika,* Abelia: Penza, 1997.

Drozdov, Yurii, *Zapiski nachalnika nelegalnoi razvedki,* OLMA-PRESS: Moskva, 2000.

Gladkov, *Teodor, S mesta pokushenia skrylsia,* TOO "Geia": Moskva, 1998.

Krasnaia Kniga V-CH-KA, *Tom 1,* Gospolitizdat: Moskva, 1990.

Levye Esery I V-CH-KA, *Sbornik dokumentov,* Kazan, 1996.

Liudi Molchalivogo Podviga, *Sbornik,* Politizdat: Moskva, 1997.

Medvedev, Dmitri, *Eto bylo pod Rovno,* Rostov-na-Donu, 1985.

O Nikh Khodili Legendy, *Sbornik,* MOF "Pobeda-1945": Moskva, 1994.

Organy Gosudarstvennoi Bezopasnosti SSSR V Velikoi Otechestvennoi Voine, *Sbornik dokumentov,* Kniga i biznes: Moskva, 1995.

Ocherki Istorii Rossiiskoi Vneshnei Razvedki, Tom 3, *1933–1941 gody,* Mezhdunarodnye Otnoshenia: Moskva, 1997.

Ocherki Istorii Rossiiskoi Vneshnei Razvedki, Tom 4, *1941–1945 gody,* Mezhdunarodnye Otnoshenia: Moskva, 1999.

Pavlov, Vitaliy, *Operatsia "Sneg". Polveka vo vneshnei razvedke KGB,* TOO "Geia": Moskva, 1996.

Synitsyn, Elisei, *Resident svidetelstvuyet,* TOO "Geia": Moskva, 1996.

Soldaty Nevidimogo Fronta, *Sbornik,* MOF "Pobeda-1945": Moskva, 1994.

Sotsialisticheskoie Stroitelstvo Soyuza SSR (1933–1939). *Statisticheskii sbornik,* Gosplanizdat: Moskva-Leningard, 1939.

Spetszadanie (Voina v Tylu Vraga), *Sbornik,* MOF "Pobeda-1945": Moskva, 1994.

Sudoplatov, Pavel, *Spetsoperatsii, Lubyanka i Kreml. 1930-1950 gody,* OLMA-PRESS: Moskva, 1997.

Trifonov, Ivan, *Ocherki istorii klassovoi borby v SSSR v gody NEPA,* Gospolitiszad: Moskva, 1960.

Voskresenskaia, Zoya, *Teper ia mogu skazat pravdu,* Respublika: Moskva, 1993.

INDEX